FAITHFUL
TRAVELERS

Also by James Dodson

FINAL ROUNDS
A Father, A Son, The Golf Journey of a Lifetime

FAITHFUL TRAVELERS

A father. A daughter.

A fly-fishing journey of the heart.

James Dodson

BANTAM BOOKS

New York Toronto London Sydney Auckland

FAITHFUL TRAVELERS

A Bantam Book / May 1998

Book design by Dana Leigh Treglia

Library of Congress Cataloging-in-Publication Data

Dodson, James.
Faithful travelers : a father, a daughter, a fly-fishing journey of the
heart / James Dodson.
p.   cm.
ISBN 0-553-10644-9
1. Fathers and daughters.   2. Dodson, Maggie.   3. Dodson, James.
4. Fishing—United States.   I. Title.
HQ755.85.D644   1998
306.874'2—dc21   98-12967
                                                          CIP

Published simultaneously in the United States and Canada

PRINTED IN THE UNITED STATES OF AMERICA

BVG   10 9 8 7 6 5 4 3 2

To Muggins

Acknowledgments

Writing any book is an act of high-wire faith and there are many people I owe a debt of gratitude for helping coax this book to life. Brian Tart at Bantam is the kind of gifted and eerily patient young editor every writer deserves to work with at least once, and Irwyn Applebaum and Susan Corcoran merit special thanks for their continuing support. While I'm at it, I must fly-cast special heartfelt thanks across the pond to Andy McKillop at Century Books in Britain, who also believed in and encouraged this book from the beginning. I'm grateful as well to my agent Ginger Barber and her colleagues, whose enthusiasm never seems to flag. A few more brief thank-yous are in order: to Geoffrey C. Ward for his brilliant book *The West: An Illustrated History*; the selected writings of Robert Bly and Joseph Campbell; the reflections of Black Elk; the staff at the wonderful Buffalo Bill and Plains Indian Museum in Cody, Wyoming; the essays of James Carse and E. B. White; and far too many poets to name in one sitting.

My close friends Pat McDaid, Hugh Kluttz, Terry Meagher, Terry Bartow, Tony Schmitz, Macduff Everton, and Mike Purkey provided deep and useful insights throughout, and a special thank-you must go to Alison Dodson, who unwaveringly encouraged the writing of this book from Day One. Also, Virginia Doty, Kathleen Bennie, Edith Hazard,

Winnie Palmer, Patti Ohmans, and Randy Jones for their invaluable support and insights from the distaff side. Gratitude of immeasurable depth goes to my mother, Janet Dodson, for her honest memories and unflinching support, and to Sharon Pitts, a true daughter of the Old West, for assisting our journey. Thanks to Reverend Ellen Shaver for her valuable insights on faith, and Reverend Ed Chalfont for his thought-provoking perspectives. Ditto the staff at Colorado Trails for taking us in on such short notice, and the good people of Hinton, Oklahoma, who know how to make a weary traveler feel right at home.

Thanks to the fly-fishing staff at L. L. Bean for putting up with my unceasing questions and queries about the second-most fascinating sport on earth, and thank you, Jerry the Mechanic, wherever you are. Thanks to you, Old Blue not only got us safely home but she's *still* running like a prairie song.

Most of all, thank you, Maggie and Amos. No man could ever have finer traveling companions. You make me laugh and *believe*.

Come away, O human child!
To the watery and the wild
With a faery, hand in hand,
For the world's more full of weeping than you can understand.

–from "The Stolen Child," by W. B. Yeats

Rivers, I suppose, are not at all like human beings, but it is still
possible to make apt comparisons; and this is one: Understanding,
whether instinctive and immediate or developing naturally
through time or grown by conscious effort, is a necessary
preliminary to love. Understanding of another human being can
never be complete, but as it grows toward completeness, it
becomes love almost inevitably. One cannot know intimately all
the ways and movements of a river without growing into love of
it. And there is no exhaustion to the growth of love through
knowledge, whether the love be for a person or a river, because
the knowledge can never be complete. One can come to feel in
time that the whole is within one's compass, not yet wholly and
intimately known, but there will always be something ahead,
something more to know.

–from *A River Never Sleeps,* by Roderick Haig-Brown

FAITHFUL
TRAVELERS

PROLOGUE

....

The Medicine Bag

"I HAD A nice dream," my father said.

"Really? What?"

"We were camping somewhere. You, me, your brother. Perhaps up in the Blue Ridge. Nice river. Good swift water. We had a big fire going. I was reading something to you boys. Like old times."

"Uh-oh," I said. "The Medicine Bag."

A dim smile appeared. He'd been sleeping most of the afternoon in my childhood bedroom. Now it was early evening in late February, the last of the day's sun streaking low across the yard out the windows. You wouldn't have known there was sleet in the forecast. My mother had gone out somewhere. His dog Molly lay sleeping on the floor. His skin was pale, nearly translucent, his hair neatly combed. My father had just turned eighty. He looked serene, almost beautiful, just an old man waking from a nap. At times he made dying look easy.

"It wasn't that bad."

"Not bad at all," I admitted. "We didn't want you to know that, though. If it got out that our old man read us Tennyson and Longfellow by the campfire we could have been socially ruined. Tough crowd, the ninth grade."

"It didn't appear to do you much harm."

"Perhaps. Dick did all right. Thanks to the Medicine Bag he was safely cured of any interest in poetry forever. I nearly took up a career writing sonnets in the woods, though."

I was pleased to see I could still make my father smile. We both needed a lift. I'd been with him for more than a month, away from my two children and out of the stream of my own life. I'd spent my days attending to his needs as he slowly faded, avoiding my work, neglecting my rosebushes, waiting on his death. My brother would come join me later for the overnight vigil, and I wished he could have been here for this bit of give-and-take. Dad's lucid moments were becoming rarer.

The Medicine Bag was what Dad called the canvas book bag he hauled along on our camping trips. He liked to say the contents were good for whatever ailed us—the poetry of Whitman, Yeats, or Longfellow, *The Just So Stories* of Kipling, Edith Hamilton's *Mythology* of Greek gods and heroes, White's *Once and Future King*, various fables, psalms, Indian legends, bits of Plato and Aristotle, stories of the Old West and the New Testament.

His roving chautauquas were pretty corny stuff, but then I found so much of what my father did and said in those days deeply embarrassing—how he'd cheerfully go out of his way to help people he hardly knew, attempt to find the silver lining in any situation, view even the smallest weekend excursion as a grand adventure, and quote Churchill on service or Emerson on joy to my impressionable teenage dates when they least expected it. For these and other high crimes of the heart I bestowed on him the nickname Opti the Mystic, a gently mocking moniker.

I admitted to him now, perhaps not too late, how much I'd loved those camping trips, the Medicine Bag, all of it, just being with him, wading in rivers, catching our supper, listening to him read to us by the fire. The world felt so large but we felt so safe. I told him I planned to take my children soon on their first camping trip. Perhaps somewhere up the Allagash or possibly to Acadia in Maine, to where the mountains meet the sea. My daughter Maggie had recently asked me to teach her to fly-fish and my son Jack wanted to climb a mountain. The sky deeply interested him. If you climbed Cadillac Mountain, I said, you could be the first to see the sun rise on the continent, the way original peoples had. I would take my own Medicine Bag, perhaps.

"I wish I could go with you," Opti said, drifting away again.

"Me too," I admitted, then added, "You will." But I'm not sure he really heard me.

Two nights later, we sat together watching a documentary on TV.

The documentary was on Yellowstone Park, which was about to celebrate its 125th birthday. The world's first national park was in deep trouble—slowly coming back from devastating wildfires, beset by problems of overcrowding and pollution, a damaged Eden due to federal budgetary cutbacks and a soaring park crime rate. Even Old Faithful, the world-famous geyser, a living symbol of America's dynamism, wasn't all that faithful anymore, rising less than half of its original height and erupting so erratically some geologists predicted it would actually cease functioning in the near future.

"That's too bad," I said, really more to myself than to Opti, because he was asleep in his wheelchair. "We talked about camping and fishing our way out there."

"I remember," Opti replied softly, opening his eyes.

I looked at him and smiled, then turned my attention back to the documentary and grumbled something about the world coming apart at the seams.

"Things change. Worlds come and go. Yours will too."

I looked at him again, wondering what he meant by such an unsettling remark. It seemed so unlike Opti. Before I could ask, though, he spoke again.

"Keep the faith," he said. "You can figure it out."

I went outside to see if perhaps there was an explanation in the stars. My father knew his constellations and I was working on mine. But no stars were visible. Clouds had rolled in from the west.

The next afternoon, as I washed his arms, we talked of Aunt Emma.

Emma was his paternal grandmother, a full-blooded Cherokee Indian woman, perhaps a foundling from the infamous Trail of Tears. No one knew her history clearly; she had been dead more than half a century. But her farm in Orange County had been my father's favorite place as a boy, and he'd taken my brother and me there as boys at Christmas to shoot mistletoe out of the oak trees that surrounded the abandoned homeplace, a house settling in the morning glory vines.

For years my father and his brothers Jim and Bob had talked of buying the property, but it had fallen out of family hands and been sold to a man who wouldn't sell. They were proud of the family's Indian blood and I reminded my father of how he was always dragging my brother and me to Indian burial mounds, all those hours we spent looking for traces of a lost race of warriors on hot summer afternoons.

I'd finished with his arms and asked if he wanted something to drink. He was really drinking only water now.

"You could still go there," he said quietly.

"Where?" For a moment I thought he meant Aunt

Emma's place in the oaks. But of course that was long gone. A cluster of condos stood on the site now, guarded by a man at a gate.

"Out west. To Yellowstone."

The sockets around Opti's eyes were deep, like small fierce craters. "Take Maggie and Jack and just go. Show 'em their history, tell 'em some stories. Teach 'em to fish and camp. Just go."

"Maybe I will," I said.

Later that night, I went to the attic in search of books from his Medicine Bag.

My father's words had touched a nerve, but I also needed something to read to get my mind off the fact that I couldn't imagine the world, however it had changed, without Opti the Mystic in it.

I found a pile of books in an old chest containing, among other things, the scouting merit badge sashes and toy armies that had belonged to my brother and me. I sat on the floor and lined up soldiers—Roman gladiators, Johnny Rebs, Greek warriors, Viking chieftains, GI Joes, Indian warriors, Deadwood gunslingers, Arthurian knights. What epic wars we'd had with them. Now their swords were broken and their bayonets bent. But I still loved them, every one. I decided I would take them home to my son Jack.

I looked through several books and brought Whitman's *Leaves of Grass* and something called *The Soul of an Indian*, by Charles Eastman, back downstairs. I read the Whitman for a while but soon found myself engrossed in *The Soul of an Indian*. Eastman, I learned, was a mixed-blood Sioux named Ohiyesa who came East to become a physician in the white man's world. He later returned to serve his people as a reservation doctor, witnessed the massacre at Wounded Knee, and wrote ten or eleven books eloquently attempting to explain the vanishing Native American ways to the conquering white race. His stated goal was to be a sympathetic bridge between two colliding worlds, a vision at which he pretty much failed. Among other things, though, Ohiyesa had a strong and lasting influence on the values of the American Boy Scouts, which he helped found.

I read most of this little book with its badly frayed cover while seated beside my father's bed. "The attitude of the Indian toward death," Ohiyesa wrote, "the test and background of life, is entirely consistent with his background and philosophy. Death holds no terrors for him; he meets it with simplicity and perfect calm, seeking only an honorable end as a last gift to his family and descendents. . . . If one be dying at home, it is customary to carry his bed out of doors as the end approaches, that his spirit may pass under the open sky."

"Is that rain?" my father asked.

"Sleet." The storm had finally arrived.

"That's okay," he assured me calmly. "It'll be fine in the morning. Go kiss your wife."

I tried to smile at him, thinking how even now he was dispensing useful advice. A few weeks before we'd had a conversation about the complications of modern family life and I'd admitted to him that something was chewing at me about my marriage—the way things had quietly gone out of focus, how distant my hardworking wife of ten years and I sometimes seemed to each other. It was curious. Our marriage was so calm and civilized and productive that no one could really see this, I said, except us. The children didn't have a clue, and neither did our closest friends. Perhaps I was just making too much of it, worrying about something that time and a decent vacation would take care of. As usual, he didn't say much except that it sounded like I was describing a corporation rather than a marriage. He added that you

could love your kids more than life itself but your lover had
to come before everything else. It was curious that he always
called my mother his lover. Curious, too, I realized later, that
he always put her first but my brother and I never felt second. How had he managed this feat?

Now I wanted to say something but I couldn't speak. Perhaps it was thank you; perhaps it was just good-bye. I really
don't know. Suddenly my mother was by his side and taking
his hand and I stepped back. They'd been married for fifty-
five years. I left them alone and he passed away a few moments later.

In the morning, just before dawn, I accompanied Opti's
body to the funeral home where his remains would be cremated. The attendant, a young man with an impatient air,
looked mildly stricken when I asked him to open the wooden
box so I could see my father's body.

Opti was still dressed in his pajamas, his silver hair swept
back. His body looked oddly beautiful, as noble as any Viking chieftain about to be put to sea on his burning longship.
I leaned over and kissed his forehead, which felt pleasantly
cool, like a marble statue. I took a small plastic figure out of
my pocket, an Indian warrior, one of my favorites, hand-
painted for war long ago by me, and placed it on his chest,
just above his clasped hands.

As I did this, Ohiyesa's words were still fresh in my mind
and a powerful thought occurred to me—a crazy wish,
really—that I could take Opti's earthly remains up to some
high Blue Ridge summit, build a great bonfire, and commit
his soul to the Great Mystery or whichever thoughtful deity
had fashioned this rarest of men from the elements of earth
and wind. With this vision of my father's death, something
seemed to be stirring and awakening in me. I wish I could
say it was peaceful and reassuring, this awakening, a vision
of comfort, but it wasn't. It was nothing short of frightening.

I was forty-one years old and this was my first day on

earth as a fatherless child, the beginning of a journey I never imagined I would have to take, a painful unraveling and unexpected rebirth.

But I couldn't possibly have known any of that then. All I knew, as I watched his remains roll to the fire, was that once again Opti had been right. The ice storm was gone, and the morning, as he'd promised it would be, was really fine.

CHAPTER ONE

....

Babes in the Woods

EARLY ONE FRIDAY afternoon a year after my father died, my children and I drove up to Acadia National Park and found a beautiful campsite by the sea.

The campground was virtually empty—strange, I thought, for the start of what a native-born pal of mine calls Luggage Rack Season in Maine, that alternately blessed and accursed time when seven million tourists lash half of everything they own to the roofs of their cars and haul it into the state. I put up our new L. L. Bean tent and suggested to my children that they take Amos, our elderly golden retriever, for a nice walk on the beach before supper.

Amos was almost fourteen, an amiable brute who was either deaf or perhaps no longer particularly interested in what anybody had to say to him, particularly me. He'd always more or less followed his own path through life and generally behaved as if I was damned lucky he didn't object to my hanging round him.

I reminded Maggie to be sure and keep our senior citizen

safely on the lead, per federal regulations, and also advised her to keep an eye on Jack, her younger brother, who was almost six and didn't realize that he hadn't quite learned to swim. Maggie was seven going on fifteen and already an excellent swimmer and advisor on matters of life and sport. But I still didn't want anybody near the water.

"Dad," Jack said, "what's over there?" He was pointing east, past Cadillac Mountain and over the ocean.

"Ireland, I think. Or maybe Portugal. Don't even think about trying to swim that far."

"Dad," Maggie said with that world-weary sigh all seven-year-old girls seem to possess. "You worry too much."

"I know," I said, smiling at her. "That's my job."

She was right. I do worry a lot. Worrying about things is my nature. Sometimes I worry about the vanishing rain forests or hidden land mines in Bosnia. Other times I worry about declining songbird populations, wormholes in the universe, and the escalating wages of Major League Baseball players—things, in other words, I'm pretty helpless to do anything about, a feeling of global powerlessness that also makes me worry. Mostly, though, I worry about my children.

As I started preparing our first camp supper, I realized I was even more worried than usual because something I once couldn't have even imagined was about to happen to our world. A few days before this trip, their mother and I sat together in the attractive office of a woman named Jennifer. Jennifer was a certified family therapist. She was a pleasant woman in her late fifties who drove, I noticed, a snazzy red sports car with vanity plates that cutely read MDLFCRS.

"I think," Jennifer said pleasantly, "it's time we stopped talking about marriage counseling and began talking about divorce counseling."

My wife looked at me and I looked at her.

"I guess so," my wife said to Jennifer.

I didn't bother answering—perhaps I merely nodded dumbly, like a stunned musk ox or something. The truth was, I was having difficulty believing any of it was really happening, as my wife no doubt was as well, because the previous year had been like one long bad dream. Three months after my father's death, we had a rare fight in front of the children and my wife suggested we take our coffee out to the deck and talk. I was anxious to talk because our lives, in my view, had drifted even more out of focus, what with her busy work schedule and mine, the needs of the children, the demands of three aging cats and two elderly dogs, a garden that never got thoroughly weeded, and a house that never felt fully clean.

I remember sitting on the deck and looking out at my woefully neglected yard—perennial beds choked with weeds, rosebushes growing like feral children—thinking how we'd been through so much in the past ten years: the birth of our children, a miscarriage, the deaths of both our fathers, working careers that always seemed to be sending us to different places. It was time to clear the air, get the issues on both sides finally out in the open. I decided it was time to propose a new beginning. Perhaps we could renew our wedding vows, take stock of our careers, go on a serious family vacation, or at least indulge in the occasional romantic "couples" weekend—the kind of stuff all old marrieds do to try and revive a sputtering flame. We'd be more lovers and less corporation. Maybe we could have a third child. We'd always talked about a third child.

But I never got the words out. My wife wiped her eyes and said she thought our marriage was about to be over.

I think I laughed. God, I wish I hadn't done that—but when all else fails I sometimes make a joke or laugh at the terrible irony of things, and in this instance the awful mistiming of our moods and revelations seemed like some darkly comic nineties version of *The Gift of the Magi*. I wanted in, she wanted out. I wanted to begin again, she reluctantly wanted to begin packing.

For a couple hours, as our coffee grew cold and the sun crossed the yard, I tried to make her see it my way, saying that we had so much more than every other working couple we knew—happy kids, a nice life, a strong house, good values, all the Big Picture stuff in sync. I said that all our friends knew how much I loved her and pointed out that through everything that happened to us, good and bad, for better or worse, up and down, broke or flush, I could count the number of genuine disagreements we'd had on one hand. Wise people learned from their mistakes, I said, and good people deserved second chances. We deserved one.

It was a nice speech and I meant it to my core. But something *big* obviously wasn't in perfect sync. She talked again, I listened, my spirits nosedived. She felt profoundly smothered, unloved, overwhelmed—by me, by life, by *something*. I knew so much of what she said was true. Her instincts were nearly infallible. There was no third party involved, no booze, no violence. Just an unshakable *feeling* tearing her up that life had drawn us inexorably apart.

Both deeply shaken by the frightening reality that emerged, we declared a moratorium and she rounded up the kids and took them to our favorite beach. I took Amos and went to a nearby lake for a cold swim and a clear think. Sometimes, the poet Wallace Stevens said, the truth depends on a walk around a lake.

Jung said we can never begin to love until we face our shadows. A year of quiet counseling had followed. We worked hard to face our shadows, shadows all couples have, shadowy histories peculiar to us. We learned, among other things, that two people who seemed so adept at communicating understood just about everything around them except each other. Most people saw nothing but an outwardly happy family seated together at church or walking together on the beach, but the truth was, our family was slowly coming apart at the seams, unraveling like a baseball in the tide. We were good, kind, civilized, Christian people, I told myself. How could this sort of thing happen to *us*? My wife talked to a psychologist named Michelle; I did a private weekly stint with a guy named Herman. We worked hard at salvaging paradise and I took it one step further by discreetly talking with close friends and family, probing their brains for clues and insights I might have somehow missed or stupidly ignored.

Marriage is a medieval mystery play. Chekhov said we only lie at the beginning and end of relationships—the middle is where the truth resides. I desperately wanted to believe this was true and that we were simply somewhere in the middle of our married journey, but the truth wasn't something I really cared to see: We were somehow mysteriously *ending*. These friends advised me to give it time, keep the faith, keep an open mind, confront my own failings honestly. These things happened to every couple, they counseled. Be patient, keep talking. If you get through this, you two can survive anything—*hard weather makes good timber*, as they say in Maine. The children heard long and sometimes tearful discussions into the night as we wrestled with this demon like Jacob and the angel, but they had no clue of the approaching meteorite about to shatter their worlds.

And so, mere days before this camping trip to Acadia, we'd come together in the presence of Jennifer, a highly recommended marriage counselor who was going to try and help us reach some final conclusions. It was only our third session with Jennifer and as I sat there pretending to be so calm and civilized I still clung to a fraying faith that we would find the words that would help us untangle the wires and redeem a decent, honorable marriage that had somehow become impossibly complicated. Most of all I wanted redemption and a second chance. I couldn't even imagine what being divorced would be like, and I didn't wish to learn.

But apparently this was a minority opinion of one. Jennifer complimented us on our great affection for each other, thoughtful composure under stress, and shared conviction that the welfare of the children was really paramount in this situation. Our children, she said, would always be our spiritual common ground—the place we discovered and celebrated the best part of ourselves. She said the goal was to make a dignified break and create a new kind of expanded but loving family. Someday, in time, she said, we would each move on and begin new relationships while retaining in memory only the best things about our time together as man and wife.

She said other reassuring things but I can't recall what they were, exactly. As she talked and we listened, I remember vaguely wishing I could take a tire tool to the hood of her nice red sports car with the cute vanity tags. The rage wasn't really meant for her but rather myself—for somehow spoiling our little paradise and then, worse, being helpless to save it.

Finally, we all stood and shook hands. Jennifer said she was sure we'd make excellent "coparents," as if a new corporation were being formed. My wife wiped her eyes and thanked her. I thanked her, too. Then we walked slowly down her carpeted stairs together like two people who had just seen the baby doctor and been told they would soon have a newborn. Our newborn was an uncoupling.

We embraced and kissed in the parking lot. It felt—or at least appeared—so horribly normal. My wife went back to work and I went to the bookstore and bought a book on fly-fishing because Maggie and I were scheduled to take a fly-fishing course together at nearby L. L. Bean the same weekend.

·   ·   ·

Amos and the children came back to our campsite.

I was pleased to see that everyone was dry. Jack, swinging a large stick, wanted to know what was for dinner. I said we would start with a lovely Ducktrap River goose pâté followed by a select bed of fine arugula greens, medallions of grilled venison served with a lively mango salsa and puree of Belgian parsnips, followed perhaps by cherries flambé, a wedge of aged Stilton, and a nice bosky Andalusian port on the terrace afterward.

"Hot dogs and beans, Jack," Maggie helpfully translated to her brother.

"Oh good." He was clearly relieved.

Maggie explained that Amos had met a girlfriend on the beach, a small poodle named Wanda.

"*Amore* happens," I said, "even to old geezers."

"Amos isn't a 'geezer.'" Maggie felt obliged to defend her dog's honor.

"He's thirteen," I pointed out. "That's ninety-one in dog years."

"How old are you?" Jack wondered.

"Two hundred and fifty-seven. Believe me, I feel every one of those years, too."

"*That's* a geezer," Maggie said, pointing out the obvious.

I sat on a log watching my children eat beans and franks by the campfire, thinking how what they didn't know really was going to hurt them. Their mother planned to move out of the house in a matter of days; she'd already rented a small cottage by a salt pond on the way to their favorite beach. We'd purchased bunk beds for their new "other" bedroom and my framed photograph was already sitting on the windowsill overlooking the pond—all the things you're supposed to do to try and soften the blow to the innocent parties of a "civilized" split-up. Jennifer would be pleased.

"Guys," I said casually, as we neared the ceremonial marshmallow-toasting course of the meal, "I've been giving some thought to this summer. I think we should take a big vacation. If we could go anywhere and do anything, except go to Disney World, what would it be?" My work as a golf writer took me to Orlando every January for the annual PGA Merchandise Show and we usually made a small family vacation out of it. It was time to expand our horizons a bit, though.

"I'd like to go fly-fishing," Maggie said simply.

This was no great surprise. We'd just finished the fly-fishing course at Bean and she'd not only been the only girl in a class of ten men and nine little boys, but the only child who earned the right to wear her graduation pin right side up for catching a small brook trout. She also displayed a natural instinct for identifying bugs and at one point startled the Bean instructors, and disgusted her male contemporaries, by identifying a dragonfly pupa and then, on a tongue-in-cheek dare from her favorite instructor, dramatically popping the small critter into her mouth and eating it. "That's a sign," the instructor whispered to me later, "of a real fishergirl." Her maternal grandfather would undoubtedly have been pleased, but then Sam Bennie had been fly-fishing crazy, a charming Scotsman who tied his own flies and chased trout all over Scotland and the Alaskan Yukon. Perhaps fly-fishing was merely wandering through Maggie's bloodline the way golf wandered through mine.

"I want to see a rocket go up," Jack said matter-of-factly. "And go to Africa."

I nodded, not surprised in the least my son would say this. We were always talking about rocket ships and Africa. Africa was the place, I'd told him, where the first human beings may have walked upright and where lions still roamed in the wild. He had loads of picture books about Africa but he was also a little boy drawn by the mysteries of space and flight. I'd painted stars on his dormer room ceiling and he was forever asking me questions about how far away the stars really were and what it felt like to fly. My nickname for him was Rocket.

I held my marshmallow over the fire and told Jack I was fairly certain we would do those things in time.

"What about taking a camping trip out West?" I tossed out casually.

"Where out West?" Maggie seemed interested.

"I dunno. Wyoming or Montana. The best trout streams in the world are out there. To say nothing about the incredible stuff along the way. We could do the Adirondacks. See the Badlands and Mount Rushmore. I've got a friend in Minnesota who wants to fish the Boundary Waters. Who knows, really."

I told them about Yellowstone Park, Old Faithful, herds of elk and bison in the wild, beautiful trout rivers I'd never seen, gorgeous desert canyons I'd never visited. It was a long way from Maine, I said, but wouldn't it be fun to drive clear across America and see what we could find? I didn't bother telling them why I was so anxious to leave home for a while.

"Are you sure we'll go see the space shuttle go up?" The Rocket was beginning to sound as worried as his old man.

"Absolutely. You've got my word."

"Pinkie promise?" Maggie was a veteran negotiator who knew enough to invoke the ultimate verbal contract on behalf of her younger brother. I reached over and we hooked small fingers, sealing the deal.

"Pinkie promise."

Then something strange began to happen around us in the pines where the mountains met the sea.

I'd just fetched *The Soul of an Indian* and started reading them a bit about an Indian child's life when the campground began to fill up with other paying customers.

A truck camper with Connecticut plates pulled into the site next to us and a man climbed out bellyaching at his wife. A baby was squalling within. We watched a pair of kids hop out and begin pestering the man for their bikes, which he unstrapped from the rear luggage rack and placed on the ground. They hopped on them and pedaled away whooping.

We watched other vehicles arrive—a caravan of campers, the late arrivals of Luggage Rack Season. They pulled into campsites and threw up tents, cranked up generators, fired up electronic bug killers. Teenage girls were now sauntering past us on the road, playing rap music on a boom box, and I watched Maggie watching them. Behind us through the trees someone else turned on a gas generator and soon we heard a television set playing—the Red Sox were hosting the Twins at Fenway. There was a raucous burst of male laughter from another direction where, through the trees, an evening poker game was under way.

"Dad," Jack said, balancing his marshmallow over the flame, "next time can we bring our TV?"

"Absolutely not," I told him, a bit more sharply than I should have. "The point of camping is not to watch television."

"What is the point?"

I told him I thought the point of camping was to get as close as possible to nature without being murdered in your sleep by mosquitoes. I said living close to nature was the Indian way.

"Are there Indians around here?" Maggie wondered.

I said there once had been—plenty of them. The Penobscot and Passamaquoddy tribes had lived here and all of the land where we were sitting had been part of Norumbega, the Indian name for Maine. I told them the first European explorers had mistakenly thought Norumbega was a mythical city whose streets were paved with gold and searched for it for many years but never found it.

"Maybe it wasn't there," Rocket said.

No, I said, Norumbega was there all right. I explained that the Europeans made the mistake of thinking that because Indians didn't build grand cities like their own, they were basically godless and uncivilized. Indians saw life through a different lens, though. To build something permanent in nature, they knew, would be the quickest way to spoil God's paradise. So they moved around all the time, making camp and living as close to the land as possible, taking only what they needed from it. I said their great-great-grandmother would have understood this thinking because she'd been a full-blooded Cherokee Indian woman, perhaps even a foundling from the Trail of Tears.

"Cool," Maggie said. "You mean we're Indian, too?"

"Some part of you."

"Me too?" Jack perhaps feared being left out but I had no intention of ever leaving him out.

"You too."

Emerson said we do not live an equal life, but one of contrasts and patchworks; now a little joy, then a sorrow. Someone else said a divorce is like the death of a small civilization.

That's exactly how I felt watching our children's faces on the morning we broke the news to them about the divorce. Jack sat rigidly on my lap and finally began to shake with tears. Maggie, sitting with her mother in my faded green reading chair, squeezed her arms and refused to make eye contact with either of her parents, staring in stunned disbelief at a bookshelf. She had combed her own hair and pinned it up beautifully; she looked like a young princess being betrayed.

Her mother spoke eloquently and bravely—it was perhaps her best moment ever, explaining how brokenhearted both of their parents were that things had come to this moment, but revealing our shared determination to create a better, perhaps even happier life from this unhappy time. Mom and Dad genuinely loved each other, she said, but they couldn't live together and didn't wish the two people they loved most to be caught in the cross fire. It was time, she added, for everybody to start healing. Then I took a turn at explaining the unexplainable, trying to calmly reassure our children that everything their mother said was true, that things would be better in time, the pain would subside, and with God's help we would all eventually heal. It was perfectly natural to be sad, I said, afraid and angry and worried.

I said these words with great conviction, and may have even believed them. But it still felt like a civilization was dying. After a little while and a lot of tears, they went out with their mother to see their new place on the salt marsh and Amos and I got in Old Blue, my truck, and drove to L. L. Bean to purchase a canoe.

A week later, around noon on a Sunday, I finished packing up the truck. The rear cargo hold was full of gear, a new Discovery canoe was strapped on top, and the backseat had just enough room for the Medicine Bag and my guitar. I put the Medicine Bag in the backseat and returned to the house for my guitar, which Maggie had specifically asked me to bring.

When I came back to the truck, two dogs had added themselves to the cargo hold. I ordered Bailey, our younger female golden, out of the truck and she obeyed because she's an excellent dog and always does what her owners command. I ordered Amos out of the truck but he stuck his head out the window and rested his chin thoughtfully on the sill, ready to see the USA in our Chevrolet.

"Look," I tried to reason with him, "we're not just going to the store for a loaf of bread. We're going out West, to the land of sagebrush and rattlesnakes. Get out. You know how you hate heat."

He yawned, implying I should shake the lead out. I carried the guitar back to the house.

The children and my wife were waiting for me at our

favorite seaside restaurant, a lobster shack on the docks at Cundys Harbor. The place had recently been written up in *USA Today* as one of "Maine's best-kept secrets," which meant it was no secret anymore and the place was crawling with tourists and summer people. They looked so lithe and happy in their fresh sunburns and new summer clothes and we looked for all the world, I suppose, like the perfectly flawed four-part family we'd been not so long ago.

Maggie was going West with me, Jack was accompanying his mother to Nantucket. That was the plan. This was the Brave New World of loving coparenting. Jennifer would be pleased but it made me sad to be leaving the Rocket behind, though he didn't seem as unhappy as I thought he might be. He was thrilled about the prospect of riding a ferry to an island and asked me again if we would see a rocket go up and I promised him we would. Then I ordered my usual fried fish sandwich, realizing I didn't have the appetite to eat it.

All travel, someone said, is a vanishing act. You decide to go and disappear down the rabbit hole.

Two hours later, we crossed the great steel span over the Piscataqua River into New Hampshire and noticed a long line of tourist traffic headed north into Maine. A few miles farther, we came to a halt at the New Hampshire tolls. Thousands of people were flooding into Maine, thousands were going home. Old Blue was running hot, I noticed, and the air-conditioning wasn't working at all. I'd forgotten to have it checked out so I switched it off. Maggie was busy unwrapping a new Trisha Yearwood cassette tape. She'd packed a small ecumenical arsenal of road tunes—country artists, Broadway show tunes, Disney themes, classical favorites. Music for all occasions and landscapes.

"Dad," she said, looking over, "please put on your shoulder harness."

I'm always forgetting to put on my shoulder harness. I obeyed and asked her if she planned to nag me about that for the next six weeks or five thousand miles, whichever came first.

"If I have to," she assured me with a big toothy grin.

It struck me, as I said the words "six weeks," that we really were *leaving home* and headed to God knows where. My truck was ten years old. My dog was almost fourteen, my daughter seven. None of them had any business wandering the roads of America. Perhaps I didn't either. I was a professional traveler and my job took me to a lot of swell places in the world, but families on bootless odysseys were another matter. Modern families didn't go on vacations like my family had in the fifties and sixties, led by the indefatigable Opti the Mystic—just hop in the car and go where the spirit leads them, with no reservations of any kind, seeing what they could kick up. They made airplane and hotel reservations, booked a car, bought the theme park tickets months in advance, made sure the restaurants accepted their brand of plastic, and bought trip insurance in case the whole thing was a flop.

The car behind me tooted impatiently. He was anxious to get his vacation safely over with. The car ahead of me had rolled three whole feet and I had failed to keep pace. On one hand, the idea of what we were biting off was downright thrilling; on another, utterly terrifying.

"Dad, you look worried."

"Do I? It's this awful traffic, Mugs. At this rate we won't make Boston by nightfall."

As usual, I was worried. Adopted Mainer E. B. White once said there is nothing sadder than a summer day, and a lovely Maine woman I knew who always buried cut flowers in her garden after they'd gone by insisted that every leave-taking, regardless of size, should be properly observed and mourned. Perhaps I was simply doing that—mourning a bit.

Often, before I went on a long trip, I swept the walk or watered my rosebushes as a final act of homage to home. But as we sat there clogged in tourist traffic, I remembered that I'd forgotten to do that, pay homage, this time.

The larger truth was, though, I was worried about the world we were leaving behind, and worrying about the world we would come home to inherit. Too sad to stay but anxious to go, I was suddenly sorely tempted to turn Old Blue around and just go straight home and water my roses, forget this nutty idea of driving all the way out to Yellowstone Park because the embarrassing truth was, I had no idea where we'd go after reaching Boston—I'd been so preoccupied with throwing together this hasty expedition that I'd somehow neglected to choose an actual *starting point* for our great camping trip West. It had never felt *real*—or for that matter necessary—until this very moment.

"Cinchy. Why don't you take another road?"

My daughter pointed to an exit ramp just ahead of us on the highway. "Cinchy" was her hip first-grade word for any question that had a simple or obvious answer.

I smiled at her, took the exit, and soon found us on a highway I once knew very well, a winding blacktop road that led us west through small towns with green commons and stone soldiers facing south, where Independence Day flags still hung from porches and geraniums bloomed in cemeteries.

Old Blue cooled down and Amos hung his big head out the window to let the rushing wind flap his jowls. Maggie sang along with Trisha Yearwood, a lovely torch song about somebody aching to hit the road after a love affair gone wrong, anxious to get out from under a rain cloud and find a way to live again. Funny how some perfect stranger can sing your deepest thoughts. The sound of my fishergirl's sweet voice made my anxiety begin to lift like Portland fog.

A few minutes later, it suddenly came to me where we

could go—someplace I'd almost forgotten about, a beautiful river where I'd once begun another life before I somehow found my way here.

Cinchy.

And with that, we slipped down the rabbit hole.

....

CHAPTER TWO

Trout Music

THE SUN WAS dropping into the hills, casting a golden
hue over the broad Connecticut River as we rambled over
its darkly swirling currents into Vermont. I'd been calmly
driving for two hours, alternately chatting with my daughter
about this and that and then being left alone to angle in the
quiet rivers of my own thoughts, still vaguely trying to sort
out some kind of reasonable itinerary. I was feeling slightly
better and Maggie, displaying the faith of a mustard seed,
seemed downright thrilled to be headed God knows where
after trout.

She asked if we could stop and fish the Connecticut and I
replied that we couldn't because I hoped to make the banks
of the Green instead before dusk. It was only a few miles
ahead and I even knew a place we might pitch camp.

"What's the Green?"

"A river. The place I learned to fly-cast by verse."

"Did Granddaddy teach you to fish there?"

"No. He taught me to spin-fish in North Carolina. Fly-fishing is something I picked up much later. Spin-casting and fly-fishing are entirely different, Mugs. Sort of like hockey compared to figure skating."

"Who taught you to fly-fish?"

I smiled at the image of his face.

"Funny old guy. Just somebody I met when I first came to Vermont." A moment more and I recalled his oddly apt nickname. "Saint Cecil."

"Was he really a saint?" We'd recently read a book about Saint Francis.

"No. Just a retired college professor. A devoted dry-fly man."

"Tell me," she said, and crossed her bare legs Indian style on the seat, anticipating the tale.

I had six weeks and nothing better to do. So I told her.

"As I frequently used to say to my overly serious first-year students at seminary, naked cameth I into this world and naked I shall surely leave it, except perhaps for the Hardy Brothers split-cane fly rod and a couple Royal Coachmen and the odd brookie in my creel. My little funny was meant to loosen them up, prepare them for a life that takes itself much too seriously, though I'm afraid it seldom had the desired effect. *The Lord loves a good joke, you know.* That's what I used to say. *Except those we see fit to elect to higher office.*"

The speaker was a powerful-looking man in his late sixties, bullnecked, sun-wrinkled, his bristly hair gone the color of new snow. He had a small audience of attractive young women drinking white wine.

"That's Saint Cecil," Dorothy whispered to me, "my late aunt Edna's husband, an old lefty preacher who's positively mad for fly-fishing. He used to teach New Testament at some Bible college down South until they ran him off. Not shy for opinions on any subject, I'm afraid. He and my aunt always came for the Bach festival in Marlboro and he's just kept coming. He'll be underfoot here at least a week." She issued a small tragic sigh, then glanced at me. I was her new tenant, having just signed the lease on the small wood-heated house she owned on the banks of Vermont's Green River. "You're from the South. I nearly forgot. *Please* tell me you adore trout fishing."

I hated to disappoint her, but she seized my arm and dragged me over to meet her uncle regardless. He threw his hand at me like a punch and nearly fractured a couple knuckles squeezing my hand.

"I know why I'm here," he declared with a booming Alabama drawl, "to soak up the two-hunnerd-year-old strains of a Leipzig choirmaster and chase *truite de mer*. That's French Canadian for eastern brook trout. Question is, why the hell are you so far from home?"

It wasn't a question I was fully prepared to answer. I didn't wish to tell him I'd run away from home at age thirty, so I smiled and mumbled something polite about taking a year off from my journalism career, a hiatus, a much-needed sabbatical before I resumed interviewing politicians and murder suspects for my magazines.

"Reporter, eh?" The revelation seemed to annoy him. "Do you fly-fish?"

I said no and explained that I used to bass-fish with spinner bait but I mostly played golf now.

"Golf's a splendid game for old men," he agreed, lowering the tide in his wineglass by half with one swallow. "Tell you what. I've got several rods with me. I'll be by and pick you up at dawn and we'll spend the day on the water. Put a whole new perspective on the situation, fly angling. I'm a dry-fly man, myself. You can keep your sinking nymphs and blast your emergers. Dry angling, in my view, is to fishing what free will is to any intelligent discussion of religion. The fun comes from the damned difficulty, you see?" He finished off his wine with a fierce gulp.

I nodded dumbly, wondering whether we were talking

about faith or fishing. It appeared useless to protest that I knew absolutely zilch about the art of fly-fishing. Saint Cecil slapped me on the shoulder hard enough to loosen a filling, barked something about wearing shoes I could get wet, and wandered away to harass a nice couple just up from the Berkshires who were thinking of opening an organic grocery store in the village.

We spent three days climbing in and out of the swift shallow currents of the Green River together, talking a little about religion and a lot about fly-fishing. Uncle Cecil was impressed I knew a little bit about the Gospels and even more pleased to have a complete fly novice to abuse on the water. The Green is a pretty, winding river in southeast Vermont, but not on a par with the state's justly famous trout streams like the Battenkill or Mad. Over three days I learned how to tie double blood knots and needle knots and how, in order to assure a good presentation of the fly, the leader must roll out "sweet as a Bach cantata" over the water. Fly-fishing was a study in natural deception, Saint Cecil said, pointing out that the world's first great fly angler had been a trout-crazy nun from a priory in Hertfordshire. Among other indispensable tidbits, I learned that Plutarch had strongly advocated using stallion hair in tied flies and that fishhooks had been found in the ancient River Euphrates. "Possibly belonged to old Adam himself. That's the location of the Garden of Eden, you know. Crack dry-fly angler."

As we stood calf-deep in the freezing stream (I was wearing gym shorts and leather boat shoes), he ran through his personal repertoire of fly casts—basic overhead cast (eleven o'clock to four), back and roll casts, false casts, the art of shooting line, double hauling—then stood back and glared with amused disgust as I repeatedly snarled my line and tied myself up in wind knots. "It won't work worth a damn to try to *bludgeon* the fish to death," he shouted helpfully at me from a distance. "Slow that rod down, sport. Nice and easy. Stroke the air. Know any poetry?"

Through gritted teeth I admitted that I knew a few lines of a few poems.

"Excellent. Pick a stanza and recite it aloud as you make your cast. That little trick may help. Nice and slow, less wrist, and let it go."

Self-conscious in the extreme, I recited a few lines from Frost's "Stopping by Woods on a Snowy Evening." *The woods are lovely, dark and deep,* I said, *But I have promises to keep* — I truly hated being called "sport" but the trick worked and I started to get the hang of it — *And miles to go before I sleep* — developing not quite a skill but something perhaps faintly resembling a skill — *And miles to go before I sleep.* I learned, too, about damsel nymphs and stone flies, great diving beetles and water boatmen, how to scour the water lines and "match the hatch," how to strip line, tie on more tippet, debarb my hook, pinch my line.

"Interesting poem," Saint Cecil thundered at me as we left the water. "Frost wrote those lines when he was in deep depression, contemplating suicide. What a miserable sod."

I guess I'd known this, I said. Or maybe not.

"You a Scotch man?"

I didn't care for Scotch but it seemed impolite to say no. He opened a pint of Highland malt and we sat on the bank for a while taking small nips of Scotch from Dixie cups he kept in his beaten-up willow creel.

"Which gospel is your favorite?"

I was startled by the bluntness of his question but probably shouldn't have been. I sputtered "Matthew," not really knowing Matthew but recalling that it was the only gospel I'd read completely from beginning to end. I'd read parts of the other Gospels but at that point in my life reading the Bible didn't rate high on my list.

"Matthew, eh? Bit florid for my tastes. Grossly embellished the whole business about the resurrection and virgin birth, you know. Mark was a much more reliable journalist. Leaves a bit to the imagination. That's the point of a good mystery story, you know—to keep you asking the right questions. People want easy answers, and that's the Almighty's wily joke on us—there *aren't* any. Salvation is a little like dry-fly fishing that way: You've got to do the work to catch the fish. Always thought it was clever of Christ to pick *fishermen* for his sidekicks. Natural-born storytellers. Hate to let *any* fish get away."

We talked further and I learned, among other things, that Uncle Cecil had been a navy cook at Okinawa during the war and had marched, against the advice of some of his colleagues, with civil rights groups in Memphis and Detroit in the sixties. A bit like the prophet Amos, he thought the church establishment was going to hell in a handbasket— more interested in building steeples than saving souls—and that Ronald Reagan and his "stooge" James Watt (then secretary of the interior) were criminal phonies who were destroying the environment and ruining America's best trout streams. Cecil said the sound of a clean-running trout stream was living poetry, a symphony in the wild—"Trout Music." And he had fished almost everywhere: for steelheads in the Boundary Waters and wild browns in Yorkshire, Scotland's Doon, and Henry's Fork in southeastern Idaho; chased salmon through the mouth of the Columbia. When I asked him his favorite place of all, he thought for an instant and replied, "Montana's good—the upper Yellowstone particularly, absolutely stunning country, though it's getting too damned crowded with well-dressed fishermen. The Snake's excellent, or used to be; haven't been there in a while. There's a canyon below the dam on the San Juan, though—that's in northern New Mexico, just as the river runs out of the Colorado Rockies. The trout are big as your arm and damned wise. All catch-and-release. Beautiful fish, gorgeous water. Edna and I were out there for a week a couple years back. She painted landscapes and I fished. A living cathedral. Real Trout Music."

I liked that. Trout Music.

We went back in the river and fished in silence. "Above all else," he mused a while later, pausing to snip a sodden fly off his line, "the thing you never want to do is outlive your beloved. Avoid that fate, son, if at all possible." His wife had been dead for two years. Just after he said this, Saint Cecil caught a nice brook trout large enough to keep, but wet his hands and released the fish back to the stream. I finally caught a trout, too, a small one, its pale pink gills pumping. He showed me how to remove the hook with forceps and cradle the fish in the water, facing the trout upstream so oxygen could quickly revive him.

On our last afternoon together, he brought me a small book called *A River Never Sleeps*, by Roderick Haig-Brown, told me to keep it a while and read it, then send it back to him in Alabama or he'd come hunt me down like a mangy yellow dog. He suggested that I read the Book of Mark, too, if I knew what was good for me; learn to ask the right question rather than seek the answer — with a little luck, one would lead to the other; and for God's sake keep my wrist out of the cast. I gave him back his loaner fly rod and we shook hands. The man could break your fingers.

I read his book and sent it back but I never saw Saint Cecil again. I bought the cheapest fly rod Orvis offered and fished the Green and other area rivers off and on for the next year. During that time I became very good at golf and fairly respectable at presenting my fly to *truite de mer*, though nowhere near in my teacher's class. I caught a few trout and let most of them go. I got a yellow pup to keep me company in streams and named him Amos, after the Old Testament prophet who thought the world was going to hell in a handbasket.

. . .

I finished this story as we bumped along a dirt road beside the Green River. The river hadn't changed much but I saw several new houses along the road where there'd been only forests and pastures fifteen years before.

"Where did Saint Cecil go?" Maggie wanted to know.

"Home to Alabama. That's where I sent his book, at any rate. I think he lived with his son. He died a couple years later. He was a pretty old guy. You'll meet people like him in your life, Mugs. People who come and go but have an influence on your thinking."

"Did you know Mommy?"

"Not then. It was just Amos and me. She came a bit later."

Dorothy's white farmhouse was still where I left it in a crook of the river across a grassy meadow. We pulled in and I knocked softly on the door, wondering if she could still possibly live there. A younger woman, looking somewhat flustered, opened the door, pulling back a strand of hair. I told her I'd once rented a house on the property and wondered if my daughter and I might camp for the night in her meadow by the river.

She studied me for a moment, biting her lip, glancing over my shoulder at the girl and dog in the truck.

"I guess that would be all right," she said. "Please don't have an open fire, though. It's been rather dry lately."

I thanked her and assured her we wouldn't have a fire. We drove down and found a good flat spot by some alder bushes, a gap through which led to the water. It was growing dark rapidly now but I still hoped we might fish a bit. Maggie carried her fly rod and walked Amos down to the river while I put up the small Bean tent and started making ham and cheese sandwiches from the cooler, on Old Blue's tailgate, thinking how strange it was to be back here with my daughter and the pup who'd now grown old, in the place I once ran away to, my own private little Walden.

Thoreau said life is simply one great circle sailing so perhaps it made sense that I'd come here again, to find the right
question if not the answer.

The summer I came here had been full of dark questions
and the irony of Saint Cecil's gentle injunction to avoid
outliving my beloved had seemed to strike painfully close to
the source of my trouble.

At age twenty, my childhood sweetheart, Kristen, was
murdered by a nervous sixteen-year-old in a botched robbery attempt of a fine restaurant, one of those sudden, incal-
culably tragic events that never should have happened, a
random act so violent and pointless it sends sane people
spinning and makes pundits wonder what the hell's going
on in America.

I'd loved Kristen and felt certain we would spend our
lives together and simply could not imagine her dying and
was not prepared to face a world without her. Thinking to
stall that moment of truth, I tried graduate school and then
quit. I considered going to seminary but decided I was furi-
ous with God. I took a job at the newspaper where I'd been
the wireboy the night Richard Nixon resigned, and six
months into the job abruptly quit and took off for Europe
with my golf bag and favorite books of poetry in tow,
searching for God knows what. I applied for a job at the
Herald Tribune, hoping I might get sent to cover a war the
way Ernest Hemingway had. War had been good for Hemingway. He'd been wounded and fell in love with a Red
Cross nurse named Agnes and found enough good stories to
write about for a lifetime. I loved Hemingway's writing
then—had since I was a boy when my father introduced me
to Nick Adams. But nobody was hiring greenhorn reporters
that year in Paris and the war in Southeast Asia was over so
I went home to work at my hometown paper again.

Not long afterward, a job offer came from Atlanta and I
moved there and began writing stories for the nation's oldest Sunday magazine about political reformers and unsolved

murders. An epidemic of homicides was raging in the city that proclaimed it was "too busy to hate," and I spent almost six years following politicians and homicide suspects around, hanging out with beat cops and bartenders, interviewing grief-stunned families and watching autopsies being performed. An autopsy on my own psyche might have proved useful, for this work was like nothing I'd ever done before and it drew me with an almost illicit pleasure. I'd finally found my private war, created a moveable feast of death and violence. I wrote scores of these stories and even won a couple awards for them. I lost myself in their unanswerable questions, their inexplicable tragedies, and never took a day's vacation in nearly six years of work.

One afternoon I was interviewing yet another grieving family member, the mother of a nice girl named Sheila who'd apparently been in the wrong place at the wrong time. Her body would never be found. After the interview we were having coffee when Sheila's mother looked at me and remarked, not unkindly, "You're so young. How can you do this? Doesn't it bother you to ask people such terrible questions?" I remember how her mascara had smudged darkly below her eyes.

The scary thing was, it didn't. Her question did, though. It frightened me to the core to think this was who I'd become and this was all my life had to offer. One night I sat straight up in my bed, rigid with fear, convinced I was as far from God as you could get and only moments from my death. I didn't want to die like that and knew I needed help. Or out. Or something.

And so, with my father's blessing, I ran away to Vermont, leaving behind confused friends and splendid career prospects, unaware that I was still simply attempting to outrun these accumulated griefs. I told myself I planned to cool out, take a break, shed a skin, try and find a door I could walk through to a new kind of life. I remember wanting to go someplace I'd never been, thought of Montana and chose

Vermont instead, wanting to find a place that finally felt like *home*. The South was my birthplace but it didn't feel like *home*. There was too much sadness there.

My brother helped me move my furniture to the edge of the Green River. I remember how he looked at the river and said it reminded him of the Blue Ridge rivers we'd fished in and camped along as boys.

After Saint Cecil and my introduction to fly-angling, I spent that first winter in my tiny wood-heated cabin trying to housebreak a yellow pup and reading everything I should have read or had meant to read for years—most of the Bible and all of Steinbeck including his interpretation of the Arthurian legend based on Malory's Winchester manuscript, enough of Faulkner to know I truly hated him, Hemingway for the umpteenth time, Emerson's essays, Plato's *Dialogues*, volumes of poetry and history, books on Eastern religion and Western philosophy, farmers' almanacs, manuals on growing roses and astronomy, Rilke's love poems, Darwin on golf, Campbell on myth.

I read clean through the Book of Mark in one sitting. I learned how to fly-fish and keep a woodstove running all night. I discovered the pleasure of splitting wood to keep warm and rediscovered the joys of golf. I took my dog to nuclear freeze meetings for fun, and ate more zucchini bread and bean sprouts than I care to try and remember. *Things change. Worlds come and go.* I realized I wasn't dying after all and maybe God would somehow find me. What a fine thing to discover.

I walked down to the river to see if my daughter was having any luck with the local trout population. I came through the alders just as she was making a fine back cast, her line and tippet making a lazy beautiful S-shaped movement through the air. She was standing barefoot in the water, mid-calf. The fly landed in some riffles and the current swept it gently

along. I had no idea if fly-fishing was just a momentary
fascination for her or something she would do with great
passion till she became Saint Muggins. It didn't really matter. For the next six weeks, she was mine.

"Nice cast. Van would be pleased. Any trout in this
river?"

Van was the Bean instructor who looked like a poster boy
for the rugged outdoors. He'd helped her learn to tie flies
and told her she had a creative talent for it. Her woolybugger came out looking like the Liberace of dry flies, spangled
with all sorts of bright pieces of yarn. It was clear Maggie
had a crush on Van as hefty as the Bean Christmas catalog.

"I think one almost . . ." She was watching the fly drift
in the current, then she looked at me and said, "I think they
must be sleeping or something."

"It is kind of late. C'mon. I've got dinner ready. Ham and
cheese. Straight from the Official Approved Foods List."

"*Dad.*"

Maggie hated it when I made jokes about her having only
seven foods on her official list, though it was pretty much
true. We walked back to camp and I lit a Coleman lantern
and opened a can of Senior Alpo for Amos and fed him two
aspirin wrapped in a piece of cheese. He was a finicky eater,
too, and had only five or six items on his Official Approved
Foods List. One of my unstated goals in life was to eat my
way around the world, never eating the same dish twice,
and the thought of all those local hometown diners preparing to feed us across the heartland gladdened my heart.

Later, a bobbing light appeared in the meadow. The
woman from the farmhouse came down to tell us we were
free to use her well. She brought us pieces of rhubarb pie,
too. The pie was tart and still warm.

By then Maggie was already wearing her sleep shirt and
had been reading *Stuart Little* by flashlight in the tent, her
first "chapter book," as she called it. The woman, whose

plain face looked long and somewhat haggard in the lantern
light, asked Maggie how old she was.

"Seven and a half," Maggie answered, then asked, "Did
you know my father when he lived around here?"

The woman looked at me and smiled. "No, I just moved
up here two years ago after my divorce."

I explained it had been more like fifteen years since I'd
lived in the neighborhood and glanced at my daughter to
see how the woman's remark had set. I half expected Maggie to blurt out that her father was getting divorced, too, but
she didn't; perhaps it was still too new to have any reality. If
so, I shared that feeling with her, part of me still refusing to
accept it would happen. Instead, she simply made a polite
but hollow pantomime of eating her pie in silence — rhubarb
clearly wasn't on the OAFL. I asked the woman if she'd
known Dorothy, my former landlady, and she said she
hadn't because a real estate agent in Brattleboro had had
the house when she bought it. The house had been empty a
while. She apologized needlessly, and then asked if we were
headed to a vacation spot somewhere in Vermont.

"No," I heard myself say. "We're fishing our way out to
Old Faithful." It was the first time I'd stated our destination
this way and seemed like a manifesto of some sort. "We're
going out West to roam around a bit, see some of the country. Try and catch some fish."

"How wonderful," she said, and explained that her parents had taken her by car out to see Yellowstone Park when
she was five. Thinking about it almost brought tears to her
eyes these many years later, she admitted. I asked her why
she thought that might be.

She shifted onto her other foot. "Oh, I don't know.
Maybe it was because that was the only big trip we ever
took as a family. That made it somehow all the more special.
You grow up so fast."

You can only ask a kind stranger so much. We shook

hands and I thanked her for the pie and for letting us camp in her meadow—then remembered to ask her name. Her name was Becky. I watched Becky walk slowly back to her farmhouse on a narrow path through the tall meadow grasses, following the swaying beam of her small flashlight. Maggie crawled into the tent and I kissed her good night. She was a quick sleeper. Her light went out.

The night was warm and still, with low clouds hiding the stars. On the Indian calendar it was the month of the Blood Moon, a time of cleansing and renewal. I didn't feel like turning in so I tuned Old Blue's radio to a local classical station that was offering Respighi's ancient airs and dances and snooped around in the truck, pretending I needed to try and organize stuff that was already organized. It suddenly struck me as foolish how much equipment I'd dragged along, the classic overpacking job, probably far more stuff than we could ever hope to need or even want.

Besides our sleeping bags and two large duffel bags filled with our clothes, I'd brought along a pair of L. L. Bean tents (one large, one small), a large Coleman cookstove, a medium-sized rain tarp, one large plastic ground cloth, two lanterns, four flashlights, one deluxe emergency road kit, two Katahdin folding cots, a large Red Cross regulation first aid kit, two camp stools, five road atlases and several folding Michelin maps, one full-sized air mattress, three large Tupperware boxes filled with various canned goods and dry foodstuffs, another smaller Tupperware box containing cooking utensils, matches, candles, etc., a deluxe Bean cooking set, one small Coleman cooler, two complete sets of rain gear, four fishing rods (two spinning, two fly), three tackle boxes, two vests, one set of hip waders, four pairs of boots (two pairs each of men's 11 and children's 2), one folding Buck knife, one new Hudson Bay ax, one bottle of Famous Grouse Scotch whiskey, and one large canvas tote bag filled with far too many books. My version of Opti's famous Medicine Bag.

Maggie had brought her own Medicine Bag, a slightly smaller canvas tote bag filled with her essential stuff. I decided to snoop and found a Pocahontas journal, a box of colored pencils, various colored hair scrunchies, a child's travel guide to America with activity pad, three Barbies, three sets of extra Barbie clothes, a plastic Magic Eightball, several chapter books and various cassettes and CDs, and one small pink stuffed bear named Susie who'd been everywhere a bear can go in seven and one half years of life.

It was a little embarrassing, all this *stuff* we'd brought. But it seemed to say there's no going back now.

The ancient airs ended and the late news came on and I sat in Old Blue listening to a report from the Long Island coast, where a TWA jumbo jet had mysteriously exploded just after taking off from Kennedy Airport a few days before our departure, killing all 230 people aboard. Recovery crews were combing the ocean waters, searching for bodies and what one official euphemistically called a "eureka piece," some shred of telling physical evidence that would either confirm a terrorist bomb or describe a catastrophic event. I could just picture the reporters doing their jobs. Meanwhile, grieving family members had gathered on the beach and were holding an ongoing prayer vigil.

I opened the Scotch and poured myself some in a paper cup, trying to imagine the unimaginable desolation the surviving parents and children and loved ones must feel, would forever feel, lives jerked inside out by the gods. I'd been there myself. A young designer bound for Paris to search for antiques had died, as had a mother flying home to France to reunite with her children, a couple celebrating their fifth wedding anniversary, a Country Music Hall of Fame guitarist, a Connecticut man taking his girl to Paris to propose, twelve kids from the same high school French club . . .

The page turned, the news rambled on. Charles and Diana had announced that their divorce agreement was finalized and the "Marriage of the Century" was officially toast. The Atlanta Olympics had opened with a gala that was more modern Broadway than ancient Greece. The pope was kicking back at a chalet in the Dolomites. America was suffering from a precipitous decline in honeybees. A man in St. Paul had been arrested for keeping his two children attached to electronic dog collars and giving them powerful jolts whenever they misbehaved. I turned off the news, the news junkie in me sufficiently sated for the moment, and sat in the silence and heard, after a few seconds, the sound of the river running through the darkness.

Trout Music.

Sorrow is holy ground, Oscar Wilde wrote in *De Profundis*, a memoir I read the summer I fled to Vermont, a story Wilde could write only after he'd lost everything he thought he valued—money, grand possessions, literary fame—and found, waiting for him at rock bottom, an unexpectedly close relationship with his Maker, perhaps even salvation. I wondered if those people clustering on the beach in Long Island would ever really come to believe that such a thing was possible, that faith could be deepened by unthinkable tragedy. Did I? It seemed we inhabited an age of unthinkables—planes falling from the sky, vanishing children, warming oceans and killer microbes and a record number of marriages failing for seemingly the thinnest of excuses. Biblical fundamentalists saw this as hard evidence that the center wasn't holding and that a tribulation of some sort was now at hand. Polls showed that more Americans were beset by anxiety about the future than at any other time in the nation's history, but a theory of newspapering held that people couldn't get enough of somebody else's bad news simply because it made their own humdrum lives feel better.

Who could say what was really going on—the usual millennial jitters or one last big giddy waltz on the orchestra deck before the ship rolled and slipped under? Lacking any talent for prophecy, I told myself that luckily, for the moment at least, I had other fish to fry and opened a road atlas and looked at New York State to see if I could find a place we could go next. Someplace a bit wilder, remoter, a bit farther from the news and ourselves. *You don't take a trip,* Steinbeck wrote in *Travels with Charley. A trip takes you.* So take us, Father, I think I prayed, to whatever spirit was floating out there in the cosmos and perhaps eavesdropping tonight. It was good to be gone. But Yellowstone still felt as distant as the Dog Star.

"Dad?" a small sleepy voice came out in the darkness.

"Yeah, babe?"

"I need Susie."

"Right. I'll bring her."

I picked up Susie Bear and carried her into the tent, where I found Maggie more awake than I'd expected.

"Are you coming to bed soon?"

"Soon. I'm just arranging a few things in the truck."

"I'm glad you told me that story about Saint Cecil," she said, "because now I know where Amos came from."

"I'm glad. I'll tell you something else, Mugs. That's not all I found here. In a sense you and your brother came from here, too."

"Really?"

"Yep. I met your mother right after I got Amos. We fell in love and a year later got married. Three years after that you came along. Then your brother. Talk about a miracle. That's how it happens sometimes. The best things come when you least expect them."

"Neat," she said in a voice growing fainter, already halfway to Nod. "Tell me . . . some more . . ."

"Okay," I said, but added nothing more; then her even breathing told me she was asleep. That was enough of that particular tale for now, and someday, when it was time, she would learn the rest. *When you really want love,* Wilde wrote, *you will find it waiting.* Coming here, I sat with her thinking, was an intelligent move. Then and now.

Back then it had saved my life and ended my grudge with God, possibly begun my slow rekindling of faith. Perhaps, in a sense Saint Cecil would have fully understood, I was born again. This time it gave us a place to begin and even if I still had no answers for why good or bad things happened in my life or anybody else's, perhaps tomorrow I'd finally catch a decent trout.

I moved and she spoke again, as if reading my thoughts from the shoals of sleep.

"Can we . . . um . . . fish in the morning?"

"Absolutely. I'll have your fly rod ready to go at dawn. I was also just looking at the map and thinking we might drive on to a place in the Adirondacks tomorrow. It's called Indian Lake. Maybe we'll catch our dinner and I'll tell you a real Indian story."

"Mmmm." Finally, gone.

I went back to Old Blue to close up the tailgate, heard a rustling, and saw Amos coming slowly through the alders. He walked straight up to me and bumped his sopping muzzle into my pants—a familiar old trick of his, wiping his mouth on me after a long drink. He'd taken himself down to the river where he'd been a pup for a cool evening drink, proving that the Greek philosopher Heraclitus was probably wrong when he said you can never step in the same river twice.

CHAPTER THREE

....

Norumbega Girl

IT RAINED SOFTLY as we put up the big Bean tent beside Indian Lake, and then the sun suddenly came out from hiding, spreading the remains of a late summer afternoon on the water. A singing redbird flitted past, searching for his choir. An elderly couple was setting out beach chairs by their fire ring in the campsite next to us. The old man kept blowing his nose and swearing. I suggested to Maggie that we launch the canoe and go fish for our supper.

"Dad," she asked as we carried our rods and vests down the steep embankment to the shore, "why is it boys act strange?"

"That's one of the great questions of the ages, Mugs. But are we speaking in particular of one Nathan G. Toothacher?"

"Well, kinda. How'd you know?"

"Just a guess, my love."

We'd been talking about Nathan G. Toothacher most of the afternoon, on the drive across the Vermont border into eastern New York, past the water parks and faded tourist haunts of Lake George, which Thomas Jefferson once hailed as the Queen of American lakes but now probably wouldn't recognize, up New York Route 28 into the heart of the Adirondacks.

Nathan G. Toothacher was a year ahead of Maggie at Woodside Elementary School and the wavy blond star of the town's thriving, if somewhat competitively cutthroat, youth soccer league.

"He stares at me a lot but when I speak to him he never says anything. He just looks kinda weird. Like he has to throw up or something."

"Ah."

The most revealing male symptom of all—the classic throw-up look. Nathan G. Toothacher was clearly in love and sick as a pup. For all that, he seemed like a decent enough little kid and it was probably a shame I was going to have to break both his legs and burn his family's wattle hut to the ground. But a Viking father does what he must to protect his firstborn child.

"Has he ever spoken to you at all?"

"Yeah, but it doesn't count. He told me to shut up once. I wasn't even talking to *him*."

"Well, darling, that's no good. Boys who tell you to shut up can grow up to become bigger jerks. He's probably too short for you anyway."

"But I kind of like him. Sometimes."

"I guessed as much. Now, pay attention. I want to go over a few basics of good canoemanship."

I launched the canoe out into the lily pads and then began a neat little orientation speech I used to make to the tender-foot scouts when I was Sporty Haislip's assistant canoe counselor at good old Camp Wenasa. I talked briefly about how a canoe moved and turned in the water, ran through the basic stroke techniques, and told her the cardinal rule of riding in a canoe: *Never stand up.* Maggie was seated on the rush seat in the bow. I noticed two boys about her age spin-casting across the cove. They noticed us and Maggie noticed them. According to a friend of mine who was tortured at a young age by nuns, the Catholic Church believes seven is about the age when a child begins to notice the world and gains the ability to reason. I reasoned it would be only a short amount of time before the boys on the opposite shore and the likes of Nathan Toothacher Esq. commanded far more of my daughter's attention than I did, so I'd better get my nice speeches about good canoemanship and other essentials of life in now, while I still had a captive audience.

"Can we take Amos?" She was interrupting an explanation of feathering the paddle which would have done Sporty Haislip proud.

"Well, uh, I suppose so." I paddled the canoe back toward the shore and motioned for him to come down and join us. The canoe was a wide Discovery model with special stabilizer beams. Amos was reclining like a Victorian poet on the top of the bank, watching us with either vague amusement or drowsy boredom. I motioned again for him to come and he reluctantly got up. Having ridden in a New Hampshire float plane and various Manhattan cabs, I reasoned, he could certainly handle a little spin around the lake in a great big canoe, especially with an experienced canoe hand like me in charge. But he picked his way down the slope like a nag being led to the slaughterhouse. I got out of the canoe to lift him up because his arthritic back legs made jumping into the craft impossible. I spread my arms around his legs and hoisted him up as you would lift a sheep. He growled at me, obviously embarrassed, legs trembling.

"Oh, shut up, you big sissy. You're a water dog, remember?"

"Dad," Maggie said, "you're hurting his feelings."

"Well, he's hurting my back."

I placed Amos in the center of the canoe beside the cooler, fly rods, and life jackets and ordered him to sit down. He looked at me as if I must be out of my mind but I pointed sternly to the floor and repeated the command. He gave another growl of protest and reluctantly sat down. I pushed off from the shore, took a seat, and we glided serenely for a moment back into the lily pads.

"Put on your life jacket," I ordered the crew.

"You should, too."

"I will. I just want to get us out into the main channel first." The boys across the cove, I noticed, had stopped reeling their lines and were watching us paddle out. A nice-looking blonde woman had joined them, perhaps their mother come to fetch them for supper, or maybe one of them had a gorgeous fortysomething girlfriend. Placing her hands on her hips, she stood there watching us, too.

The canoe began to wobble a bit as I clumsily reversed stroke to try and turn it around. Unfortunately, my paddle snagged in the lily pads and the bow drifted back toward the shore in the light current. Amos took this positive development as an indication that the idiotic boat ride was over. He abruptly stood up and prepared to leap for terra firma, and I stood up to make him sit back down.

What happened next, I fear, would have deeply aggrieved Sporty Haislip. The canoe rocked wildly as my old dog made a violent lurch toward land. He landed with only the smallest splash and lumbered safely up the bank. I stood momentarily pinwheeling my arms in a highly unsophisticated canoeing maneuver I feel certain you won't find in any manual on the sport. Then I fell backward into the water.

When I resurfaced, still wearing my hat, Maggie was clutching the side of the canoe, red-faced, uncertain whether to be terrified or burst out laughing. The boys on the opposite bank, however, had no such doubts. They were howling like town drunks. The attractive woman was laughing, too. Even the elderly couple from the next campsite briefly abandoned their beach chairs to come peek over the bank and see what all the commotion was about. The old woman put her hands to her mouth to suppress a giggle. The old man blew his nose, turned around, and left, obviously disgusted.

"Dad, that was *great,*" Maggie said, deciding it was okay to laugh. "I can see why you're not supposed to stand up in a canoe."

"Good," I said, slogging to the shore, glaring up at my triumphant dog on the bank. "And let that be a good lesson to you both."

Once upon a time in America, the central Adirondacks were a fly angler's paradise, the natural home of the eastern brook trout. Two dozen rivers drained in all directions from a pristine wilderness sitting astride the Precambrian remains of the oldest mountain range on earth, flowing either toward the St. Lawrence or the Hudson-Mohawk river system.

The first men to cast flies there were probably British army officers stationed on the Mohawk who learned the gentleman's sport of fly-fishing back home in Izaak Walton's England and began pushing to the region's wild interior in the mid-1700s. Roughly 125 miles wide and 160 miles from north to south, forbiddingly cold in the winter and difficult and dangerous to traverse in summer, the Adirondacks, originally devoid of year-round inhabitants and unexplored by white men until after the Civil War, were sometimes indicated on a map by a large blank spot.

Fur trappers were first to penetrate the wilderness for economic purposes, followed by lumbermen looking for hemlock and tanners who found an abundance of tannic acid in the coffee-colored lakes and pools of the region. Those same pools were home to plentiful brook trout, and upon the arrival of railroads the newly opened paradise was within easy striking range of Manhattan anglers, who'd pretty well depleted fish stocks in the Catskills. They came north in droves, staying for weeks at a time at scores of rustic hotels and lodges that sprung up in the 1870s. According to trout historian Nick Karas, by 1875 no fewer than two hundred such establishments were catering to a new species of tourist clientele—the traveling angler. Due to the tannic waters, Adirondack trout were no monsters, rarely growing larger than five pounds in size, but they were so plentiful and full of fight that magazines and journals began to extol the virtues of the northern brookie.

"By the 1880s," Karas writes, "the Adirondack wilderness was a thing of the past. The mountains, lakes, and rivers had been badly abused by loggers, miners, railroads, tanneries, and water-oriented industries. The latter at first demanded canal water and later hydroelectric water. Tourism and hotel building on an unprecedented scale also took their toll on the pristine aspect of the area."

Ironically, as Karas notes, it may have been the endangered speckled beauties themselves who ultimately saved the wilderness from extinction, as fishermen first raised the public alarm to rescue what was left of this special ecosystem. Sportsmen, hikers, birders, campers, naturalists, and even artists like Winslow Homer and Frederic Remington, eventually joined the popular chorus to save the "North Woods" and before long politicians began to see the political wisdom of hopping on board the idea of a legal preserve. One early champion of the cause was Governor Theodore Roosevelt, who'd fished and hunted the Adirondacks as a young man. In an effort to bring back depleted trout stocks, Adirondack rivers and streams were stocked with more prolific-breeding rainbow trout and black bass species—to the detriment of brookies. In 1894, an area containing roughly 5,300,000 acres, still the largest such reserve in the lower forty-eight, was set aside in perpetuity by the New York legislature and named the Adirondack Forest Preserve.

We paddled down the southern shore of Indian Lake for a while, passing what seemed to be miles of tent campers, then hung a left and disappeared behind a promising hemlock-topped rock island, whereupon we found a group of people frolicking in the buff.

I smiled politely as we tooled by the nudists, who much prefer to be called naturists, but are naked people any way you care to look at them, which I tried not to do, particularly the lady with the mammoth physique wearing only a big friendly smile and water-stained Mets cap.

"Hi!" she chirped at us. "Great weather at last, huh?"

"Very nice indeed." The weather, I meant to add.

A skinny naked guy fiddling with a camera on the shore lifted his hand to wave, and several other unclothed people smiled sweetly at us as we glided past. I thought about apologizing for intruding on their private Kodak moment but decided to just keep paddling for dear life. The second we got safely around a corner of the island, Maggie jerked her head toward me, blushing and grinning.

"Dad, did you *see* those people? They were all *naked!*"

"Really? I guess I failed to notice. Actually, darling girl, I think the proper polite description is *buck nekid*."

"Dad!"

"Okay, okay. I saw the Mets fan was missing her top. What's the big deal? You and the Rocket trot around naked half the time and I'm pretty sure the Mohawk Indians who used to live here probably swam without encumbrance of loincloths most of the time. They weren't the least bit modest about their bodies. Good thing we left old Amos back at camp, though. He's such a prude."

"What's a prude?"

I explained that a prude was somebody who lived in the eternal hope of being offended by somebody else's idea of freedom. The irony, of course, was that the worlds of art, literature, and religion were full of naked people. Half the public squares in Europe had naked people frolicking in their fountains and much of the artwork of the Renaissance, including religiously themed masterpieces, used depictions of unclothed men and women to convey a sense of their human vulnerability and intimacy with God. I explained to her that in ancient times there was a widespread belief that nakedness enhanced the power of a woman and reduced the power of a man, which perhaps explained why the magic of men was said to dwell in their garments—the vestments of war they put on, the armor of battle and badged uniforms that signified their position and rank in society, and so forth.

"Cool," she said, looking back to see if the naturists were still in view.

I *almost* explained to her that the Roman Catholic Church eventually condemned any ceremonial rite involving nudity as a pagan rite because a medieval priest named Saint Jerome took the hard line that women should be ashamed of their bodies and cover them up lest they distract saintly men from pure thoughts and good work habits, effectively rendering women second-class citizens of the church and their bodies the objects of self-loathing for the next five centuries—something every modern shrink treating an epidemic of bulimic Kate Moss wanna-bes undoubtedly already knew. But again, this was one of those complex discussions perhaps best saved for a later date and her mother's thoughtful insights. As I had this thought, it suddenly struck me how much more complicated such discussions would be in the near future—one family spread across two households, with a wilderness in between where words, explanations, and insights could easily get lost, poorly translated, or simply misunderstood.

Happily, Maggie herself changed the subject and asked about the Indians who'd lived on Indian Lake, and I knew a bit about them. The fierce Hurons who inhabited the northern fringes of the wilderness had found the interior so inhospitable they were literally forced to eat bark off trees one winter in order to survive—hence the park's name.

Adirondack meant "bark eaters" in the native language of the competing Mohawks, their neighbors to the south. The Mohawks, I explained, were part of something called the Iroquois Confederacy, six tribes which peacefully came together in the 1770s in what was called the Great Peace to establish property boundaries, laws governing disputes, and codes of living; they even practiced a rudimentary form of voting democracy—the Western world's first example, many believed—which Thomas Jefferson, among others, studied before setting pen to parchment and creating the Declaration of Independence.

"Did they believe in God?"

"Of course they believed in God," I said. "Don't you remember when I read you *The Soul of an Indian* about the Great Mystery and Watan Tonka and the Circle of Life?"

"You didn't read us that," she pointed out, delicately dipping her paddle in the dark brown water, and I realized she was correct. Just as I'd started to read about that to her and Jack by the fire at Acadia, the circus had arrived at the campground.

"You're right. How about if we read it later by the fire?"

"Sure. Can we have marshmallows later, too?"

"Of course. We'll invite the naked people over, if you want."

"*Dad.*"

We found a good spot to fish, tucked in a narrow cove where the sunlight was slanting through low-hanging boughs of tall evergreen trees, stately as a chapel, a setting straight from Longfellow's *Evangeline*. We pulled the canoe up on rocks and got out. I pulled on my hip waders and Maggie sat on a rock tying a floating nymph to her leader tippet. She was good at making Duncan knots, much better than her old man the Eagle Scout, and soon had her gear ready to go. The rod she was using was a Bean Guide Series six-weight graphite with a British-made Silver Guide fly reel equipped with a click drag and right-hand retrieve, good for making short, tight casts as well as longer casts up to forty yards. It was easy to handle and had good smooth action. She got up and stepped lightly over the large, water-polished rocks, studying the surface lines for hatching bugs as she'd been taught to do. Down the shore a bit, she paused and nimbly leapt a few yards out to a large smooth rock and began making easy fly casts, finally dropping her line nicely on the water.

Watching her, I thought, not for the first time, how effortless and natural her ability appeared, a gift perhaps, unlike my own, which was a slow-learned process of self-conscious wrist flicks and elbow bends punctuated by the occasional, but rare, unexpected throw of brilliance. Plato advanced the interesting idea that we all know our destinies and possess certain skills before birth and that helpful "spirit" guides called daimones are present to usher us sympathetically along the cosmic birthing canal, sometimes even permitting us to select the people who will become our parents. Several Indian creation myths speak of this same idea, noting that we are closer to the Great Spirit at the moment of our births than at any other time during our lives—and simply forget, as we age, where we really came from. We come trailing clouds of glory, as Wordsworth chose to describe it in "Intimations of Immortality," and the rest is but a sleep and a forgetting.

Whenever I looked at Maggie I saw a yellowing photograph of my mother, whom she resembled at her identical age to an almost eerie extent—even down to the dramatic gestures, the occasional flaring sulks, and the way she wore her fine light brown hair pulled back just so. It was probably far too soon to know what if any elements of her mother and me would manifest in her approach to the world—elements that were perhaps the reason, *Père* Plato might have said, she and her daimones had opted to choose us as earthly guardians in the first place—but she clearly possessed her grandmother's physical beauty, deep sympathy for others, and lush-spiritedness. I saw powerful traces of her maternal grandfather Sam Bennie, the Scottish fly angler, beginning to emerge as well. It was more than the natural fly-casting gene that had even been apparent to the instructors at Bean; she had the restless curiosity of a traveler and the refiner's fire of a truth-seeker. If you asked her, she would inform you without the slightest hesitation that she intended to be a film actress *and* a scientist. Madame Curie meets Meryl Streep.

When Maggie was still in her mother's womb, Sam, a renowned expert in the field of electromagnetics, had while traveling the world for ITT begun collecting stuffed animals from every place he visited—some new but most old and dusty—and nicknamed this ragtag collection of worldly castoffs the Stardust Fan Club. It was strangely sentimental behavior for a self-professed agnostic and man of science. Maggie was Stardust and the only one of his eight grandchildren Sam ever got to hold because he died of throat cancer fourteen months after her birth. Something had clearly passed between them, though, I'm convinced, something only the two of them knew about. I once caught him showing her a photograph of a trout.

I went into the water, wading in nearly to my waist before making my first cast. I was using a four-weight Scott rod with a Hardy Brothers reel that belonged to my oldest friend, Pat McDaid. It was nine feet long but light and had splendid action and more than a little sentimental value. Pat bought the rod when he was poor—it was sheer extravagance, he said. As success came, he'd accumulated more expensive rods but always came back to his first fly rod, and I was honored that he'd offered to lend it to me, saying it was a regular trout harvester.

The water was the color of just-steeped tea. I could feel its coldness compressing the neoprene waders against my bare legs. The air was warm and calm, the surface of Indian Lake mirror-still. Small clouds of pale-winged bugs skittered over the surface. I made a clumsy first cast, dropping my Hare's Ear nymph on the surface just a few yards ahead of me. I stripped several feet of line from the reel and flicked my wrist and the rod lifted to one o'clock. *The woods are lovely, dark and deep. . . .* I flicked it and the line arced forward and sent the fly twenty yards farther into the cove. *But I have miles to go before I sleep.* That was better. Not a bad presentation, all things considered. Perhaps even Saint Cecil would have approved.

Fly casting in still water is sometimes disdained by purists because trout aren't nature's smartest fish, but neither are they the dumbest, and perhaps they're the most practical. In still water they carve out territories and follow familiar feeding routes, and the rule of thumb is if you can see them they can see you and you might as well plan on hamburger for supper.

This late in summer, the trout would be swimming low, feeding around the large boulders, the tops of which were visible five or six feet down. Practical anglers would have been using sinking nymphs, but this was a dry-fly expedition in search of a proper salvation, and though it would have been nice to catch our supper on a fly, it really wasn't mandatory. I had chicken breast marinating in white wine and cumin seed back at camp, guarded by Sirius the sleeping dog. Even so, as we'd had no luck on the Green earlier that morning, catching a trout or decent black bass would be a nice start to the expedition.

I flicked again and watched my fly settle. Maggie's line whisked softly through the air.

"Keep that rod tip low," I commented, my voice carrying easily across the cove.

I'd forgotten how relaxing fly angling could be. I'd quit doing it the year I met my wife—life happens, someone said, while you're waiting to go fishing. That was fine, but now, being brought back to something so peacemaking by my own daughter had a nice touch of cosmic irony and neat circularity I'm certain the electrician Sam Bennie would have appreciated. His favorite expression to me—which I always took as a kind of personal manifesto—was entirely true to his scientific nature, but tinged with the ambiguity of the spiritual empiricist: *Keep the faith, Jimmy. It'll all evolve.*

A kingfisher flew past and vanished in the hemlocks. The air smelled moist and piney from them, rearing up around the small cove. They made me think of the druids of Celtic mythology, ancient stories in which large trees were considered the wisest elders, the true giants of the earth. Disney appropriated this same myth in the recent film *Pocahontas*, by making the heroine's "grandmother" a willow, and Merlin the Magician of the Arthurian legends I so dearly loved as a boy used the deep forest as his classroom, often assuming the form of an oak tree himself. Oaks were the central figures of the ancient Druidic cults that swept across Europe before the fifth century and legend holds that St. Patrick himself was educated by a Druid. Some Scots to this day believe a feminine presence inhabits trees, perhaps a holdover from medieval times when virgin brides took to the forest to pray for decent husbands.

Maggie must have been having similar pagan thoughts because she suddenly commented, "This is really cool. Check out those trees, Dad."

She wondered if they were a thousand years old. I said they were probably less than a hundred because the forests around these lakes were the first to go when lumbermen pushed to the heart of the Adirondacks. At one time, though, I pointed out, before European colonists came to North America, a red squirrel could climb a hemlock here on the shore of Indian Lake and travel all the way to Minnesota before coming down again. I remembered reading this somewhere in a serious-minded book, though it may have been a complete load of romantic rubbish.

I told her about a Native American origin myth in which the world's first couple were trees; snakes freed their roots and when they toppled over people were permitted to crawl out and inhabit the earth at the Great Spirit's direction.

"That sounds like Adam and Eve."

"It does. Every group of people has its own stories, and if you examine them you'll find they are, for the most part, remarkably similar. We have the same yearnings and desires. Same hopes. Same fears and failures. That's why you should always respect somebody else's religious traditions. These stories are the same in every land because they are linked by the same human spirit."

Nice speech, Dad, I thought; now shut your cake hole and just fish. But then I heard my mouth open and begin yakking again. I told her a wise philosopher named Plato believed that the presence of God was manifest in groves of trees and that another man called Buddha, who founded a great Eastern religion, discovered enlightenment—truth, wisdom, awareness of sorrow—while sitting beneath one. The fruit of forbidden knowledge that got Adam and Eve into such hot water with their Maker came from a tree, and in the fairy tales she and her brother loved woods always held mysteries, divinities, sprites, and nymphs. Thieves were always hanged from the stoutest oaks in ancient times, and the Song of Songs records that Christ's face was fairer than the cedars of Lebanon. The legend of the dogwood tells how Christ perished upon, and ascended to Heaven from, a tree.

"Why did they cut down the trees here?"

"They thought it wouldn't harm things, I guess. They needed the lumber for houses. But some people took it too far."

I explained that in other places in the world, rain forests were still being systematically removed, possibly creating a worrisome process called global warming, which prompted her to interrupt me and explain she already knew about this subject. She gave me a vigorous impromptu site lecture on the critical need to preserve South American rain forests for their impact on global air quality and medicine and I just listened with great pleasure, thinking, again, that Sam Bennie, wherever he was, must have been pleased to see how Stardust was evolving.

"Cool," I said when she was finished.

"Do you know any more old stuff about trees?"

I smiled and admitted that pretty much was the extent of my tree lore. But I had once met a man in a Shropshire pub who had been arrested forty-three times for trespassing on construction sites where old forests were being systematically removed. He was one of Britain's most celebrated tree activists and nothing like the tree-hugging crackpot he'd been depicted as in the tabloids. He was a no-nonsense corporate accountant by trade and his argument was surprisingly practical, more geographical than spiritual: To say nothing of the incalculable loss of valuable topsoil that accompanied removal of ancient tree roots, if we cut down all the old trees our physical identity as a people, the necessary sense of who and where we are as a species, would be invalidated in the process.

"What's *that* mean?"

"Never cut down a tree unless you have to."

"You built our house of trees," she reminded me, as always able to spot the log in her neighbor's eye.

"True. I did." Ours was a post-and-beam house whose beams had come from a great Canadian hemlock forest. "But I built it on a hill in the center of a great woods and I've never removed a tree without planting something to replace it—at the very least a nice rosebush." I sometimes sat in my den and studied the thousands of knots and meadering rings of life in the beams overhead, wondering what wonders they'd witnessed. When my house creaked and groaned with the north wind, it almost seemed to speak.

"Dad."

"What?" My head was still in the trees.

"I caught one."

She had indeed; a small trout was flipping around at the end of her line. She reeled it in and we got it to the net. A pretty little trout with black spotting and iridescent lines below the gills. Unfortunately, I'd forgotten to debarb our hooks and had to use my artery forceps to remove the hook. The damage wasn't too severe, though. I passed the little fish from my wet hand to hers.

"Our first trout," I said, and almost made a joke about how much that little critter had cost to land. The wife of a trout-crazy buddy of mine named Bill once calculated that the salmon he brought home from his annual fishing trip out West cost $375 a pound. You could buy fifty pounds of salmon at the grocery store for that, Paige had pointed out. "True," Bill had calmly retorted, "but they weren't caught on a dry fly."

"Do you think he has a name in the fish world?"

"I don't know." Did fish name, or even know, their progeny? "We could give him one, if you like." I explained that her great-great-grandmother Emma taught her grandfather that Indians always named things as they saw them—people, animals, even places. They believed everything you saw had a spirit and a life force and deserved to be given a name, a transcendental view that crept through the side door of American theology via people like Henry Thoreau and Walt Whitman. Naming was important, I said, so let's name everything we see as we go. Captains named their ships, aviators their planes. I didn't see why we couldn't name this little fish, too.

We named him Ishy—short for Ishmael—and let him go, wished him a long life, then headed for the canoe.

"While we're at it," I said, "let's name our canoe, too. She's a sturdy craft. Even if some of us have had a problem staying in her."

"How about Norumbega?" Maggie suggested.

"How about Norumbega Girl?" I countered, hoping I wasn't *too* transparent.

A nice smile.

"Cinchy."

Amos was dozing on the bank above the cove where we'd left him, though as he lifted his head at our approach I had the distinct impression he'd been nosing around a bit, a fear that was immediately confirmed by the appearance of the old man from the adjacent campsite, who marched up as we made landfall and scolded me for leaving a dog untied and unattended in a state park.

"It's against the rules," he fumed. "You can get fined, you know. It's not my business but I don't want that dog around my property."

"I'm sorry if he bothered you," I said mildly, thinking how I must finally be maturing because part of me really wanted to tell him to stick his snout in a tree stump.

"Oh, he didn't bother us," the elderly woman said, suddenly appearing and smiling a little embarrassedly. She'd come over to hand her husband his vomit-green windbreaker. I heard rather loud accordion music playing from their camp radio and was reminded of the old saying that a true gentleman is somebody who can play the accordion, but doesn't. "He seems like a very friendly dog." She bent over and scratched Amos's head for a moment and her husband stalked back to their camp. The polka music stopped, the woman straightened up and said good night, and a few minutes later their red pickup truck sped away. I could imagine the sharp lecture he was giving her on the way to supper for undermining his civic duty to God, country, and the State of New York.

"What's for dinner?" Maggie asked.

"Something from the Approved Foods List," I assured her. "Green peas, applesauce, and Chicken Norumbega."

"What's Chicken Norumbega?" She sounded as if she thought it might be raw baby yak meat served on a bed of poison ivy greens.

"Grilled chicken breast with cumin."

"What's cumin?"

"An herb. The Indians believed it gave you the gift of second sight."

"What's second sight?"

"An ability to see through things to their hidden meaning. Lots of saints and mystics had it. So does the IRS. It's also very useful if you ever decide to go on *Jeopardy!*"

I built a fire and Maggie sat on a log to write in her Pocahontas journal, no doubt recording everything that had been said in the past couple hours, including the swimmers au naturel and my exchange with our bossy neighbor. She had her mother's extraordinary memory and talent for recall and, with all due respect to Professor Wordsworth, once told me she could actually remember the moment of her birth. When I questioned this, she sighed and said matter-of-factly: "Okay. Here's what happened. Mom handed me to you and you carried me into that little room where they weighed me on that little scale. It was, like, *really* cold." "Oh really? How did you know it was actually *me*?" "Because," she answered, as if I'd been born yesterday, "who *else* could you be?" I was forced to concede the point.

I watched her take her first bite of my exquisite Chicken Norumbega.

"Well?" I said, hovering like Pascal the chef.

She chewed and nodded, forced a taut little smile. "It's really good, Dad," she said, and then spit lightly. "Except mine's got some dirt on it."

"That's the cumin."

"Oh. Sorry."

At least she ate the applesauce and a few peas. Amos ate the remains of her Chicken Norumbega uncomplainingly and we finished with a nice warm cup of Swiss Miss by the fire as the first sprinkles of rain fell from the darkness. Out on the lake I'd seen mares' tails in the northwest sky, a sure sign back in Maine of approaching weather, and I knew from the radio earlier in the day that a series of large and violent rainstorms was sliding toward us from the Great Lakes. I feared we'd seen all of Indian Lake we were going to see this trip. My hope was to make a motel somewhere near Buffalo by the next evening, ride out the storm, and maybe leave early enough to go see Niagara Falls before slipping across into Canada and heading for Michigan. I'd never driven to the West and part of me couldn't wait to actually *be* there.

While I cleaned up the dishes, Maggie hooked Amos up to the lead and took him for a walk. The red pickup truck came back and the elderly couple disappeared into their camper, shutting the little door firmly. The old man bugled his impressive nose again and then it grew remarkably quiet save for the pleasing croak of bullfrogs. A frog's croak is essentially an amphibian equivalent of foreplay and an impressive barbershop chorus of lonely male frogs was searching for mates that night. Back home in Maine, on what's popularly called Big Night, which comes in the early spring, another buddy of mine named Earl and others like him loved to don waders and slog into marshlands with flashlights, looking for giant singing frogs. Down South where I came from, people loved to "gig" frogs and eat them fried in butter, but Earl, an unromantic lobsterman by trade, only loved to search for them, find them in their habitat, and briefly revel in their deafening love song, an act of mobile poetry that connected him in ways he couldn't have imagined with the ancient Egyptians. The Egyptians considered bullfrogs sacred symbols of fertility, a symbol of the fetus, associated with the goddess Hecate, Queen of Heavenly Midwives, and the song of the frog in ancient times meant something was about to be resurrected. It was a great wake-up call.

Dog and girl returned. Girl yawned, dog sprawled by the fire. I'd planned to read some of Ohiyesa's writings to her from the Medicine Bag—what better setting than Indian Lake?—but the fatigue of the day had caught up to us all again. So we toasted a few marshmallows, I fed Amos his evening aspirin wrapped in a piece of cheese, and we watched the fire sputter down.

"Dad, did you know Aunt Emma?"

No, I said. She died half a century before I was born. My father had been around fourteen.

"How did she die?"

I said she possibly died in the great influenza epidemic that claimed twenty million lives in the 1920s. There's one way life had changed, I said. People rarely died from the flu these days.

"Did she have a husband?"

I said of course—Uncle Jimmy. His picture hung in the entrance foyer of our house, remember? The old dapper gent in the blue suit shiny with age, with the carnation flower in his lapel and bowler on his head. The photo was taken when he was a very old man, shortly before his death.

She nodded. "Do you think he loved her a lot?"

I said I was certain he did. They were pioneer people. There were no airplanes, no TVs, no electricity when they were children. Love took a different shape, too. After she died, he never finished building his house. He lived in the old homeplace till it came down around him. The story was, he had an old bull who kept him company and occasionally attempted to gore him. Uncle Jimmy died before the bull.

I poked the fire with a stick, wondering if my nose was growing.

I had no doubt Jimmy had loved Emma and spent years grieving for her. Recently, though, my second cousin Roger, the family's de facto historian, a retired missionary, had told me something utterly astonishing. Aunt Emma Dodson had committed suicide by hanging herself from the rafters of the house Jimmy was expanding, undoubtedly the reason he never finished the place. I'd asked Roger if he had any clue why she'd done it and he merely looked at me and shrugged. Suicide was extremely uncommon among Christian settlers but Emma had come from the Indian world before she became a Methodist—perhaps that duality accounted for whatever demons possessed her. Her grandsons had adored her and she'd always seemed content and happy. The suicide, at any rate, became the family's darkest secret for generations—yet another tale to be told somewhere further down the road.

"Dad," said Norumbega Girl as I tucked her and her pal Susie Bear into her sleeping bag, "you really shouldn't feel bad about your cooking."

"I don't. You do."

"Well, at least Amos liked it."

Something else seemed to be on her mind. I asked what it was.

"Well. I was kinda wondering. What do you think happened to the bull?"

"Hard to say." It probably wouldn't have made her feel any better to say somebody probably turned him into a nice freezerful of steaks. "I'll bet he missed Uncle Jimmy, though."

She nodded. There was something else hanging fire. So I asked what that was, too.

"Could we, like, call Jack and Mommy?"

A few moments later, I used the cell phone in Old Blue to connect us with the hotel room of my wife and son on Nantucket. They'd just returned to their room from dinner. The stars were out on Nantucket; they'd gone for a ride on a bicycle built for two, walked the beach collecting shells, and made friends with some nice people and their two children at supper. I eavesdropped as Maggie happily revealed to her brother that I'd fallen out of the canoe and she'd caught the trip's first trout, a fish named Ishy. I was sure she'd mention the naked people but she didn't.

Was this indeed the new world awaiting us? If so, it didn't feel quite as bad as I'd imagined it would, though being lost in the Adirondacks probably helped.

CHAPTER FOUR

....

Maid of the Mist

WE TRIED OUR luck in Indian Lake once more in the morning and, proving luckless, broke camp in a deepening mist and fog and drove to Speculator for lunch.

A couple and their young son were at the table next to us and a conversation started up. They were up from Washington for the week, a pair of schoolteachers in running clothes named Mark and Robin and their three-year-old son, Josh. Mark taught social studies at a junior high near Bethesda, and Robin, who taught earth science, explained that she'd been coming to Indian Lake since she was born because her grandfather had owned one of the first wilderness camps on the lake before the government opened up the area to developers and ruined the lake. She was only thirty-five but could remember when going to her grandfather's place felt like going to Alaska. The camp had no running water or electricity and you had to drive on a dirt road for nearly two hours to reach it. She saw her first bald eagle there when she was six.

Mark volunteered that Robin's grandfather had hunted and fished with Teddy Roosevelt.

"Who's that?" Maggie asked.

"He was president of the United States," Mark told her. "Though not then. After he went out West."

"We're going out West," she informed him.

"Really?" Mark smiled at her. "Maybe you'll be our first lady president."

"Thanks, but I think I'll either be a scientist or a country music singer or maybe a movie actress," she primly explained. I looked at Maggie. The "country music singer" bit was new and I wondered if it was just to please me. Once upon a time, as she knew, so long ago it sometimes felt as if it had happened to somebody else, I'd seriously considered striking off to Nashville to try and find a career making what an overeducated pal of mine called "goat-ropin' music." We all have our dark little secrets. Mine was goat-ropin' music. Her mother had one, too.

From the sidelines, I added: "Maggie's mother went to Harvard but secretly always wanted to be a *Solid Gold* dancer."

"*Dad!*" Maggie was mortified that I was blabbing family secrets.

"It's nice to have so many talents," Mark told her with the smile and grace of a good teacher, and she rewarded him with a shy smile over her hot dog.

Once we were back on Route 8, headed south to connect with the New York Thruway at Utica, the mist and fog turned into a light rain and the Beatles sang about love in a yellow submarine. Amos slept on the rear seat, and Maggie sat Indian style in her shoulder harness practicing a cat's cradle with a piece of red yarn. We were following a yellow Ryder van with New York plates and Maggie wanted to know more about Teddy Roosevelt. I explained that he'd been America's first conservationist president and that, because of his intense love of the outdoors, perhaps originally kindled here in the Adirondacks, he was responsible for establishing the nation's system of national parks—a visionary feat of leadership that got his head put on a mountain in South Dakota. Yellowstone, our destination, had been the model for the entire federal park system, I pointed out.

"Can we go there?"

"That's the plan, babe." The plan was finally taking shape.

"Why did he go out West?"

I thought about her question for a moment and explained that Teddy Roosevelt went West because of a personal tragedy. Almost unimaginably, his wife and mother died on the same night, only hours apart, in the same house on the Hudson River just down from Albany, the state capital. His mother had been ill and his wife was giving birth to their first child, a little girl he later named Alice.

"Did the little girl live?"

"Yes." I explained, though, that Roosevelt was so devastated by the dual tragedy—"This house is cursed," he said to his brother Elliott—he decided a radical change in his life was in order. Among his peers in the corrupt New York General Assembly, where Roosevelt aimed to make his mark as a moral legislative reformer, the energetic young man was considered a force to be reckoned with, but also something of a dilettante and a dandy—a rich boy, as I explained it, who'd never gotten his hands dirty. His wife's death changed all that. She was twenty-two, the light of his life, and she died on the fourth anniversary of their wedding engagement. It was Saint Valentine's Day.

"That's a really sad story," Maggie said feelingly.

"I know," I agreed, thinking how maybe every person's life has a pivot point like that. Roosevelt's had. Emma's had. Opti's had. Ditto son of Opti's. My daughter's surely would, too. *Sorrow is sacred ground.* The question was what you did with the sorrow, I said—learned from it or cursed your bad luck, let it pry open your heart forever or shut it down for good. With this kind of lyrical right-brain think-

ing, I'd probably have made a helluva goat-ropin' songwriter.

"What did Roosevelt do?"

I explained he ditched politics, bought a cowboy suit
made by Brooks Brothers and a hunting knife from Tiffany,
then bolted West. *Black care rarely sits behind a rider whose pace
is fast enough,* he wrote to a friend from the Dakota Badlands, where he took up the life of a rancher. Only a fair
horseman and an average shot, and a poor rope handler, TR
never publicly spoke of the tragedy that had changed his life
but caused him to shed the "dude" label forever by proving
his courage in the West. Mark had probably been right—it
made him a good president, too.

I started to say something meaningful about good things
coming from bad things when something bad nearly ruined
our nice little chat and ended our own trip West.

As we rounded a rain-slick curve where the black rock
face of a mountain descended like a ragged wall to the right
shoulder of the highway, I noticed the yellow Ryder van in
front of us begin to lose control. The rear wheels slid left
and then slithered back to the right as the driver, obviously
going too fast for conditions, fought to regain control of his
vehicle. He went into a terrible fishtail and for a second I
was certain he was going to roll the van. Instead, he veered
off the highway to the right, slamming off the mountain's
rock face with a shuddering crunch, then spun back onto
the highway directly in our path.

I had only a second or two to react, cutting the wheel of
Old Blue sharply to the left, which threw us into the oncoming lane and narrowly permitted us to avoid ramming the
van but placed us in the path of an oncoming Cadillac, the
owner of which was laying on the horn. As we slid around
the stalled van, I turned Old Blue's wheel back the other
way and missed the Caddy's front bumper, I think, by a
mere whisker of the driver's chin. Fortunately there was no
one following the Caddy because our rear end slithered

dangerously to the left and we were suddenly wildly fishtailing, too. For several seconds I steered into the direction of the sliding wheels and finally coaxed the slowing truck back under control as we hit the loose gravel on the left shoulder and barreled down a small incline into a little grassy creek.

It was over faster than you could say *Bully good piece of driving, Pops.*

I switched off the truck and turned to look at Maggie. She was sitting rigidly in her shoulder harness with her bare legs still crossed, ashen, clutching Susie Bear on her lap and the string between her fingers. The Beatles were now singing "Ob-la-di, Ob-la-da. . . ."

"Are you okay?" I felt my heart pounding the bars of my rib cage like a drunk in a holding tank demanding his rights.

"Uh-huh." She nodded slowly. "I think Susie Bear fainted, though."

Amos was on his back on the truck's floor directly behind us, struggling like a sea turtle to get back up on the seat he'd tumbled from. I unbuckled my seat belt and tried to assist the old gent back to the vertical but he growled at me as if to say his lawyer would soon be in touch with mine.

The truck's left wheels were mired several inches in the Adirondack mud but there didn't appear to be any other structural damage. I locked the hubs, shifted into four-wheel drive, and cranked the engine, really expecting to go nowhere fast. But Old Blue surprised me. Spewing mud and grass, she clawed her way back up to the shoulder of the road, where I once again got out to survey the damage. There didn't seem to be any. She would need a nice warm bath and perhaps some chamomile tea to soothe her jangled nerves, but we'd been incredibly lucky. I could have kissed the chairman of General Motors or, at least, his secretary.

We drove back to the highway to where the Ryder van was now parked beside the road, its right side caved in like a crushed beer can. Two men stood beside the vehicle, both pale as mackerels.

"That was pretty close. You fellas okay?"

The younger man nodded. He was skinny, probably about nineteen, with acne, very short hair, and two small silver rings in his nose. His oversized black T-shirt read: *Live Fast. Die Hard. Fear Nothing.* He'd nearly done just that, and appeared to be mildly in shock as a result.

The other man was overweight, about my age, wearing a blue work shirt with the name *Paul* in red script above the left breast. "That was close as shit," Paul said, shaking his head. "A goddamn miracle nobody got killed." He tried to smile and then saw my daughter hop out of our truck and looked at me and mumbled, "Sorry."

I didn't know if he meant sorry about the language or sorry about nearly killing us. "Don't worry about it," I said. "The important thing is that nobody got hurt. I guess we'd better call a cop."

Paul looked at me, then my truck, then me again. "If it's all the same to you I'd rather not. I mean, if your truck is okay and all. We can limp on down to Utica. The truth is, the kid had a couple open beers in the cab." I looked at Paul's eyes to see if that meant he had a couple open beers in him but his eyes looked clear and I stood for a minute trying to think what to do. "That was a piece of driving you did," he said, resorting to simple flattery. "I thought you were gonna nail us for sure."

"Fur sher," echoed the kid, who was perhaps rethinking his ambition to live fast and die hard.

"We were all lucky."

Two passing cars slowed. I turned and looked at a woman who was frowning at us as she passed. The third car to pass was a New York state trooper. He pulled over and got out and walked slowly toward us. I was relieved because the decision was no longer mine to make. Paul immediately began explaining what happened, babbling about the rain and the slick road. The trooper calmly asked for his license and registration and then checked mine. He looked at my truck and at me. He asked me how fast I thought we were going. I said probably about forty, forty-five tops. He glanced at my daughter and smiled a little bit. "What's your name, honey?"

"Maggie."

"That your dog in the truck?"

"Uh-huh. He's old."

The trooper asked me if we were all okay. I said we were. He asked us to return to our vehicle and wait for him to come take down our statement. We went back and sat in the truck. "Dad," Maggie asked nervously, "are you going to be arrested?"

I glanced at her and smiled. "Of course not. He just wants to make sure he knows what happened." Amos began to fidget, obviously had to pee. I asked Maggie to walk him over to some bushes on the lead so he could do his three-legged balancing act. Why did talking to cops make me so uncomfortable? I'd had only a few traffic tickets in my life and lived an embarrassingly dull life well inside the paint of the law.

Perhaps I had been going a shade too fast for the conditions, and perhaps even following the van too closely, but I wasn't going to admit that to the trooper because, God knows, life was complicated enough. No harm, no foul, we were lucky, let's leave it, shall we, and just go on? "Ob-la-di, Ob-la-da, Life goes on," as the other Paul had been singing. The trooper came back and listened to my explanation of what happened.

"Maine, huh? Nice place. Lived there your whole life?"

Not yet, I almost replied, remembering the old joke.

Instead, I said I was from North Carolina but had lived in Maine for a decade; my children were from there, though. Born and raised. I added that to a real Mainer this alone didn't make them native Mainers, though, because as they say in Maine, *Just 'cause your cat has kittens in the oven don't make 'em biscuits.*

The trooper smiled. He liked my little Maine funny.

"Where are you all headed?"

"Wyoming. Goin' fishin'." That had a nice innocent ring to it. Unless you're the fish.

"Trout?"

"If we can find some."

He handed me back my license and registration.

"I'm a bass man." He told me he had a bass boat with twin Johnson outboards which he kept on Lake Erie and was fishing in a big Bassmaster tournament that weekend. I wished him good luck. We were suddenly brothers of the Holy Order of the Rod and Reel and it was like we were having small talk outside a diner. He even told me a pretty lame fishing joke. *How can you tell if a fisherman is lying? His lips are moving.*

Maggie and Amos came back. The trooper scratched Amos's head and told us we were free to go. He said we should have a nice trip and hoped we caught some real hogs.

As we pulled out, I glanced back at Paul and the kid standing beside their crumpled truck. Paul was gesticulating and I wondered what kind of fish tale he was spinning for the trooper.

"Nice driving, Dad," Maggie complimented me quietly, resuming her leg position and yarn game. I could almost hear her brain whizzing as it processed everything she'd just witnessed. Then she giggled.

"What's so funny?" I asked.

"That policeman," she replied. "He thought we were going to catch pigs or something."

We drove across upper New York State in a sensational thunderstorm, unable to see much through the rain-streaked windows except lightning bolts pounding the earth. I taught my daughter the redneck goat-ropin' way of measuring the lightning's distance by saying "one-Mississippi-two-Mississippi" in the gap of silence between the flash and the boom. The closest strike was a mile away and actually seemed to make Old Blue shudder.

I thought of Jack, how I sometimes lay with him at bedtime telling stories during electrical storms, how storms of any kind really frightened the Rocket. I'd always told him that his fear was quite natural and storms deserved our respect and explained that at his age I'd feared them, too, until my father told me that thunder was nothing more than the gods bowling and lightning couldn't hurt you if you outsmarted it by staying put in your cave, the way the ancients did. Perhaps a thunderstorm was really nothing more than the random collision of hot and cold air molecules, the violent electrical nexus of negative ions and positive protons. Or maybe, as I explained to Jack as my father had explained to me, a rocking thunderstorm was good old Zeus hurling lightning bolts at philandering chaps while neatly overlooking his own indiscretions in that category. In any case, I sure hoped Jack was having better weather on the Cape.

"Dad, are we going to fish in this rain?"

"Do you want to try?"

"Well . . . maybe. I dunno."

I'd hoped we might stop long enough to toss a line in Onondaga Lake, where a Manhattan sportswriter friend of mine assured me the smallest smallmouth bass was the size of an average NBA sneaker. But the rain was coming in such torrents I honestly didn't see how that would be any fun. Lakes are like golf courses that way — best to steer clear of them when there's fire in the sky. I suggested, instead, that we crank up the radio and push on for Buffalo — my parents had some friends there who hoped to take us out to dinner — and Maggie vouchsafed the plan. After all, she'd safely replenished her stock of Blow Pops and Wild Blue Raspberry Gatorade and Patty Loveless, one of her favorite singers, was wailing about some no-good cheatin' ole deadbeatin', two-timin', double-dealin' mean mistreatin' sorry sumbitch she'd left in her dust.

"Why is it in most country music songs," Maggie wondered aloud, "that the men are always leaving the women and the women are kind of glad to see them go, or else the women leave the men and the men are, like, you know, sick and angry and stuff?"

I explained this was a universal theme in art and music, as irresistible to the seventeenth-century Venetian opera librettist as to the twentieth-century Nashville songwriter. Someone, I noted, had called it the battle of the sexes.

"You mean they *like* to fight each other?"

"No. It's just that men and women are made so differently that sometimes the same things that attract us to each other also cause a few problems." I realized, as I said this, that we were veering dangerously close to our own situation. She and her brother had overheard more arguments in the previous year than they'd heard in their lifetimes and I knew it frightened the daylights out of both of them. Well, it had frightened us, too. "The trick is to learn how to see eye to eye. To honorably disagree, respect the other's viewpoint, and get over it and on to something better," I said, thinking this was apparently where her mom and I came up a bit short—or maybe not. Time would tell.

"Right," Maggie said confidently. "You mean sex."

I rolled an eye in her direction. "What do you know about sex?"

"It's what people do when they're in love and get married. To have babies. It's very normal, Dad."

"Ah. I see. . . ."

I nodded, worrying. We'd never had a discussion of sex before because it seemed like only moments ago that my darling daughter was trying to decide which guy she really, really, *really* liked the most, Bert or Ernie. The Big Talk loomed in the not-too-distant future, but a rain-swept interstate highway in western New York didn't seem like the time and place to open up this Pandora's box. Besides, Maggie was only seven, more interested in fly-fishing than boys, right? When the time was right, she'd ask even more unsettling questions and I'd sit her down and tell her exactly what she needed to know about men and women, the battle of the sexes, human reproduction, etcetera and so forth, and where babies *really* came from—which, as everyone knew, was from lily pads in an enchanted pond somewhere beyond the clouds.

Mercifully, she decided to clamp on headphones and listen to a Roald Dahl book on tape, leaving me once again free to drive along a rainy road with my thoughts. Out of habit, I tuned Old Blue's radio to a local public station and found a learned head talking to the National Press Club about the crisis of fatherlessness in America. Thirty percent of the kids in America, he said, went to bed every night without a father in the house, and most of the nation's escalating social ills could be traced to the curse of the absentee father—the alarming rise in teen violence, the growth of urban gangs, the shocking rate of unwed births. America, he predicted, would soon be the most fatherless society on earth.

Under the circumstances, this was a thesis I didn't need or wish to hear more about so I turned the knob again and learned, on a more cheerful note, that oxygen had been discovered on this day in 1831. It was also the fortieth anniversary of the U.S. interstate system, which I vaguely knew, and the fiftieth anniversary of the bikini, which I didn't.

The hourly news came on. A bomb had gone off at the Olympics and a security guard named Richard Jewell was being questioned in regard to that incident. I had a first cousin named Richard Jewell and vaguely wondered if the suspect might be him, then decided it probably wasn't. Elsewhere, the Republicans were getting ready to nominate Bob Dole for president in San Diego and some windbag senator was urging Dole to embrace the idea of getting rid of the U.S. penny, a piece of antiquated currency, he said, that had "outlived its usefulness to society." The Democrats, who were about to convene in Chicago, were saying pretty much the same thing about Bob Dole.

The rain stopped in Buffalo just as we checked in to the Lord Amherst Motor Inn, named for Baron Jeffrey Amherst, the famous British army officer who gallantly fought the French for Fort Ticonderoga and cleverly gave disease-infested blankets to the local Indians, introducing half a dozen European maladies to the North American landscape.

It was our first motel night in six days. We needed firm beds and warm showers and the motel accepted pets as long as you kept them off the beds, which explained why Amos immediately lumbered up on one double bed and made himself comfy while Maggie jumped on the other one, grabbed the remote, and quickly switched on the television to see if Nickelodeon had managed to stay in business without her, reminding me that it had been at least "a whole entire week" since she'd seen an episode of something called *Clarissa Explains It All,* which rather explained it all.

Seeing Maggie and Amos reminded me why my plan was to try and stay in as few motels and avoid as many big cities as possible on our freestone fly-ramble out to Yellowstone. If I didn't, we'd all become overweight couch potatoes in no time because, let's face it, pretty soon I'd start watching CNN and The Weather Channel and we'd never reach Old Faithful and the Yellowstone River.

I washed my face and dialed my parents' friends who lived somewhere on the south side of town, hoping they could give me useful advice on the best way to see Niagara Falls on a crowded summer morning at the heart of wedding season. I was secretly excited about seeing Niagara Falls. It's such an icon of American culture. A decade before, returning from our honeymoon to Quebec City—the "Poor Man's Paris," as it's called—Maggie's mother and I had briefly considered driving over to the Falls for a quick look and perhaps a self-conscious laugh at this living cliché of connubial bliss, but lack of time and money had prevented it. We'd veered south to Vermont instead.

Don Hoffmeyer was an old friend and business associate of my father's who'd once taken me trapshooting at his club on a hill in Buffalo. He was also a devoted fly fisherman. Don invited us to meet him and his wife, Joyce, for dinner and during it asked me how my mother was holding up since my father's death. He seemed pleased when I told him my mother was doing well, having more good days than bad. "I'm sure she misses him. We all do. Your dad was a special guy," Don said. "You must miss him, too." I admitted I did. More than he could ever know. The fourteen months since his death sometimes felt like fourteen years.

Don started talking about fly-fishing in Canada and I eavesdropped on Maggie, who was busily filling Joyce in on our death-defying escape on the road out of the Adirondacks, how she'd caught the trip's first trout, and my half-gainer out of Norumbega Girl. Joyce appeared charmed. She inquired about Jack and I said Jack was just fine—riding bikes and learning to swim with his mother on Nantucket, as it so happened. "How marvelous," she said, "that you can each take separate vacations like that and enjoy it."

"It works for us," I replied cheerfully, avoiding my daughter's solemn gaze.

She ordered angel-hair pasta. I ordered chicken wings. Don, who had a T-bone steak, ordered another round of drinks and started telling me about a staggeringly expensive shotgun he once bought on Regent Street in London, then suggested that we get to the Canadian side of the Falls before noon because the view was better and the parking could be murder if you waited too long.

·   ·   ·

The next morning around ten, we crossed through Canadian customs. The stern lady clerk examined Amos's rabies certificate and then studied Amos for a moment, perhaps thinking he might be a cleverly disguised fugitive from Interpol's most-wanted list. Then she studied me to see if I was a deranged individual trying to snatch an elderly dog and a small girl calmly doing yarn games from the bosom of their homeland. The border official bore an uncanny resemblance to my fourth-grade teacher, Miss Wettington, who had an impressive mustache and carried a riding crop on school field trips.

She asked me—none too friendly-like, either—where exactly we were headed. I said we were headed to the Canadian side of the Falls and she looked prepared to slap me for being such a wise-mouth. In the nick of time, I mended my ways to say we were taking a shortcut across Ontario to the Upper Peninsula of Michigan, where we planned to camp and fish in Hemingway country.

"Poor Woody Ham," I said as we were finally waved through Checkpoint Wettington.

"Who's Woody Ham?"

I told Maggie the sad story of Woodrow C. Ham. Woody Ham was a meek round-faced boy in my fourth-grade class who never made a peep. One day somebody wrote something pretty harmless about Miss Wettington on the tiles of the boys' bathroom—*Miss Wettington is really a man.* Miss Wettington responded by lining up every boy in the class and interrogating us one by one beneath the glow of an intense reading lamp in the janitor's closet. Woody Ham, of all people, fessed up to the graffiti and was soon led away for summary execution. Miss Wettington had a four-foot wooden paddle with nine holes in it—nine holes, it was rumored, for those victims who'd *died* from it. The legendary paddle actually whistled, I explained to my daughter, and today it resided in a special exhibit on frontier-era child abuse in the Smithsonian Institution in Washington, D.C.

"Wow. Where is Miss Wettington now?"

"I don't know. With any luck she's waxing her mustache and doing twenty-five-to-life in the state prison."

We parked the truck in a large asphalt parking lot and hooked Amos to a long lead, then headed toward the main set of Niagara Falls viewing buildings, where several thousand other tourists were milling about in the bright sunshine. It was a fine summer day, with giant white battleship clouds serenely anchored overhead. I do hate to sound like a complete hayseed from Maine, but I'd honestly never seen anything quite as impressive as Niagara Falls—the way an *entire* river rushed over the precipice and the mother of all mist swelled up from the churning tumult below.

It was suddenly obvious to me why the Falls had been such a sacred spot to Native Americans. Long ago they offered crops, game, weapons, and other personal possessions to try and appease the god of the thundering Falls, and the most famous story was the legend of the Maid of the Mist, the beautiful virgin girl who was annually sacrificed to the Falls in a white canoe filled with flowers and fruit. She would calmly guide her canoe into the vortex, it was said, assured of her place in Heaven. The last young woman to give herself to the rite was the daughter of a powerful chieftain, who was so grief-stricken over his daughter's demise that he steered his own canoe over the Falls. Supposedly their spirits still dwelled in the caves beneath the Falls, a tale guaranteed to pierce the heart of any daddy parent.

I stood looking at the Falls, enthralled by their mystery and power, remembering how as a child the thought of losing one or both of my parents was my darkest fear; realizing, too, how as a parent the thought of losing one of my children had an even more potent terror attached to it. *The joys of parents are secret,* Francis Bacon wrote. *And so are their griefs and fears; they cannot utter the one, nor will they not utter the other.* Undoubtedly there were people on a beach in Long Island having thoughts along these same lines.

"Dad," Maggie said, interrupting these sober thoughts, "what are you *doing*?" I realized I was standing on a bench, leaning far over the rail—just the sort of dumb fool thing you scream at your kids for doing. Amos was seated on the pavement panting as a small crowd of admirers made a fuss over him. A toddler kept desperately trying to kiss his nose.

"What a nice puppy," the toddler's mother cooed.

"He's not a puppy," Maggie said. "He's thirteen."

"Really? He doesn't look all that old."

We chatted with the Donahue family from Atlanta. They'd leased their house in Midtown for the Olympics and vamoosed north to see America while the rest of America was busy watching the Olympics. I didn't tell them I'd lived there once upon a time and I wondered if they were perhaps traveling in a bus because there seemed to be two or three dozen of them, a team of Donahues all wearing the same Atlanta Braves caps. They were headed to the new Rock 'n' Roll Hall of Fame in Cleveland next, then maybe to Chicago for a Cubs game or two, where they would fill up most of the outfield seats.

It's believed about a million newlyweds a year still come to pay homage to the thundering gods at Niagara. A few moments later, two of them asked me to snap their picture. They were a handsome Chinese American couple from Baltimore, Ken and Natalie. Cute kids in matching Georgetown T-shirts, recent grads who had just gone to work on Wall Street. They were drinking diet Cokes held in identical blue plastic holders. I pictured them having two of everything in their long and prosperous married life—two nice kids, two luxury automobiles, a pair of handsome matching investment portfolios, and twin marble bathroom vanities.

Ken explained that they were about to head down and board the *Maid of the Mist* for a jaunt beneath the Falls. "The *Maid of the Mist*, you know, is one hundred and fifty years old this year," he said, and Natalie added that speaking of birthdays Tupperware was forty.

A rangy black guy in a Bulls basketball shirt loped up
and patted Amos briskly on the back and said, "Man oh
man. Great dog. Let me *ride* this guy."

"He's too old," one of the minor Donahues told him from
somewhere beneath a baseball cap.

Maggie asked if she could unhook Amos because he
didn't like the lead. I said she could but she had to watch
him or else he'd be drinking from the Falls or, worse, peeing
in it. A tubby geezer in a tank shirt that read *Living Sex
Symbol* laughed and asked me if we'd been down the street
to the Daredevil Hall of Fame yet. I admitted we hadn't but
said we were thinking of taking a ride with Ken and Natalie
on the *Maid of the Mist.*

"Don't waste your time," the living sex symbol said. "The
lines are a mile long and it's kind of a rip-off. If it was me,
I'd go to the museum. Remember that nut Stephen Trotter?
He's there."

Actually, I did remember Stephen Trotter, the last American to survive the 180-foot plunge over Horseshoe Falls,
and the youngest ever, a teenager from Rhode Island whose
courage matched Woody Ham's, one of only five individuals
who survived the plunge among the sixteen daredevils who
made it over. When the Victoria police hauled him out of
the slosh he had only a slight scratch on his arm. "It was
real cool," he told the local paper.

I caught up to Maggie on the steps by the gift shop,
where she was still talking to the Donahue matriarch, apparently giving her our entire family history.

"Maggie," I said worriedly, "where's your dog?"

"Oh." She looked around and then pointed to the open
gift shop door. "I think he went in there."

I went in the gift shop and found our elder traveler waiting patiently in line behind a large red-haired woman buying caramel corn. The woman looked a bit like Sarah
Ferguson, the celebrity-crazed Duchess of York; perhaps it
was even her. I tapped my dog on the head and indicated

that he should follow me, but he refused to budge. Amos has a sweet tooth that easily eclipses that of an overweight British royal. Just then, Maggie appeared, flush with an apology.

"Sorry, Dad. I just kind of forgot."

I grumbled something about learning to accept responsibility, then realized Amos was really *my* responsibility and apologized. It was too damn hot, too damn crowded. I suggested we get soft-serve ice cream—Amos loved ice cream—and hit the road for Michigan.

The red-haired woman whipped around with flashing eyes. "Where did you find ice cream?" she demanded with a fruity and unmistakably upper-crust British accent. "I simply *adore* soft-serve ice cream."

We fished late that afternoon on the Thames south of London. London was a town in the southwest corner of Ontario, less than an hour from Michigan. Before we reached the river, we stopped at a convenience store for Gatorade and candy bars. The store sold fishing licenses and I casually asked the elderly clerk if that river out back had any decent fish in it and he replied, "Only pike a foot long, eh?" He smiled as if he might be lying through his dentures.

We found a convenient sandbar ten miles south of the city near a provincial boat launch. Due to the currents, I didn't fancy launching Norumbega Girl and having to face a three- or four-mile portage back upstream after an hour's idle fishing. We would fish from the river's shore, like Ike Walton's original East Sussex anglers. The river was wide and had a greenish cast, whether from municipal sewage upstream or late summer algae bloom it was impossible to tell. I'd never fished for pike, which are a freshwater species related to pickerel and a carnivorous fish equipped with formidable teeth that feed on smaller fish, snakes, and other aquatic life, are known to eat four times their weight, and are sometimes called jackfish in Canada. I had a friend who grew up near Ontario's famed Shelf Region who claimed the northern pike was, ounce for ounce, the most tenacious game fish on earth. I decided to try my luck against the brute by using a spinner rod with a silver minnow lure. Maggie stayed a fly-rod purist and after I tied a lighter leader and Bristol Emerger on her tippet, so she could fish just below the surface film, or what's sometimes called the meniscus, I watched her wade into the shallows wearing her old canvas sneakers.

"Hey, not too far out. Those currents look a bit tricky."

A short nod.

She made a cast that immediately snarled due to the crosswind. She tried to untangle the wind knot but finally gave up and asked me to come over and help. I set down my rod and waded through the shallows to the sandbar. Her line was badly snarled. I took out my clippers and snipped off the mangled line, then unwound more tippet from a spool in my vest. We sat on the sand and I tied on a new leader and fly for her, greasing a new elk-hair emerger with float dope.

"Dad, can I ask you something?"

"Sure. As long as it's not about Miss Wettington. I've spent thirty years trying to forget that woman and her whistling hardware."

"Did you, like, enjoy getting married to Mommy?"

Take a romantic fishergirl who remembers her own birth to Niagara Falls, I thought, and you get exactly what you deserve: ten million questions about matrimony and none you'd care to answer. I didn't wish to talk about it, but she obviously needed to.

"Oh, absolutely," I said, and then told her about the sensational wedding party we'd thrown in the salt marsh north of Boston. My southern redneck buddies came bearing cowbells, bourbon, and barbecue. Her Maine and Harvard friends came wearing dark wool and bemused expressions.

A Sicilian baker from Gloucester who spoke no English made the cake; Amos ate five pieces. We held the reception under a tent during a real Atlantic gale. The orchestra bravely played "Pennies from Heaven" while the wooden dance floor sank half a foot in the yard muck. Local ladies from the village served the food and one of them told me I'd married the most beautiful woman on earth. She also told me that rain on your wedding day was a good omen because it meant you would someday be rich—rich in love, rich in babies.

"She was right."

"Do you still love Mommy?"

"Of course. I'll always love your mother. She's a wonderful woman."

Perhaps I shouldn't have said this, I thought, as I said it. This might give her false hope. Or me.

"Could I, like, hold your wedding ring?"

I nodded and put down her fly rod. The ring took some work to get off.

My finger had grown. She sat down on the bank holding the ring and looking closely at it, squinting to see the tiny date inscribed inside the narrow gold band, forgetting the pike entirely. I picked up my rod and sent the silver minnow arching far out into the river. I began reeling slowly, occasionally jigging the rod tip to make the minnow dance.

Those who want the fewest things, Socrates said, are closest to the gods. What I really wanted most at that moment was probably impossible to obtain—simply for us all to be safely beyond this unexpected sadness. I wouldn't have minded landing a nice fat pike, too, so I moved off down the sandbar a bit, working my line against the currents, trying to focus my mind back on fishing and wondering if we could make a state park campground at Bay City, as planned, by nightfall.

I was pleased to see Maggie eventually pick up her rod and begin making casts. The casts looked halfhearted, though, and it was clear to me that the heat and adventures of the day had taken the shine off fishing. The pike weren't happening. Maggie walked slowly down the bar and asked if she could go sit in the truck with Amos and listen to her book on tape. I said yes and reminded her there was a fresh supply of Wild Blue Raspberry Gatorade on ice in the cooler. I asked if she would give Amos a drink of water and she said she would.

"Take your time," she said, and I watched her cross back through the shallows and climb the weedy bank. She had her rod in one hand and my ring on one of her fingers and God knows what thoughts going round in her head.

She gave me back the ring just before we crossed the border back into the United States at Port Huron.

"Thanks. It's a pretty ring."

"Yes. It is."

I slipped it into my shirt pocket and fastened the button, thinking as I did that maybe I'd someday have a necklace made out of it and give it to her. Would she consider that a touching gesture or an unspeakably cruel one? At that moment, I honestly didn't know. I turned on the radio to see if I could find a weather forecast for the evening and learned that provincial authorities planned to forgive the phone bill of a ninety-six-year-old man who'd run up $90,000 in charges with a phone sex company.

Then we crossed a blue bridge back into America and I happened to glance at my hand on the steering wheel and the finger on my hand, unringed for the first time in a decade, a telltale pale line where the band had been. It looked strange, I thought, eerily exposed and even a bit accusatory. As jewelry wasn't my thing, it had taken me a year or two to get accustomed to wearing the ring. Now I wondered how long it would take me to get used to its being gone.

CHAPTER FIVE

....

Touching a Trout

WE MADE WALLOON Lake in Michigan early and in tranquil sunshine, a relief after having endured a wild night of howling winds and thunderstorms off Lake Huron that buckled our tent and caused a comic moment of confusion in the darkness as man fell over dog who fell over girl who woke with a yelp of terror. Heaving the saturated tent and our gear into the cargo hold of Old Blue, we fled the state park at Bay City before dawn and pushed on toward Grand Traverse Bay. Maggie shivered beneath a damp blanket and quickly fell back asleep. Amos lay on the backseat smelling like a wet dog and staring at me as if I'd stoop to any cheap stunt to keep us moving. I drove listening to the tail end of a Strauss waltz, dearly wishing I had a fresh-brewed cup of Starbucks Sumatra premium octane, and suddenly remembered I had friends in the Grand Traverse area, which has become something of a top-drawer golf destination of late. But then I remembered we didn't have golf clubs or reservations and weren't on that sort of expedition anyway.

We drove straight through and headed up Highway 31 to lovely Charlevoix, a charming place hemmed in by lake waters and full of geranium blooms, then on to Petoskey, where Victorian summer houses sat on pretty bluffs above the surprisingly calm surface of Lake Michigan and a few sails were already out like canvas hands folded in prayer. A bell knelled softly as we rolled into town. People were walking in shirtsleeves and summer dresses toward the Catholic church, where morning mass was about to begin, and we thought of going but stopped in the restored downtown district for breakfast instead. I bought the Grand Rapids paper and ordered scrambled eggs and black coffee and Maggie ordered her usual plain bagel and chocolate milk, which might have discouraged her mother but her mother was thousands of miles away and we were on vacation, damp and rumpled and faintly redolent of *Canis familiaris,* so I ordered a chocolate milk myself and opened the paper.

I was surprised to read that Ernest Hemingway's granddaughter Margaux had been found dead in a one-room apartment in Santa Monica. Suicide was suspected. She was about my age, with a steeply declining career in low-budget films behind her. Suffering from bulimia and alcoholism, she'd recently been at the Betty Ford Clinic and a mental hospital in Blackfoot, Idaho, the report said, and had sought spiritual guidance from the Dalai Lama. She'd been hearing voices and was unable, according to a source close to the family, "to separate fantasy from reality. I'm afraid she never really found her own identity." There was wide speculation that the approaching thirty-fifth anniversary of her grandfather's suicide had played a part in the tragedy. I sipped my coffee, shaking my head. It seemed almost too ironic.

Maggie was giving me a funny look over her Pocahontas journal, which she sometimes wrote in at breakfast. I explained the story to her. She'd never heard of suicide and an hour before she'd never heard of Ernest Hemingway. I told

her he was a writer who probably influenced more writers
than anybody else in the past hundred years and she asked
if he wrote about golf and I said no, he wrote about . . .
what exactly? . . . and had to stop and think how to tell
her. "He wrote a lot about hunting and fishing. This is
where he spent his boyhood summers, though. He got to be
very famous and traveled all over the world but no place
ever meant more to him."

"You mean here?" Kids are so literal. She looked a bit
wonderingly around the coffee shop.

"Well, in this area. His family had a summer cottage on
Walloon Lake. There's a state park near here. I thought
we'd make camp there and then go fish the lake. See if the
trout are interested."

"Cool."

Once upon a time I'd been extremely taken with Ernest
Hemingway. My father was to blame. I was about fourteen
when he suggested I read the Nick Adams stories for a
school book report, so I did, saw in them what I imagined
was a spiritual brother, and kept reading. I read and reread
everything he wrote and never quit reading Hemingway
until my friend Kristen was murdered, at which point I quit
reading him because I realized I wanted to lead his life, not
mine. It wasn't until I ran away to Vermont and took up fly-
fishing that I could read his works again with the necessary
detachment. I was changed. And, luckily, his stories no
longer had their hypnotic hold over me. I no longer wanted
to be Ernest Hemingway.

Earlier that morning, following my finger across the road
map, I'd come across the name Walloon Lake and the name
had jumped out at me like a water siren calling, opening up
a host of old feelings and curiosities. If it's true that geography makes poets of its sons and daughters, this place had
made Hemingway as surely as any café on the Left Bank or
bullring in Spain. In fact probably more so. He wasted an
inordinate amount of oxygen denying the Nick Adams sto-

ries were autobiographical, but he idealized this lake and the towns around it in some of his best writing and spent the balance of his life, according to his many biographers, either trying to outrun the life he had here or restlessly attempting to find Walloon Lake's spiritual match, a familiar grounding place, a safe and uncomplicated shore. He became, in the process, impossibly famous and a miserable sod who abused alcohol and four wives, betrayed most of his best friends in print, hated Harvard men, won the Pulitzer Prize, was extremely vain about his hair, and blew his brains out at age sixty-two when he could no longer bear up under the weight of his own mythology. America never produced a more perfect literary icon than Papa Ernest Hemingway. He haunts American manhood and leans over American letters the way a weathered hemlock shades a summer lawn.

But I wasn't on a search for Papa Hemingway, and my daughter probably couldn't have cared less. We were on no sacred literary pilgrimage here. Leave Papa to the package tours shuffling among the six-toed cats at the late great man's hacienda at Key West; we were just sympathetic strangers passing through town and pausing to say hello and sample the food. It was Nick Adams or maybe fifteen-year-old Ernie Hemingway who shot the blue heron and touched the trout in the current and rowed out in the lake with best girl Marjorie and later, by the fire on the shore, broke her heart and was unable to tell her how much he loved her and foolishly let her row that boat out of his life—that was the fellow it might be nice to find traces of, I thought idly, flipping through the rest of the Sunday paper.

We raised the big Bean tent at Petoskey State Park, a beautiful park fringed with hemlocks and mature hardwoods. While Maggie took Amos for a brief constitutional, I fell into conversation with an interesting couple just cleaning up their breakfast dishes in the adjacent campsite. They were traveling in a small wooden wagon that looked like something from which a nineteenth-century medicine man might have peddled miraculous tonics, elixirs that cured everything from crabgrass to plantar warts.

In fact, Jerry and Toni Bowman were Canadians and practicing Mormons taking a year off from their computer jobs in Toronto to join up with a wagon train re-creating Brigham Young's great Mormon exodus West. Their horse was stabled at a farm a few miles away. I admitted that I was impressed by the scope of their undertaking. Jerry explained that three travelers (counting the horse) was small potatoes compared with what other Mormon families were doing at that very moment, crossing America as their forebears had in search of a New Jerusalem, inching toward the high desert country around the mother church, mothers and children and grannies and dogs hoofing along after covered wagons, heading out of Illinois and Missouri with the aid of motorized support vehicles, but essentially performing a real pilgrimage, a hard walk of faith. The Bowmans' tidy little wagon, at least, had Monroe shock absorbers. Jerry told me this with a smile; he'd built it himself.

"How old is your daughter?" Toni, folding towels, wanted to know. I saw a Bible on the table, where they'd obviously been reading it.

"Seven going on fourteen." I explained that yesterday my daughter asked out of the blue to purchase rum raisin fingernail polish, claiming her mother had given her permission to paint her toenails. I'd said no.

"Well, you better get used to it," Toni said with a laugh. "Seven or eight is about where it starts with girls. Is your wife with you?"

"Not this trip," I said, looking at her. "She couldn't get away."

.   .   .

In *Big Two-Hearted River*, following a big flapjack breakfast with apple butter, Nick Adams tidies up his camp and heads into the river with his eight-dollar fly rod. He places a live grasshopper on the hook and makes his first cast, stripping enough line from the reel to allow the fly to drift almost out of sight in the current. He feels a strike and reels in a nice brown trout, wets his hand and holds the wiggling trout, gently unhooks the fly, and drops the fish back into the stream.

He hung unsteadily in the current, then settled to the bottom beside a stone. Nick reached down his hand to touch him, his arm to the elbow under water. The trout was steady in the moving stream, resting on the gravel, beside a stone. As Nick's fingers touched him, touched his smooth, cool, underwater feeling he was gone, gone in a shadow across the bottom of the stream.

He's all right, Nick thought. He was only tired.

For years, I thought that was one of the most hypnotic passages in all literature, better than just about anything I'd ever read. I was thinking of this passage as Maggie and I gathered our gear and went off to find a spot to put in the canoe.

Unable to find a public access to Walloon Lake, we drove back to fish Lake Charlevoix and put in near the small town of Horton Bay, another tramping ground of young Ernie Hemingway, then paddled down to a promising cove overhung by large trees. The afternoon breeze was rising, turning the surface of the lake gray with small waves, making fishing out on the lake in a drifting canoe difficult, but the cove was slightly sheltered and someone had a nice weekend house sitting in the hardwoods up a three-tiered flight of wooden steps leading down to a dock. We pulled the canoe on shore onto the rocks next to the dock and I looked up to see if somebody might object but nobody seemed to be home.

I put on my waders and went into the lake. Maggie walked to the end of the dock to fish.

"Why do you think that girl killed herself?" she called over after we'd been fishing a while.

"I don't know, Mugs. Life can be tough sometimes. Her grandfather had the same difficulty. I guess they ran out of hope that things would get better. Whatever happens, you gotta hold tight to hope."

"I hope we catch a big fish."

"Me too."

I realized this might be an opportune moment to expand a bit on Aunt Emma's tragedy but then thought better of it. The family secret had kept nicely for sixty years; it could keep another five or six. Yesterday, my daughter had never even heard of suicide or Ernest Hemingway. Tomorrow she might forget them, though I rather doubted it.

I told her, instead, how Indians used to live in a settlement near here—a collection of shanties, really—in the woods near Horton Bay, and often appeared at the Hemingway summer cottage bearing buckets of just-picked blackberries to sell. They made a huge impression on Ernie Hemingway, leaving as silently as they arrived.

Making a longer and slower cast from the thigh-deep water, I suddenly caught my first decent trout. He took the fly and headed for deeper water, a good-sized fish to judge by the fight. The rod tip bowed and I lowered it nearly to the water's surface and flipped on the drag to let the fish run a bit, then remembered that the lake's deeper currents would only help him. I lifted the rod and maintained the tension and reeled in my stripped line and soon had the fish working toward shore. Maggie came down from the dock and within a minute or two had him in the net, a two-pound lake trout with black markings. He was large enough to keep and I briefly considered having him for supper. Then I wet my hands and took out the hook and told her about the trout-touching passage from *Big Two-Hearted River*.

"Do you think he really did it?"

"I don't know. May have just been a story. Want to try it?"

"Sure." She gave me a little grin.

I held the trout in the water for a few seconds, waiting for him to breathe again, then released my fingers. He hovered a second or two more but didn't sink. His caudal fin moved slightly. Before I could even move my right hand toward him, though, he was gone.

"They must have gotten a lot swifter since Hemingway tried this," I said with a laugh.

Maggie laughed, too. At least we had fresh hamburger on ice.

After supper, I washed up the dinner plates and put on water to scald them, then fed Amos his aspirins in cheese. A screen door slapped up at the lighted shower building and the Mormon couple came back from having their evening showers. I introduced them to Maggie, who was headed to the showers with her towel, soap, and toothbrush. When she was gone, Toni Bowman brought over fresh-made coffee and an extra cup. Jerry followed his wife, buttoning up a flannel shirt. The night was surprisingly cool off Lake Michigan.

"We made too much and hate to pour it out," she explained.

We chatted for a while about their trip and ours and I admitted to them that Maggie's mother wasn't with us because she and I were getting divorced. I suppose part of me thought of this confession as a little test. I wanted to see how they would react, how a Mormon who didn't accept the idea of divorce would take this news, how any stranger would. Perhaps I'd not yet stated the words aloud because part of me clung to the belief that they simply weren't true. Just the prospect of going through a divorce makes you feel so unclean, so anxious to try and explain that you're really not an awful person. *Everybody's got a casserole for the widow,* Rev. Barbara Cawthorne Crafton has written. *But nobody wants to stand too near someone going through a divorce.* I half expected them to whip out their Bible and lecture me in that cheerfully pious manner some Mormons have about God and family values. But the Bowmans were either too considerate or maybe just didn't know what to say. They only offered hot coffee and a bit of sympathy, for which I was grateful on both counts. Jerry said they were fetching their horse and rolling out in the morning, too, hoping to make Holland by the weekend. "The town," he said with a pleasant wink at Toni. "Not the country."

We said good night and a little while later my daughter came back from her shower and asked me to comb out her hair, which I was delighted to do. She hadn't asked me to comb out her hair in what seemed like ages. First I tossed on another log, sending up a burst of sparks, and then put on the radio softly, though no news this time. Central Michigan University was playing Copland's *Appalachian Spring,* a bittersweet anthem based on Shaker melodies which had its world debut on the same day fifty years ago that the war ended in Europe. My father had been in that war, had seen things as awful as Hemingway had, and it had changed him, too. Strangely, it made him more determined to be kind and optimistic.

The Copland piece was one of my favorites. It reminded me of my home in North Carolina and I suppose I loved it for that, though not as much as I loved combing out my daughter's sweet-smelling wet hair and not as much as I loved being lost with her in the Michigan woods with a storm rumbling like a timpani drum or maybe the gods bowling far out on Lake Michigan, heading, like us, for the Upper Peninsula.

"Dad?"

"Yeah, babe?"

"Do you think that fish remembers that we caught him today?"

I smiled to myself and complimented her for asking such an interesting question. Soon she would have her own chair in philosophy at Yale—or at least a great country band. Did fish have memories? Only she would ask such a thing. That trout we'd caught and let go was two pounds of muscle, fin, membrane, and sinew, a few thousand strands of taut nerve endings and survival instincts as old as stone, one of the most efficient eating machines on earth—amazing, I said, when you thought about it, for a creature whose brain was just slightly larger than a fresh green pea. She reminded me that we'd had fresh green peas for supper and hamburgers shaped to look like trout and said there must be room in there somewhere for a bit of memory. I smiled again, kept combing, and explained to her that the Psalms say memory is immortality and I would remember that fish a long time even if I'd failed to touch him and he forgot me the moment I let him go. God gives the solitary a home, the Psalms also say. A little girl gives you hope, I would add.

"I think that trout will be a little bit smarter next time. That's how small fish get to be big fish."

"Did he feel pain when you caught him?"

"Yes. It hurt him to get caught. Every living thing feels pain. But you know what?"

"What?"

"It made him feel better to be set free. I bet he won't remember the pain."

CHAPTER SIX

No Small Miracle

"DAD, MAY I ask you a question? It's really important."

"Of course."

What burning question of the ages would it be this time, I wondered, glancing at my precocious fishergirl. My head was starting to ache from trying to answer so many Big Picture questions about fishing and life, stuff I hadn't even begun to figure out yet. Her bare feet were propped on Old Blue's dash and a large grasshopper was balanced on her knee. Did the grasshopper know he was traveling with fly anglers and thus was potential fish bait?

"You really don't like Barbie, do you?"

"Who?" The prairie wind was roaring past one ear and Paul McCartney was wailing about a long and winding road in the other. For a minute I thought she'd asked me which Beatle was my favorite. We'd been playing our made-up game called Beatle Challenge in which someone announced a Beatle song's title and the other person had to sing at least twenty words of it or risk being made the laughingstock of an entire generation. Maggie, naturally, was well ahead on points.

"*Bar-bee.*"

"Ah." I nodded and smiled, stalling for time. Aside from the fact that Barbie was older than the oldest Beatle and never visibly aged, had plastic bullet breasts, a brainless smile, and represented an impossible ideal of womanhood I dearly hoped my daughter wouldn't aspire to, I thought Barbie was fine, probably fairly innocent stuff. After all, through much of the sixties I'd wandered around with a pair of cheap six-guns strapped to my person pretending I was Hoss Cartwright, and even grew up to vaguely resemble him, but I had never had the slightest inclination to gun down anybody. Barbie was the perfect little capitalist icon, a doll originally modeled after a German fräulein who looked a little bit like a hooker, but I figured her allure would probably pass and we wouldn't have to build an extra wing on the house to accommodate Barbie and all her accessories.

"What makes you think I don't like Barbie?"

A faint shrug. "I don't know. You looked kind of annoyed at that mall."

"It was more the mall than Barbie, Mugs."

The mall in question was the Mall of America, just south of Minneapolis. Being a couple hayseeds from the slow lanes of Maine, we'd gone there with friends to see what all the hoopla was about and found packs of teenagers in floppy clothes and face metal wandering through the Food Court and fake palm trees of America's biggest mall. Seeing it made me glad the state of Maine has only one mall to speak of, a large edifice we seldom feel the need to visit, and I confessed to her that malls in general made me worry a bit about what was happening to the America I grew up in because they all smelled and looked alike and you could never tell where you were in them or whether it was night or day, dry or raining cats and dogs outside, to say nothing of remembering where you parked your dad-gummed car —

which, I supposed, was the point of having a bunch of chain stores under one roof and why most people really liked them. Malls had surgically killed off much of Main Street America, and I started to give her my full dreary dinner speech about the related declines of gas stations and neighborhoods — how gas stations were now convenience marts where the clerks, inconveniently, couldn't give you decent directions to the next street corner and how neighborhoods weren't what they used to be because of the explosive growth of "gated" communities. But I realized in the nick of time that I was veering dangerously close to achieving Whining Old Fart status and decided to keep the banter light.

"Next question," I said. I was sure there was a next question because with my fishergirl there always was.

"Okay." She took a helpful slug of Gatorade and thought for a moment. I sensed a good Beatle Challenge question coming. Perhaps she'd foolishly toss "In My Life" at me and I'd volley it triumphantly back across the net, showing her I might be an Old Fart but wasn't an entire disgrace to the Fab Four generation.

"Do you, like, believe in miracles?"

"Depends on the miracle," I said, marveling at how nimbly a girl with a freeloading locust on her knee could shift the general floor discussion from the ridiculous to the sublime. On the other hand, my children and I talked often and freely about the subject of God and faith and they knew or sensed I had strong feelings about the spiritual side of life and that I encouraged their own wanderings in this realm. My son went through a period where he believed with the simple faith of a mustard seed that God was the sun. He had no doubt about it whatsoever, was as sure as any ancient Egyptian and child of Ra. For her part, my daughter was of the unwavering opinion that everybody had a guardian angel appointed by God and that God would agree to let you come back as the animal of your choice if you were nice to all His creatures while here on earth—hence her worries about causing fish pain. I haven't a clue where such otherwise pleasant Christian children got such embarrassing heretical notions, though I'd half made up my mind to ask the Almighty to come back as a Boothbay Harbor seal and perhaps the Episcopal church we attended was a bit more ecumenical than we even knew.

The simple truth was, I didn't quite know what to make of miracles—not in this modern Age of Reason where people or their legal representatives demanded to see the physical evidence before rendering a legally binding opinion. Myths were full of wondrous healings and gospel accounts of Jesus' miracles were deeply moving and, to me at least, believable—spit that opened a blind man's eyes, seas calmed by the solemn lift of a hand—but perhaps because I'd been a street reporter for far too many years, relating modern tales of man's inhumanity to his neighbor, modern miracles seemed a bit irrelevant or simply too flashy to be believed, like vulgar parlor tricks designed to make the prayer lines ring off the hook and keep the tithes flowing. Much of my own Christian religion seemed, at times, from the vantage point of a dirt road in Maine, far more obsessed with raising steeples than advancing human hopes, erecting ambitious satellite ministries than feeding hungry people, curing budget deficits instead of suffering, promoting political agendas in place of faith. But there I was about to make another speech to the Old Fart Convention. *I will put a muzzle on my mouth,* says one of the Psalms. Good advice.

"Well, like what for instance?" she demanded.

I explained that miracles were different things to different people and that the miracles I'd witnessed, if you could call them that, tended to be on the small side—things you might just as easily overlook. The fact that my lavender plants came back every year on the heels of a fierce Maine winter seemed almost miraculous, as did looking out our window back home one summer morning recently and seeing a gorgeous ten-point buck standing in the yard. When the Braves won their first World Series, I was convinced it was a minor miracle, and I'd had a few putts to win golf matches over my old nemesis Pat McDaid that fell neatly into that category. I explained that Christian mystics, Buddhists, and Native American holy men maintained that miracles were constantly happening around us but we just refused or were unable to see them. Catching a trout seemed a little bit like a miracle. So was riding in an airplane. Ditto duct tape and the Phillips screwdriver. If I could somehow get telemarketers *not* to call the exact moment we sat down each evening to supper—that would surely be a miracle to match the fish and the loaves.

I laughed at my own irreverence, but Maggie didn't. Come to think of it, the locust didn't look all that amused, either. Perhaps the locust was the reincarnation of my Southern Baptist grandmother who always insisted on hauling her suitcase-sized pocketbook to the communion rail with her because, let's face it, theologically and otherwise, Lutherans really couldn't be all that trusted.

"Well," she countered, "that guy Paul said it was a miracle we weren't killed and I wondered if it really was."

A prairie flicker darted across the highway in front of us and it came to me that she didn't mean Paul on the road to Damascus. She meant Paul on the road out of the Adirondacks, the Paul who had some big-time explaining to do at the Ryder rental counter in Ithaca. Indeed he had said it was a miracle we weren't killed and for all I knew perhaps he was right.

"What about that boy?"

"Boy?"

"The boy on Meadow Road. The one on the sled."

"Oh. Right." Three years before, a few days before Christmas, I'd run over a boy on a sled who came out of nowhere. He'd lived to tell the tale, and perhaps it was a miracle that he survived. His family certainly believed so.

An angel had descended from the blizzard to save the day. Jesus had waved an unseen hand, preventing disaster. Or perhaps it was merely dumb luck—a near-miss of colliding molecules—that we'd both walked away unhurt, though certainly not unchanged, from this powerful and strange encounter. The event had been so shattering, to tell the God's truth, I was *still* trying to make spiritual heads or tails of it.

"I suppose that might qualify as a miracle," I admitted uneasily to her. "Tell you what. Let me think about it a bit and I'll get back to you." The first rule of being the parent of an inquisitive child is this: When in doubt, stall for time.

We were on the edge of the Great Plains and would not fish again for at least two days, not until we reached Wyoming. It was late morning and we'd just passed through Blue Earth, Minnesota, stopping to buy some Prairie Girl ears of corn on the edge of the prairie from a woman at a roadside stand. The corn was beautiful, the color of new pearls, six ears for $1.46. The woman, adjusting her hair bandanna slightly, said it was grown in her father's field in Worthington. He'd just had a stroke but wouldn't give up his corn patch. Nearby, a man was gassing up his Harley. He was wearing faded jeans and fringed buckskins and had an American flag tattooed on his neck, a single silver earring, military shades, a Rockies baseball cap, and a beaded Lakota vest.

I saw Maggie watching him. A modern rider of the High Plains, he told us he was headed to the big Harley rally in Sturgis, South Dakota. Two hundred thousand bikers were already there, as he put it to me, "hanging out and getting high on fumes." He measured us with a low slow smile. Dakota Territory lay dead ahead, the vastness of the Great Plains, the ever-widening sky.

Pulling out from the farm stand, we learned on the radio

that sprinter Michael Johnson had just set a new world record for the hundred-meter dash at the Atlanta Olympics—a kind of miracle, if you thought of it that way—but that there'd been another suicide bombing in the Gaza Strip and a thirty-eighth black church had been torched by unknown persons in northern Mississippi. So, in a sense, the daily tote board was a spiritual loss. A few moments later, however, Paul Harvey revealed that Madalyn Murray O'Hair, America's most famous professional atheist, the woman who chased God from the Republic's classrooms, was herself missing and suspected of socking millions of her foundation's funds away in Swiss accounts before hitting the bricks to parts unknown. You could hear in his voice that Paul Harvey was tempted to declare a national day of celebration.

I turned the dial to South Dakota Gardener's Hotline with Norm Evers out of Pierre—properly pronounced "peer"—and learned, more interestingly, about the early warning signs of corn smut and how to protect a garden from an infestation of "Creeping Charlie." I'd never had a case of Creeping Charlie, so far as I knew, but a vacationing rose gardener can't be too complacent about these matters.

A large highway sign announced that the "world's best coffee" lay just ahead in Mitchell, "home of the world's only Corn Palace," and another one a short time later advised us: "We Dakotans reject animal activists. Fur, fish, game, and livestock are our *livelihoods*!"

It had been three days since we threw fly lines and I missed it, but heavens, what possible minimiracles of American ingenuity and culture we'd beheld in a thousand miles of the Republic! In Michigan's Upper Peninsula, we'd fished a second Indian Lake on the shores of the Hiawatha National Forest, then gone into Manistique to eat lake perch at a nice diner and attend the Schoolcraft County Fair and run slap into the outgoing Miss Schoolcraft County, who was hoofing across the dusty ball field in her starched white ball gown, dabbing her eyes every few steps, a pretty made-up farmgirl named Arlene—a real-life Barbie!—who stopped and chatted enthusiastically with my daughter about how you had to say only positive things about life and America's youth and how you should remember to always smile if you wanted to win beauty pageant titles and then explained to me, when I asked, that what she would miss most about her reign as Miss Schoolcraft County, she guessed, was singing to the old people in rest homes and inspiring the kids who might never have the opportunity to leave Manistique. She was about to do that herself come fall—she was headed to dental school in Akron—and when I pressed her about whether she might someday come back, she glanced around, spotted some approaching neighbors, produced a spectacular smile, squeezed their hands as they passed, then turned back to me and said with a tearful sniff, "Probably not."

Across the border into Wisconsin—America's leading cheese state!—we stopped for cheese in a town that had the largest iron skillet in the world, right there in the main drag for all comers to admire, and I wondered to a waitress named Ruthie how the town could possibly resist the temptation of going for broke after the world's biggest cheese omelette record, and Ruthie, sloshing more coffee in my cup, told me it was my kind of big thinking that made the Packers the best team in pro football. She told me I could be a Cheesehead, talking like that. Then we moved on to a place near La Crosse that, if you can fathom it, boasted the world's largest six-pack of beer. A short time later, we removed what might have been the world's largest snapping turtle from a busy country road, perhaps sparing him a visit to some hungry Cheesehead's soup pot au gratin, then pushed on to St. Paul and stayed for two nights with my old friends Tony and Patti, who lived in a racially mixed inner-city neighborhood called Frogtown. There we got to have breakfast on the Mississippi River, tour a swell state history museum, watch the Frogtown community parade, and then walk around a multicultural food and music fair where everything I ate made me proud to be an American, if not a Packer Cheesehead.

Later, while our daughters rode bikes around the block, Tony and I sat on his porch on Van Buren Street drinking beers and talking about our fathers. Mine, Opti, with a little luck, was playing a golf course somewhere in Valhalla. His, Emil, was a retired garage owner and widower who lived in the small lake town west of Minneapolis where Tony grew up.

I had pleasant memories of Emil at Tony and Patti's wedding, the reception of which was conducted in Emil's garage due to the uninvited arrival of a sudden ferocious thunderstorm. As we stood there watching the sky empty itself, Emil explained to me the proper way to disassemble and rebuild a Plymouth Fury engine, highly useful information I'd unfortunately never been able to put to much good use. I asked Tony how his father was doing with his mother being gone.

"Oh, fine, I guess. I think he's lonely and misses her a lot, but he never really lets on about it. It's a different world for him, though."

"Does he fish?" I had memories of Emil talking about the killer walleye in the land of ten thousand lakes.

"A little bit. I think he enjoys gambling more these days. Once a week he gets in his car and drives out to a casino on the edge of the prairie run by the Indians. He loses a bit of money and comes home a well-contented man."

Tony, who ran Frogtown's little community newspaper now, was my closest reporter chum from my Atlanta years and we both had swapped big-city stories for small-town lives and now shared fatherhood and gardening and news of blood drives and bean suppers and drank our beers in contented silence for a moment, waiting for our daughters to pedal back as a blue dusk settled over Van Buren Street.

Maggie had never ridden a bike on a city street before and I was visibly nervous about her maiden sortie — "Relax," Tony deadpanned, "we haven't had a drive-by shooting in, oh, at *least* two weeks" — and I took his word on faith and was eventually rewarded by the sound of two girls coming around the corner, their voices floating ahead of them on the night. I smelled something sweet from Tony's garden and said I would take that second beer after all.

"I sometimes think there's a bit of poetic justice in my father's heading out to the prairie to gamble," he said, getting up slowly as we watched the girls park their bikes on the walk. "We took their fathers' land and now they take our fathers' money."

Just across the line in South Dakota, we stopped at the "world-famous Corn Palace" in search of coffee and a pee, depositing the grasshopper in a small park behind a rank of large motor homes, and wandered into the Corn Palace, which disappointingly turned out to be just an auditorium with a lot of corn husks creatively arranged on its walls. While I waited for Maggie to inspect the plumbing, I busied myself reading a brochure about the place and tried not to be mistaken for one of the elderly sightseers who were gathering to take the official guided tour of the premises. They looked gaunt and agitated, as if they'd merely stepped into the building to escape the fierce Dakota sun and had then been asked to serve on a hanging jury. According to the brochure, Mitchell was such a pleasant boomtown because it was located on part of the Oregon Trail and a couple enterprising real estate men had come up with the idea of creating the Corn Palace to try and drum up business and convince settlers passing through on their way West that Mitchell was really someplace they ought to stop and put down stakes. By the look of the small town's congested main street, though, only junk jewelry dealers and T-shirt shop owners seemed to have been impressed enough to stick around. We bought coffee and soft-serve ice cream and fled down the highway to Chamberlain, where we suddenly saw the Missouri River for the first time, wide and brown and glittering majestically in the late afternoon sun.

Many of those same settlers had believed this was the start of the real West, the great high grassy inverted bowl of the plains leading to the Dakota Badlands and the sacred Black Hills and the very feet of the Rockies beyond. The thought of passing through such an unbroken and forbidding place, I thought, surely must have made more than a few of them wish they'd never left home, and surviving this barren windswept world must have been no small miracle.

I suggested to Maggie that we try and get a glimpse of what it might have been like heading alone through the desolation of the prairie. She looked at me and smiled. A bowl of melting vanilla ice cream was on her lap, her bare feet were safely propped against the dash, Mary Chapin Carpenter was singing about stones in the road, and Amos was busy ignoring the Great Plains in back. She was practicing the Eiffel Tower with yarn, having already established a world record for doing cat's cradle in five-point-two seconds flat. "That would be cool," she said, casually looking out at the sere landscape to the north.

We followed Route 50 up a dry canyon through the Creek-Crow Indian Reservation, passing through the run-down junction town of Fort Thompson, which boasted a sky-blue post office, an Indian-run casino called the Lode Star, a tribal school, and a modest subdivision with brown yards, several liquor shops, and a boarded-up bingo hall. We stopped at the post office to mail postcards from the Corn Palace and I casually asked the white clerk what people did in Fort Thompson to help make the time pass. The sound of locusts filled the open door, making the air outside electrified.

"Think about moving someplace else," he replied without

even looking up, calmly sorting mail. He told us there was a campground across the Big Bend Dam, right on the river's edge, pretty good fishing, especially near the dam. We drove on and crossed the Missouri and found the campground, a dusty patch of cracked-open earth with no freshwater facilities. The temperature must have been closing fast on one hundred and no one was about except the locusts. I opened the road atlas on the hood of Old Blue and considered following the Missouri farther north to Pierre, where there was another state park and we could camp and fish before dark, but suddenly the heat and the dust and the vast isolation felt a bit too overwhelming and I thought it would be no small miracle to put up a tent and unpack the gear and find a decent night's sleep in this godforsaken place. I suggested to Maggie that we push on to a town called Murdo and maybe find an air-conditioned motel room with a pool and a nice home-cooked dinner.

We rolled on, encouraged by the thought of a swim in a pool but silenced by the relentless heat and openness, rising after what seemed like half-hour intervals to the summits of long grass hills that simply afforded us more views of brown hills and baking grasslands.

The radio station faded out. I told Maggie about a man I'd once visited out here on the High Plains for an interview, a rancher whose family had been on the land for over a hundred years. He'd grown up in a predominantly Norwegian Lutheran household but his great-grandfather had been a full-blooded Cheyenne Indian medicine man, a survivor of the massacre at Wounded Knee who practiced the "old ways" and taught his grandchildren the Ghost Dance.

"What's a Ghost Dance?"

I explained that the Ghost Dance was performed in a circle, a ritual dance that sometimes lasted over several days, with participants holding hands and dancing until exhaustion dropped them into a deathlike trance. The participants believed the ceremony would summon their dead

ancestors back to the earth, along with the vanquished buffalo herds, thereby restoring life to the way it was before the
white man arrived with his bullets and new religions. Warriors believed it would also make them invulnerable to the
bullets from soldiers' guns.

At its height of popularity in the late 1880s, I explained,
inspired by the visions of a Paiute prophet named Wovoka,
thousands of disaffected Indian youth began performing the
ritual dance in a desperate attempt to assimilate Christianity
into their religion, in defiance of U.S. government laws forbidding them to practice it. Frightened by rumors of new
Indian hostilities, the government's response to the Ghost
Dance was to dispatch *half* of the entire U.S. Army west to
the plains reservations, resulting in a massacre at a place
called Wounded Knee where 146 men, women, and children
were cut down by drunken soldiers of the Seventh Cavalry.
On New Year's Day, their frozen bodies were tossed into a
mass grave and hastily covered over.

"That's a terrible story," she said. "Did they really kill
children, too?"

"Afraid so." I explained that those children who survived
Wounded Knee and many other Indian massacres like it
got sent either East or to special Indian schools on government reservations, where they were whipped for speaking
in their native tongue and even sometimes killed if they
got caught worshiping anything but a white Christian
God. The idea was to transform them into something
they could never be—white Christians. I reflected that
Aunt Emma, her great-great-grandmother, the Cherokee
foundling, had undoubtedly endured such a fate.

As I said this, it suddenly hit me that perhaps I'd stumbled upon the answer to the family's most perplexing and
troubling mystery, a possible explanation as to why Aunt
Emma had finally removed herself the way she did. Out
here on the plains it suddenly seemed to add up. The world
of her childhood had been utterly destroyed, her people

marched West at the point of a soldier's gun. The world she was asked to live in as an adult belonged entirely to someone else. She'd had great courage and wisdom but no true spiritual home and maybe the imbalance of nature was simply far too much to bear and so, unafraid of death, she eventually followed the path of her ancestors home.

Maggie gazed out the window for a moment and asked if the rancher I'd visited showed me how to do a Ghost Dance.

"No. But he drove me out to a spot on the plains where he believed his grandfather was buried. There was a cluster of cottonwoods and the wheat grass was very green around a small creek. He showed me a steer skull that had been bleached white in the sun and warned me to watch for rattlers. He said there was no marker because Indians didn't believe in marking graves the way white men did because they felt they belonged to God's earth, not God's earth to them. He knew it was the spot, though, because he claimed he could 'feel it.' "

"What did it feel like?"

"I don't know. To me it seemed kind of empty. All you could hear and feel was the wind."

I made a serious miscalculation in Murdo, expecting a pretty High Plains town with a few nice shade trees, a good diner, and perhaps a clean motel with Mom and Pop Birdsong catching the evening breeze in lawn chairs, sipping a cool iced tea by the pool. But Murdo was your basic interstate trucker town, full of noisy big rigs and cheap motels and dust-covered tourist cars gassing up for the all-night haul across the Badlands.

We took the last room at the kind of neon motel where the management changes the sheets daily—at least room to room—and ventured out to try and scour up some grub at the nearby Buffalo Lounge. Buffalo burgers were the spe-

cial that night and there was a noisy group of bikers
yukking it up under beer lights in the back room. There
was an all-you-can-eat salad bar with nothing much you'd
care to eat, so I ordered the buffalo special. The waitress
wrote that down and then stared hard at Maggie. "Better
try that burger, sugar," she said, snapping her gum.
"It's some tasty."

"No thank you. Are you really going to eat a buffalo?"
she asked me somewhat incredulously.

"Well, not all of it."

She shook her head. "I don't care for anything, thanks."

Something was chewing at her—the heat, the dust, the
Bates Motel, the waitress who did her evening facial in ce-
ment, perhaps even the story I'd told her earlier about Indian children being shot by cavalry soldiers. Maybe that
had been a mistake, one story I should have kept in the jar.
It probably didn't help that her parents had decided to get
divorced, either. Some sadness you can't outrun.

"If you could have anything in the world right this moment," I said, "what would it be?" I was afraid she was
going to say McDonald's chicken nuggets or for her mother
and father to get their act together.

"A swimming pool," she replied without hesitation. Our
luxury roadside spa, alas, didn't have one and the Mom and
Pop running the place looked as if they might be blood
relatives on their last stop in the federal witness relocation
program.

Just when you think you've got somebody neatly pegged,
though, they go and change everything. The waitress gave
us a sweet sympathetic smile. I noticed that her canine tooth
was perfectly edged in gold. "You know, hon, there's a nice
community pool up on the hill. My niece swims up there
every night. I think it stays open till dark."

I thanked her, left a five for her trouble, and we drove up
the hill and discovered a beautiful pool full of clean cold

water. A group of teenagers on bikes was hanging around by the admission table. Bats or flickers swooped low in the purpling evening sky. The view was sensational. I asked the teens how the water was. "Pretty good," a large boy with acne replied. "But that was this morning 'fore all the little kids pissed in it." He pronounced it "kee-ids."

The teenagers giggled.

"What kind of dog is that?" a tall and gangly girl wondered, pushing stringy hair behind a sunburned ear.

"Old and hot mostly," I said. Amos had already deposited himself on the cool wet pavement by the entrance to the changing rooms.

"A retriever," I added.

"What's he retrieve?" More giggles.

"Not much." Amos had never been one for fetching things. If you threw a stick, his view seemed to be that you ought to go pick it up instead of wasting his valuable time.

We swam laps. The water was a real surprise, cold as a Maine lake in July and thoroughly refreshing. I got out and sat on the side of the pool until Maggie begged me to come back in and race her. She was a splendid swimmer for seven and I suppose I let her win, though it wouldn't be too much longer before she would have to let me win. I got out of the water and flopped in a plastic chair while she padded toward the diving end of the pool, where a pudgy nut-brown Indian boy wearing cutoff shorts with a belt was doing cannonballs off the low diving board. There was a large splash. The kid did good cannonballs.

I opened a book from the Medicine Bag called *Dakota: A Spiritual Geography*, by poet Kathleen Norris. I'd been re-reading this lovely memoir of faith slowly for weeks, snatches here and there, an account of Norris's return to an ascetic life on her family's bleak ancestral lands in northwestern South Dakota. Maine was extreme, I thought, but nothing quite like that.

The idea of personal transformations and Norris's description of killer blizzards, combined with Maggie's question earlier that day, made me think of the boy I'd run over three winters ago. He was about the same age as the Indian kid doing cannonballs. I'd gone to the store at the start of the season's first good snowstorm, a real Atlantic howler, in a deep holiday funk, just needing to get out of the house for a while to try and clear my head. Something was gnawing at me but I couldn't figure out exactly what.

Perhaps it was that I was about to turn forty, but I didn't think so. So much in my life seemed, by anyone's standards, almost idyllic—children who were healthy and happy, a career that finally made sense, a sturdy house I'd built with my own hands, surrounded by rose gardens and a beautiful forest. In two days' time I was scheduled to play my classical guitar during the annual family Christmas Eve service at Settlemeyer's barn. All of which made this sudden Christmas funk even more maddening and intolerable.

I drove out into the blizzard to try and figure out what was making me so miserable. The supermarket was virtually empty because anyone with any sense was already safely home. I bought a box of Cheerios, a quart of Diet Pepsi, four lightbulbs, two cans of cat food, and a newspaper, and checked out behind an elderly woman who was buying a potted plant and a copy of *Time* magazine, the annual year-end special that summarizes the year's total of natural and man-made disasters, celebrity deaths and marriages, hot movies and holy jihads. "Isn't it beautiful the way the snow covers everything?" the elderly woman suddenly said to me. I looked out at the empty parking lot, at the prehistoric shapes of the few vehicles still out there, and may have nodded. "You'd think people would slow down and notice all that beauty, wouldn't you?" I smiled at her as you would at any unbalanced person, noticed that she was wearing only cheap running shoes, assumed she was perhaps someone "from away" or simply unacquainted with the ferocity of Maine winter storms. I confess I thought: *Crazy as a widow loon.*

I got back in Old Blue and drove along Meadow Road. I turned on the radio and suddenly heard Bach's *Sleepers Awake,* the very melody I was preparing to perform at Settlemeyer's barn. And then the words of the crazy lady floated back into my head; I cut my truck's speed nearly in half, noticing the way the snow slanted across the fields as I approached my favorite old homeplace on the hill. I'd never seen the people who lived there.

As I rose over the small knoll between the house and the barn, though, a shape suddenly materialized out of the storm, a boy bouncing on a sled. I cut the wheel sharply to the right but saw him vanish beneath the wheels, heard a small cry, and felt a sickening crunch. The truck tilted on its side as it slid down the embankment. This took only an instant to happen and I was still strapped in my seat harness, which for a change I'd worn, staring at the ruptured Pepsi bottle spraying cola all over the dash and the small round oats of Cheerios scattered everywhere. For a moment I sat, dumbly suspended in my seat harness, trying to comprehend what had just happened, and then I heard another cry and was scrambling like a madman to get out of the truck and up to the boy. I found him lying on his stomach in the middle of the road. I touched his head and asked him if he could move. *My legs,* he said with a whimper. *I can't feel my legs.* I picked him up and moved him to the side of the road, fearing the sight of a snowplow roaring over the knoll. I told him not to move and said I would go get help. Just then, the door to the farmhouse swung open and a heavyset woman came plunging down the snowy yard, wailing and out of control. She fell in the snow and struggled to get up. I went to help her and, as I gripped her arms, we briefly did an absurd minuet of terror on the slippery county road. I had never seen such grief in a mother's eyes. She was thinking the unthinkable. And then her eyes suddenly changed, softened somehow in wonder. I turned around. The boy was standing up. *It's okay, Mom,* he said, rubbing his back. *I think I'm okay.*

There was another large splash. The Indian boy had done another cannonball.

"That's my grandson. I think he's trying to impress your daughter."

I shielded my eyes from the low sun to see the woman seated just a few feet away. Maine winter was gone, Dakota summer was back. The sun was behind the woman's head but I could see she was an Indian woman, I guess about sixty or seventy, fully dressed with a large floppy straw hat on, also reading a book. I wondered what she was reading but couldn't quite make out the title, though for some reason I imagined it was something by Rosamunde Pilcher, a fantasy of English cottage life, taking her about as far from here as you could get.

"Those are some splashes. I'm sure she'll be impressed."

"She's quite a swimmer. Y'all headed West?"

"Yes ma'am." I wondered vaguely if I was right to have addressed her as "ma'am," a holdover from the days when among my greatest ambitions was to make a good cannonball.

"I figured that. Where to?"

"Yellowstone. Maybe into Idaho. We're kind of wandering, to tell the truth."

"Nice. Will you go to the Pacific?"

"Perhaps. My daughter would probably like to see it."

"She's not alone. I'd like to see it, too."

She went back to her evening reading and so did I. Norris was now talking about how in the Dakotas you are about as far from the sea—any sea—as possible. You are in a world turned upside down, she says, a place where angels drown.

The boy on the sled was named Matthew, like the author

of the gospel. He was thirteen. His father was the sexton at the big Catholic church in town. The boy sat in a wooden chair by the kitchen woodstove, sobbing nearly uncontrollably, overwhelmed by the immensity of what had just happened. The kitchen was extremely warm. The constable was outside watching a wrecker winch my truck from the ditch. His mother turned to me and said, with the conviction of a true witness: *It was a miracle. I have no doubt about that at all.*

I had doubt, plenty of doubt—doubt about it being a miracle, doubt about my sanity. A little while later, I drove home, made myself a large Scotch, and sat in my favorite chair in the den, numbly staring at chickadees dive-bombing the bird feeder, where I'd just put out new seed. Under normal circumstances the chickadees would have given me great pleasure. They amazed me—the way the smallest creature in Maine is able to stand up to the worst that winter can dish out. Their will to endure was astonishing to behold. The storm ended and my wife took the children out to do some Christmas shopping in Freeport. I remember Maggie, then almost three, pausing as she left to kiss me and to ask if we could make a real snow angel when they returned. I promised we would, though I didn't really believe it.

"Dad?"

That same voice, older now, brought me back to the High Plains.

The Indian boy was in the water and Maggie was standing on the diving board, watching him, waiting with her hands on her slim hips. I noticed, for the first time, how the land fell abruptly away behind her. You couldn't see the dusty little town below and nothing was visible but the tops of a few treeless bluffs in the purpling distance. She was framed by the dimming sky, pleats of gold and rose.

"Dad, watch!" she called out, and I called back, "I'm watching."

The woman was watching, too, and so was her grandson.
Maggie stood erect for a moment, releasing her hands to her
sides. The board was perhaps three meters high. I was
pretty sure she was going to jump, because she had never
dived and had always jumped.

She loped slowly toward the end of the board, bounced
lightly once, then rose upward in the arc of a dive. For a
split second she hovered in the air, like a girl diving into the
sky. I couldn't believe what I was seeing.

It wasn't a perfect dive but it was her first dive and I
know I'll never forget it. She surfaced a second or two later,
spitting water and grimacing with either pain or joy.

"My God, Maggie. That was great!" I got up to go see
how she was.

The Indian woman clapped her hands. "Wonderful.
Really *wonderful*."

A couple of the teenagers even turned their heads to see
what had happened. The Indian boy was smiling, too.

After the accident, I sat in my darkened den watching the
chickadees dive-bomb the feeder for nearly two days, trying
to figure out what the hell had happened or was happening
to me. You read about people having nervous breakdowns,
unable to shake a feeling of impending doom. My malaise
wasn't quite like that—it was more anger with myself, and
anger with that damned old woman who put it in my head
to slow down. After all, if I hadn't slowed down I wouldn't
have nearly killed the kid. Finally I gave up and called my
father, recounting every detail of the incident to him and
admitting it was one of the worst moments of my life.

"Maybe so, maybe not. Maybe it's the best day of your
life. You obviously want to change something."

The remark was so like my father, so Opti the Mystic. He
was asking me to turn the proposition on its ear, consider
the problem from another angle. I went back to my chair

and thought about that possibility for a while, staring at the chickadees. The chickadees flitted up, flitted away.

The mules angels ride, poet Wallace Stevens said, come slowly down from Heaven. Something happened I wasn't even aware of at first. It really took weeks to notice, perhaps even months. My mood perceptibly changed, brightening with the days, and I realized I felt an almost palpable hunger to move deeper into the stream of my own life. The children, my work, the house—all were fine but none of it was enough alone. I needed something deeper, a stronger connection to my own life, a truer place to be, a genuine knowledge of where I stood on earth.

Perhaps I was seeking a mystical experience. I'll never know. Something happened, though. Something changed. It wasn't at all what I hoped and prayed for—our carefully constructed world was beginning to fall apart and I didn't even know it. *Careful if you ask for true enlightenment,* goes an old Eastern saying. *For God will set your hair on fire.*

"We're going for ice cream," the Indian woman said, gathering their things. "Would you two like to join us?"

We all went together down the hill into Murdo and I learned the woman's name was Helen. She was the boy's grandmother, visiting from Sturgis. Her husband, Bill, was helping her son raise a barn but she and Bill always liked to get out of town when the Harley bikers converged on Sturgis; last summer they'd gone to Yellowstone. The boy's name was Vern but they called him Lootie. I congratulated Lootie on his cannonballs and asked his grandmother, a little awkwardly, what tribe they hailed from. My terminology felt stiffly self-conscious, like that of a dude straight from Beantown.

She smiled and said they were Crow-Creek. In the old days the Crow were fierce enemies of both the Lakota Sioux and the American horse soldiers, which may explain, she said, why they vanished first. We were all eating cones of chocolate ice cream at the convenience market, except Lootie, who was having cookies and cream.

"Of course," Helen said, with immaculate timing, "we never really vanished. That's the joke. We're still here."

She asked me what I was reading. It seemed she worked in a bookstore in Sturgis. I showed her Norris's memoir and she nodded. Lootie and Maggie were down the aisle looking at water guns now. She'd read Norris's memoir and thought it was excellent, particularly the bit about South Dakota's being a place where whites and Native Americans live alone together, with a windy silence between two worlds. In books, she'd found, some turn of phrase simply catches you. That one had caught her and seemed so true. I asked what she was reading and she showed me—a paperback edition of Ralph Waldo Emerson's essays.

We smiled. How amusing. I was reading a poet of the West, she a poet of the East. I admitted I loved Emerson but hadn't read his stuff in quite a while. She handed me the paperback.

"Here, take it with you," she said. "I've got half a table back home covered with these things. This guy almost sounds like an Indian."

The plains where we lay in the darkness had once been a prehistoric seabed. What an astounding thought. That world had changed, too. Vanished before someone's eyes.

"Dad. Are you awake?"

"Yes, babe." I was lying with my hands behind my head, a sheet covering my sweaty skin, staring at the darkness and listening to the Bates Motel air conditioner wheeze. My unquiet mind was churning. Had I unearthed my own eureka piece here on the remains of an ancient seabed somewhere near the exact heart of North America?

"You told Lootie that you liked his cannonballs."

"I was just being polite. He's a kid who probably doesn't get much encouragement from strangers."

"Did you like my dive, too?"

"Maggie, I thought your dive was awesome. I really mean that. Did I forget to tell you? I'm sorry. I've never seen anything quite like it."

I caught myself before I said it. Then I went ahead and said it.

"In fact, do you remember asking me if I believed in miracles?"

"Yes."

"Well, I do believe in them. I think I saw my very first one tonight. That dive, kiddo, was a real miracle."

CHAPTER SEVEN

....

Silent Sam

Dear Pocahontus,
Today when we traveld a cross Ameraka with Amos we wnt to
Mount Rushmore which was good because we saw a poodel
with a leather jacket and a helmit on. The man who had the
poodel had a beard and talked to Dad a long time showing him
his mothercycle. Mount Rushmore was so big and cool and I
like president Teddy Roosyfelt the best because he came out
here too and did stuff like wear doing. I wanted a picture and
some guy took the picture for us and he loved Amos and held
his leed while Dad and I walked up to look at the presidents.
Then we went camping and stayed in a cool cabin by a lake
where the Sue Indians used to live and thot the world began. I
would never be able to count all of the hells angels on there
mothercycles but later we met a buffolow and named him Stan
like my cat and Amos touched his nose with his nose and well
that's my part of the story for now, Love, Maggie.
> *P.S. Tumorrow we are going fly fishing again.*
> *P.S.S. I Love you, Love, Maggie (Dodson)*

"It ain't one damn bit like it used to be, man. I shit you not. You got all these rules and regulations now, cops who'll bust your ass for havin' an open beer. Fancy little dudes walkin' around with walkie-talkies. No more weed, no more whiskey. It's like one damn big Amway convention or something."

"It's a wonder you can bear to come anymore."

"Hey, it's America. I got a right. It was mine before theirs. See that dude over there?"

I looked at the guy he was pointing to, a guy decked out in black leather, with a filthy bandanna on his head, a hook earring, and several days' growth of beard. His vest had a nice embroidered skull on the back. He was talking to a blonde biker moll in tight-fitting jeans.

"Know what that sucker does for a living?"

I almost said he murdered families in their sleep. But it would only have been an educated guess. Instead, I shook my head.

"Dentist from Ohio. No shit. I met him last year. Him and his wife come out to Sturgis every year, hauling their Hogs on a trailer behind their big shiny Suburban. They park the truck fifty miles east of here and ride in like real bikers. Toy bikers, I call 'em. Turns your goddamn stomach, don't it?"

I was chatting with an aging Son of Thunder who was concerned about what the annual Harley Bike Rally in Sturgis was turning into, one big friendly costume party for dentists and proctologists. The Son of Thunder had a large mane of flowing gray hair like an Old Testament prophet's, a faint aura of the King of Beers, and real knife-wound scars on his face. Beyond that, he seemed like a perfectly nice sort of person and even graciously offered to take our photograph and hold Amos's lead while Maggie and I hoofed up to the main observation deck at Mount Rushmore to view the presidents' heads. The long walk up would be too much for the old fellow to negotiate in such

heat and I considered the man's offer, remembering that
Jesus had called his disciples Sons of Thunder. When I said
yes, Amos looked deeply relieved and immediately took a
seat by the man's Harley, which was parked under a leaning
pine tree. As we walked away, I heard the biker ask him if
he'd care for a Budweiser.

The Black Hills were crawling with bikers from the rally
ninety miles away and we'd followed a noisy line of cyclists
and their molls all the way up to the monument's main parking lot, where we found several hundred more cyclists already parked and milling around, including a man who had
a standard poodle straddling the seat behind him. The poodle, wearing a leather vest and aviator's goggles, seemed
perfectly at ease on the back of a Hog.

The four presidents, half a mile or so distant, seemed
strangely detached from this scene and deeply embedded in
their own thoughts. George looked slightly prim and disap-
proving while Tom was gazing heavenward as if in a kind of
dreamy trance; Teddy's chin was set in a no-nonsense manner, his eyes looking a tad suspicious, while Abe merely
looked as if he'd seen a ghost. They looked unreal or perhaps
unnatural and a great deal smaller than I'd expected. I also
wondered why none of them had been depicted smiling. In
the natural rock to George's right, I could almost make out
the face of Mr. Magoo, but maybe I was just seeing things.

We walked up for a closer inspection, weaving through
the dense crowds in the hot sunshine. I was anxious to keep
moving because we had a reservation for a cabin on Sylvan
Lake near Harney Peak in Custer State Park and Maggie
wanted to try and see a buffalo before dark and I wanted to
put Norumbega Girl in the lake and get back to slinging a
line and tippet for trout.

We stared up respectfully at our four great presidents for
a few minutes until Maggie asked, "Why isn't there a girl up
there, too?"

"Good question. Probably because we haven't had a

woman president yet. My guess is, you'll be the first. When you're safely in the White House just promise me that your old man can have unlimited access to the presidential putting green."

"Okay. But I think I'd rather be a movie actress or a scientist instead. Would you mind?"

"No problem. Maybe Aileen will be the first Mrs. President." Aileen was her best friend back in Maine.

Maggie nodded and smiled, then demanded to know what each of "those guys" had done to warrant having his likeness carved on a mountaintop. I gave her a thumbnail sketch of each president. Washington was "father of our country" and had declined the option to be named king. He supposedly refused to lie about hacking down his father's cherry tree (a double lie, as it turns out, because it never happened), once supposedly tried to toss a dollar coin across the Delaware (ditto), suffered grievously from gout, the effects of wooden dentures, and a stiff back from sleeping in too many fine country inns. The truth was, I didn't know much about George Washington, though the more I gazed up at him, with his bobbed hair and prim mouth, the more he uncannily resembled my old nemesis Miss Wettington.

Jefferson was a different story. I'd read virtually everything written about him. He was, in my view, to borrow a phrase from a certain Son of Thunder, the most impressive *dude* America had ever produced. Tall, cerebral, a philosopher farmer, wine lover, creator of the most liberating document in human history, devoted father, slave owner, visionary architect, restless house builder, an old soul but a new gardener, a lonely theist who created his own Bible by editing down the Gospels, a man who lost virtually everyone he loved and died nearly penniless, an aging statesman who made lists of ordinary things to try and escape grief and beat depression. A true American original—and enigma. John Adams called him "the Shadow Man."

Call me crazy but I could relate to Jefferson a bit. He tore down his house on a hill at Monticello and rebuilt it several times, never quite content with its arrangement, and never finished it as a result. I'd built my post-and-beam house on a hill in Maine and was forever changing something about it, too. Like Jefferson's, my flower gardens were an endless source of joy and frustration, and like his my children were the primary source of light in my life. My faith was of the same eccentric bent, and I also compulsively compiled lists of things — things to do, things I didn't wish to forget; things upon things. The first stories both our fathers told us, mine when I was about six, were Indian tales, and the older Jefferson got the more he just wanted to sit and read philosophy and religion and watch his roses grow. I hoped all similarities ended there, though, because I couldn't bear the prospect of outliving my children, as he had.

During our trip through the Adirondacks, I'd filled Maggie in a bit on Teddy Roosevelt — why he went West to find a new life, how he rediscovered himself in the Dakota Badlands and became a pretty swell president, creating, among other things, America's first national park system based on the success of Yellowstone. And Lincoln she already knew a fair amount about thanks to the good offices of Louise Colburn, her first-grade teacher. She knew Abe Lincoln was a man of the people who'd freed the slaves and held the Union together during its greatest period of trial, then been shot and killed by a fool who did the one damned thing that could finish off the South. She knew his likeness was on the American penny, which some idiot in Congress was determined to try and scuttle. What she didn't know was that Lincoln suffered woefully from migraines and nightmares and was subject to periods of the blackest despair, or that his wife went crazy as a widow loon after his death and the country drifted into rancorous stagnation for nearly thirty years.

"Dad, can we go see a buffalo now?" She had her heart set on seeing a live buffalo—and, come to that, I'd never seen a real one, either. The best part of wandering through America, I was learning, was that we could simply go when we'd had enough.

"Sure thing, babe," I said, still gazing up at maybe the four most famous sad guys in American history, holding my daughter's hand amid the bikers; then we went back down and discovered the aging Son of Thunder and our dog dozing peacefully side by side beneath a leaning lodgepole pine. I almost hated to disturb them.

The bikers still outnumbered us at Sylvan Lake, where we stopped at the general store near the cabin to provision for the drive in the morning across the Bighorn Mountains into Wyoming. The bikers were having a cookout on the lawn and I saw Maggie eyeing the hot dogs with a wistful remembrance of wieners past and suggested she and the big guy go get one while I used the pay phone to check my messages back home.

We'd been down the rabbit hole sixteen days and I hadn't felt the slightest desire to check my messages even once. There were twenty-six messages waiting, mostly from people I could safely forgo speaking with until autumn or the next century, but one call from the wife of an old college friend that couldn't be ignored. I heard tremendous anxiety in her voice.

"Hi, Jim. It's Maureen. I'm calling because of Robert. I think he really could use a phone call from you. He's having kind of a rough summer. Could you give him a call sometime?" Curiously, she left her work number, which suggested to me she wouldn't mind speaking to me first. I hung up the phone and dialed her number.

My friend Robert was a successful lawyer who lived in Savannah. We'd known each other in college and kept in

touch over the years. He'd built a thriving practice on
marine law and had a beautiful wife and two teenage daughters, a big house on the Isle of Hope, a cozy summer place
in the Carolina upcountry, a collection of vintage shotguns,
and he belonged to the best golf club and a hunting club on
Pamlico Sound where he and other lawyer types went every
autumn to massacre ducks. He knew I'd quit hunting long
ago but invited me every year, for old times' sake, I think. I
asked Maureen, when she came on, how Bobby, as I called
him, was doing.

"Fine, I guess, if you discount the fact that I found him
sitting in the dark in the basement last Saturday afternoon
holding a loaded shotgun saying he thought he might have
to shoot himself."

I swallowed dryly at this news and gazed around at the
bikers eating their hot dogs in the Black Hills sunshine. My
daughter was having two hot dogs, I noticed, then realized
she was breaking off pieces and hand-feeding them to
Amos.

"He reminds me," she said, "of that statue you guys put
underwear on up at Chapel Hill. Remember? The one that
just sits there holding his gun and saying nothing?"

"Silent Sam," I said. Silent Sam was the popular name
for the statue of a Confederate soldier that *stood* on a grassy
quad on the university campus, a lone sentinel holding his
musket and watching out for returning Yankees. One night
after a fraternity party twenty-five years before, a group of
us had put a jumbo pair of gent's underpants on Silent Sam.
It was pretty lame and innocent stuff but we found the stunt
to be fall-down hilarious—a soldier going to war in his
Skivvies. No wonder our side lost.

Maureen explained that she'd persuaded Bobby to go to
the hospital, where they'd placed him in an observation
room and called in a psychiatric specialist. The diagnosis
was acute clinical depression and Bobby still wasn't saying
much except that there was no way he would take any an-

tidepressant medicine of any kind. At one point, he'd calmly
told her his life wasn't worth living and to go home and he'd
figure out how to dispose of himself so the insurance company wouldn't ask any questions. The thing was, he seemed
almost rational about his clearly insane plan. Maureen was
nearly at the end of her rope as a result, she admitted, and
the girls were terrified, and she wondered if a call from an
old friend might help—help him see the wisdom of taking
the medicine or help him see how valuable his life was or at
least coax him out of his scary silence a bit. She seemed to
remember I'd gone through a rough time after a friend of
mine was killed and wondered if it might help Bobby to
hear about that.

I promised I would call him and she gave me the hospital
number. Then I said good-bye and hung up the phone,
slipped the paper into my pocket, and stood there for a
moment wondering what I could possibly say to my old
friend that would help him. Mental depression is scary business and I knew several men in their forties and fifties
who'd been cruelly afflicted by it, seemingly out of the blue,
without warning, almost randomly, at the fullest stride of
their lives, madness sent down by the gods. None of them
had succumbed to it but a couple were still borderline cases.
I think I'd had a spot of it myself after Kristen's death and
after running over the boy on the sled.

Medical science understood a fair amount about what
caused the disorder—a depletion of several naturally occur-
ring chemicals in the brain, perhaps triggered by stress, and
an increase of other hormones that caused a wrenching fluc-
tuation in the brain tissue, a literal brainstorm that first
depleted the brain of its resiliency and ultimately attacked
the rest of the body as well.

That was depression on paper. Profile of a silent killer.
An idiopathic fog that settled on one's world, scrambled
neurotransmitters, and turned the brain agonizingly in on
itself with cannibalistic intent, what the ancients called "a

sickness of the soul" or acute melancholia, a pervasive sense of personal loss accompanied by systematic physical exhaustion, a despair beyond despair, the wind of the wing of madness, as Baudelaire was supposed to have described it. It had driven Roosevelt West and killed Hemingway. Given time and proper analysis, certain drugs could alleviate some of the symptoms of the disease, keep demons at bay, and perhaps even make life once again more than tolerable. Though some researchers were firmly convinced the critical factors that caused the onset of acute systematic depression in adults lay buried in their childhoods, the bottom line was that science, for all its technical brilliance and impressive pharmacology, probably understood more about the origin of the sun than about the root causes of depression.

I'd recently read in *Time* that more Americans than ever were believed to be suffering from some form of mental depression and that twice as many women as men typically sought medical assistance for it. Men, it was believed, typically attempted self-medication through various outlets — addiction to work or booze, playing golf or the commodities market; perhaps even fishing was a form of self-medication. According to the statistics, twice as many men as women killed themselves, though, which led some experts to believe that the numbers of people who suffered from the disorder were probably about equal. Women were apparently just smart enough to seek help.

On that cheerful thought, I chased away my own brain fog and realized that the guy using the pay phone beside me was none other than the same tough-looking hombre the Son of Thunder had pointed out at Mount Rushmore, the dental biker with the skull on his back.

I couldn't help overhearing his end of the conversation. "Hi, Chrissie!" he chirped pleasantly. "It's *Daddy*! Are you being a good girl for Nana? Mommy and Daddy are having a wonderful time on Daddy's motorcycle. We'll be home sometime on Sunday afternoon, sweetie pie! We'll bring you something nice. Okay, Chrissie, let me speak to Nana again . . . thank you. I love you, too. Bye, sweetie!"

I smiled a much-needed smile, wondering if his earring was really a clip-on.

Late the next day, we saw our first bison.

He was standing alone in a grassy meadow near a shallow stream off what's popularly called the Loop Road, an eighteen-mile stretch that meanders through scenic open grasslands and pine forests in the southern half of Custer State Park. We were returning from Deadwood, where we'd gone to spend the afternoon after an unproductive fishing expedition on Sylvan Lake. The trout weren't sipping flies so we left the canoe chained to a tree and became Black Hills tourists. Deadwood was full of bikers throwing money away in casinos but I wanted to see the town because it was where James Butler — Indian scout, sometime spy, stagecoach driver, bullwhacker, sheriff, and gambler — was murdered by a young drifter named Jake McCall, shot in the back while supposedly holding two aces, a pair of eights, and a nine of diamonds, known thereafter as the Dead Man's Hand.

Thanks to an afternoon walking tour, Maggie now knew a little bit about Wild Bill Hickok, as Butler preferred to be called, and the sad strange woman who some say loved him, Martha Jane Burk, aka Calamity Jane, an illiterate alcoholic whose checkered past included jobs as an army scout, mule skinner, nurse, prostitute, hotel cook, and Wild West Show performer. She drifted into Deadwood in 1876, at the beginning of the Black Hills Gold Rush, dressed in men's clothing and boasting of her exploits as a Pony Express rider, and died penniless there in 1903. Her last wish was to be buried next to Bill Hickok in the town cemetery. In 1889, the year South Dakota gained statehood, the residents outlawed gambling, in large part because Deadwood had become such a raunchy hole of betting parlors and brothels, but exactly a century later the state legislature passed limited-stakes gambling, creating a second gold rush that brought in big gaming casinos and drove property taxes through the roof, chasing a number of longtime residents straight out of town in the process.

One of the more recent arrivees was Kevin Costner, the movie star who owned a part interest in the Midnight Star Casino and promoted a well-financed campaign to raise betting-stakes limits from $5 to $100. But the citizens of the state, sounding almost sensible enough to be Mainers, handily voted down the measure. When I asked why, our young walking guide, a local high school honor student named Cindy, paused and solemnly glanced around to see if the telegenic star of *Dances with Wolves* or perhaps a representative of the Chamber of Commerce might be loitering within earshot, then confided: "Well, I think it's because South Dakotans are a pretty independent breed and aren't too impressed with movie stars. My grandfather says Kevin Costner's no Jimmy Stewart and the only wolves he ever danced with wear nice Italian suits." I told her with an attitude like that, she could move straight to Maine.

The buffalo watched us park the truck. He stood perhaps thirty yards away in the tall grass, an old bull with a shaggy prehistoric face.

I got out to take his photograph and Maggie got out, too, prompting me to tell her to get back in the truck because, as park authorities constantly warn visitors, the tranquillity of the American bison can easily lure you into a false sense of security. Observing them during his passage West in 1829, Meriwether Lewis wrote in his journal: *The buffalo are so gentle we pass near them while feeding, without appearing to excite any alarm in them, and when we attract their attention, they frequently approach us more nearly to discover what we are, and in some instances pursue us to considerable distance apparently with that view.* But as Lewis learned, the peaceful looks of Amer ica's largest mammal can deceive. The average bison, weighing up to a ton, can run faster than a horse, turn on a buffalo nickel, and gore you quicker than you can say, "Kevin Costner's sure no Jimmy Stewart."

I told this to Maggie as we stood there, face-to-face, so to speak, with a ton of hair on the hoof. She didn't seem particularly worried and neither did the buffalo, so I moved forward a few feet, crouched, and snapped a photograph. The bull even helpfully turned his head a bit to the right so I could get a better profile shot. Maggie crept forward too, kneeling in the grass beside me. It's believed that at the end of the fifteenth century, I whispered to her, close to fifty million bison roamed the Great Plains, and apart from their having been a steady meat supply for Native Americans, their fur and hides were used for clothing and shelter, their bones for weapons, utensils, and toys, their droppings for fuel. It's possible no other animal on earth was ever as intricately woven into the lives of humans as the buffalo was into America's native people's, which explains the bison's high spiritual standing with Indians. The Lakota believed, for instance, that the universe began when the Great Spirit caused the bison to emerge from a wind cave in the earth, and the Blackfeet held the holy beast in such reverence that they developed a ritual dance they performed before every hunt.

"Can you do the dance?" she asked solemnly.

"Sorry. White guys can't dance. Except with wolves, of course."

Funnily enough, though, I told her, I remembered the origin myth of the buffalo dance from my Boy Scouting days (and, knowing we might soon see a buffalo, I'd boned up on it from a book of native myths I had in the Medicine Bag). In the Blackfoot legend, the plains tribes are facing a difficult winter when the beautiful daughter of a chieftain offers herself in marriage to the head buffalo if he will only persuade his brothers to stampede over the jump—thereby assuring the tribes a winter supply of furs and meat. The buffalo complies and the tribe's holy man informs the girl she must now go off and live with the buffalo as his wife.

"I don't think that's fair. A girl should get to marry who she wants to marry."

"I agree. It's just a story. Feel free to marry the man of your choice, sweetheart, as long as you're both over thirty and have legal written consent forms signed by both your parents, and he's been fully cleared by the Securities and Exchange Commission and the FBI."

Maggie socked me on the arm and I continued the tale. The girl's family rises in the morning to find her gone. They are very sad and worried. So the father takes his bow and sets off after her across the plains, followed by a magpie. The magpie explains to him what has happened and leads him to a buffalo wallow, where he encounters his daughter's new husband. A struggle ensues and the buffalo kills the father and tramples his bones to dust.

"That's really sad."

"I know. I'll avoid the temptation to say that another good man bites the dust. But luckily it's not the end of the story."

"Continue," she said evenly.

Shattered by this news, the Indian wife tells her buffalo husband she can never really love him because of what he has done and the buffalo, perhaps feeling remorse, informs her that if she can restore life to her father, he will release her from her promise. The magpie finds her a bone and she performs a revivifying dance that brings her father back to life. The buffalo husband is astonished by what he has witnessed, but also saddened. He asks the girl and her father why they have never done this dance to help his people, the buffalo. They see his point and agree that from this moment on, before every hunt, warriors will perform the buffalo dance to ensure that each buffalo always returns from death.

"How did the dance bring them back to life?" Maggie was wiggling her fingers at the buffalo.

"Well, that's not really explained. It's part of the mystery, what the plains Indians called the sacred hoop of life. Indians did everything in circles. They traveled with the seasons in a kind of circle, set their tepees in a circle, performed all their ceremonies in circles. A circle symbolized the unity of everything, man and nature, life and death. Death comes from life, life comes from death."

"Like the story of Jesus."

"I hadn't thought of it that way," I admitted. "But you're right."

"Dad," Maggie said, "he's coming toward us."

It's true. He was. The big brute had moved a few steps toward us, shifting his massive girth and working those big moist black prehistoric nostrils, scenting us. I was about to herd us safely back to Old Blue when I realized the buffalo wasn't moving toward us at all. He was coming toward Amos, who'd lumbered out of the open truck door and was calmly wobbling toward the bison and perhaps the golden retriever happy hunting ground.

"*Amos!*" I hissed at him. But, of course, I might as well have been talking to the wind.

The dog headed slowly down the slope and moved into the shoulder-high grass as if he and the buffalo were merely two old sons of the prairie saying howdy. He stopped a few yards shy of the buffalo and lifted his head to sniff. The buffalo turned his head slightly and advanced a step, lowering his own snout to sniff. Amos edged forward. The buffalo advanced, too. A moment later, their noses inched close enough to touch. A flurry of sniffs ensued. Then Amos turned around and walked nonchalantly back to the truck with a visible spring in his step, as if to ask *What's the big deal, pards, about befriending an American bison?*

"Cool," Maggie said breathlessly. "Can I go touch him, too?"

"Don't even *think* about it."

We decided, at least, to give him a name to remember us by and on the spot came up with "Dances with Dogs" and "Too Big to Fit on an Indian Nickel" and finally settled on "Stan the Man" in honor of Maggie's favorite cat but also her first heartbreak, a big silver tabby who showed up at our house one November night and made himself at home for almost two years. A teenage house sitter forgot to feed him for a week ("Geez. Like I'm sor-*ree*. Okay? But, like, can't cats find something to eat in the woods or something?") and Stanley had left us, perhaps feeling we'd abandoned him. Maggie had wept inconsolably for a few days and I'd been forced to make up a neat fiction about Stanley going back to his original owners—which may, in fact, have been the case, and I certainly hope so because it was my best hope, too. Perhaps one reason we tell ourselves stories is to simply offer grief a place to go.

We bid good-bye to Stan the Man and drove back to Sylvan Lake and went swimming in the fading sunlight below Harney Peak, the tallest place in South Dakota. My daughter dived from a rock and I saw trout rises on the lake's surface and seriously considered fetching my fly gear but we went up to the Lakota dining room instead and ate fabulous Black Hills trout next to an elderly couple who were relentlessly determined to fix each other's flaws after all these years. He slurped his soup. She couldn't read a road map worth beans. We heard them murmuring soft imprecations at each other over their plates. A woman I knew who'd been a summer waitress at Bar Harbor once told me her theory that people revealed their true selves while on vacation because there was no social pressure to be polite— no benefit, as it were, to be derived from holding your tongue in the presence of someone you'd never see again. Vacations, she believed, exposed our strongest likes and dislikes and either made us, as a result, extremely happy or pains in the ass to be around. It was an interesting theory—

something, as I told her, some cranky intellectual at Harvard ought to look into when he'd returned from snapping at waitresses in Maine.

"Dad, do you think Stan the Man will ever come back?" I was tucking my daughter into bed at our cabin above the lake. Her hair was combed, her teeth were mintily scrubbed.

I'd feared that the mention of Stan's name would open the floodgates of feline remembrances.

"It's hard to say. Sometimes I think he will. I'm certain he knows how much you loved him. He obviously loved you, too." I decided not to tell her I sometimes saw a cat on our road that resembled Stan. And once or twice I'd even caught a glimpse of a silver cat watching our house from the edge of the woods. But he always vanished when I stepped out.

"Too bad," she said, "there's no dance that would make a cat come back."

"The world could use it."

I rose before dawn and pushed the canoe out into the lake, producing silvery fantails on the surface. I hadn't slept well, unable to shake thoughts about my troubled friend. I pictured him sitting like Silent Sam in an air-conditioned hospital room in Savannah, too addled to shave, trying to remember who he used to be, staring at the fine grass-cloth walls. *How do we mediate,* asked the poet Robert Penn Warren, *our self-divisions?* I decided I would call him when we reached Wyoming, perhaps tomorrow night. That would give me time to try and think of what to say to him.

I paddled across the lake, to the spot where I'd seen so many rises the evening before. On my fourth or fifth cast, using a #16 Hairwing Caddis, I caught a small brown trout, unhooked him, and dropped him in my water bucket. I made another cast and caught another fish. The caddis was working beautifully. The water was so still I decided to ignore the cardinal rule of responsible canoeing and actually stood up and stripped line at my feet and made several casts that grew longer with each pass overhead, the line softly sighing. A figure appeared on the shore, a woman out for a dawn walk. She waved and I waved and then a large fish broke the surface off to my right and I flicked my line and made a slow, long cast in that direction.

The sun was just reaching the summit of Harney Peak, where the Oglala Sioux holy man Black Elk had experienced his astounding Great Vision at age nine. The spirits of his six grandfathers swept him away to this sacred spot in the center of the *Sapa Hapa*, or the Black Hills, which were considered the center of the universe by the plains people, an Indian Eden untouched by the *waichus*, or white men. He was led away by dancing horses that changed into animals of every kind to a tepee made of cloud, with a rainbow for an open door. *And the oldest of the grandfathers spoke with a kind voice and said: "Come right in and do not fear." And as he spoke, all the horses of the four quarters neighed to cheer me. So I went in and stood before the six, and they looked older than men can ever be—old like hills, like stars. . . . I knew that these were not old men, but the Powers of the World.* The Powers gave Black Elk the power to heal and destroy, the power to make things flourish, the power of the cleansing wind. They showed him the flowering hoop of the world, but also a black road that led to the thunder beings, the coming of the *waichus* and the iron horse, *a fearful road, a road of troubles and of war.* He saw his people dancing with great joy and weeping with great sorrow. He learned it was his destiny to travel and heal, and he woke from his Great Vision smote by sadness, with both his parents hovering over him.

Perhaps it takes a poet to really understand madness or to fathom why a man's life suddenly breaks apart. Mystics believe there is divine purpose in true madness, a shattering of the old self that permits entry to enlightenment—a power we all possess but fear to unleash. It took a Nebraska poet named John Neihardt to record Black Elk's extraordinary mystical experience, which eerily mirrors the story of Buddha's saga of enlightenment at the foot of the bodhi tree, and even Christ's journey into the desert.

At the moment of his enlightenment, his transformation into a healer, Black Elk's people were already doomed. Four years before, gold had been found in the Black Hills and the U.S. government had illegally seized it, breaking all of the existing treaties it had made with the Siouan peoples in order to allow white prospectors and fortune hunters to flood their holy land. Horse soldiers were sent to protect the newcomers and among other atrocities a policy of systematically exterminating the bison was undertaken to remove the spiritual life source of the Indians.

The beginning of the end came on June 17, 1876, when the combined forces of Cheyenne and Lakota warriors under the leadership of Crazy Horse attacked General Crook at the Battle of the Rosebud. Crook claimed victory but beat a hasty retreat, while more warrior groups streamed into the area, assembling twelve hundred tepees strong, an estimated fighting force of nearly two thousand warriors, near the banks of a Montana stream called the Little Bighorn. The newspapers of New York and Washington created a golden-haired hero-god out of George Armstrong Custer, portraying him as excellent presidential timber despite the fact—or perhaps because of it—that his ruthless treatment of Indians and his thorough disregard for legal treaties caused native peoples to call him "the Chief of Thieves."

On June 27, Custer's command of 210 soldiers was surrounded on a small rise of land and wiped out in less than an hour. Exact Indian losses remain unknown.

As Black Elk recounts, by the fall of 1883, seven years after the battle at Little Bighorn and three years after his Great Vision on Harney Peak, below which I now sat flicking my fly line, *the last of the bison herds was slaughtered by the waichus. I can remember when the bison were so many that they could not be counted, but more and more waichus came to kill them until there were only heaps of bones scattered where they used to be. The waichus did not kill them to eat; they killed them for the metal* [gold] *that makes them crazy, and they only took the hides to sell. Sometimes they did not even take the hides, only the tongues; and I heard that fireboats came down the Missouri River loaded with mountains of dried bison tongues.*

The terrible vision Black Elk had been shown on Harney Peak finally came to pass when settlers and fortune seekers poured into the Black Hills, panning for gold and slaughtering as many as fifty *million* bison. A single green hide could fetch $1.25 in the West, while a finished buffalo robe sold in the salons of Europe for $100, and shopkeepers couldn't keep them on the rack. Waichus like Buffalo Bill Cody made glamorous names for themselves in dime novels and newspapers back East by shooting buffalo and scouting for the army as it subdued the last holdouts and herded remnant tribes onto reservations. Cody himself, according to one popular legend, shot over a thousand buffalo in one day. *All our people,* Black Elk told Neihardt, *now were settling down in square gray houses* [federal reservations] *scattered here and there across the hungry land, and around them the waichus had drawn a line to keep them in. The nation's hoop was broken.*

Black Elk's response, under the circumstances, was an interesting and brave one. Like Ohiyesa, he decided to venture into the world of the waichus to see if he could create a bridge between the victor and the vanquished. Buffalo Bill, whom the Indians called Pashuka, sent word to the Oglalas that he was looking for a band of warriors to perform in his Wild West Show. *They told us this show would go across the big water to strange lands, and I thought I ought to go, because I might learn some secret of the waichu that would help my people somehow. . . . Maybe if I could see the great world of the waichu, I could understand how to bring the sacred hoop together and make the tree bloom again at the center of it.*

Black Elk joined the show. He saw the sights and met the
citizens of New York, London, and Paris. His winter in
New York was particularly painful. Between shows at Madison Square Garden, he wandered the streets of Manhattan
dressed in waichu clothing. *I felt dead and my people seemed lost
and I thought I might never find them again. I did not see anything
to help my people. I could see that the waichus did not care for each
other the way our people did before the nation's hoop was broken.
They would take everything from each other if they could, and so
there were some who had more of everything than they could use,
while crowds of people had nothing at all and maybe were starving.
They had forgotten that the earth was their mother. This could not
be better than the old ways of my people.*

After nearly three years on the road, during which he met
"Grandmother England" (Queen Victoria) and got lost for a
time, wandering alone through Europe, he decided to go
home to the Black Hills. He felt his holy powers were gone,
dried up, his heart dying. In a vision, he saw his parents'
tepee and longed to be there. Bill Cody gave him $90 and a
boat ticket home. *Then he gave me a dinner. Pashuka had a
strong heart.* Arriving home, Black Elk found the American
government had taken even more of his people's lands, but
his mother and father's tepee was exactly where it had been
when he left. *My parents were in great joy to see me and my
mother cried because she was so happy. I cried too. I was supposed to
be a man now, but the tears came out anyway.*

I was floating in my canoe on the lake below Harney
Peak, reading bits of Black Elk's memoir between casts,
glancing up from time to time to look at the rock peak,
which grew yellower by the minute from the rising sun. I
thought of the famous psalm that said the sun comes forth
like a bridegroom from his chamber. Pretty soon there
would be spandex-clad rock climbers scaling the peak,
which is one of the premier mountain-climbing experiences
in the West.

I put down the book and made another long cast and

thought about Silent Sam, how the hoop of his world had suddenly just snapped. That's when I saw a white dog standing on the shore. It was Amos. A moment later, Maggie appeared, waving. I paddled over and showed her my two little trout in the bucket. One by one, we let them go.

"I'm sorry I left you at the cabin," I said. "I hope you weren't afraid when you woke." She smiled and shook her head, then looked down at the last fish, her oval face still softly dented from sleep.

"That's okay. I wasn't scared. I knew you were here, even before I woke up."

"How's that?"

"I dreamed it."

"How interesting," I said. "Indians believe their ancestors communicate through dreams."

"Maybe Aunt Emma told me."

CHAPTER EIGHT

....

Cody

WE LEFT THE Dakota grasslands at 9:05 Mountain Standard Time and began our ascent into the Bighorns on Route 16, passing a sign that said WYOMING — LIKE NO PLACE ON EARTH! and stopped in Upton for gas. The Conoco station appeared to be the only functioning business in town, half a block from a sun-faded sign that read: WELCOME TO UPTON. BEST TOWN ON EARTH.

I asked the clerk at the Conoco, directly across the asphalt from the Cowboy Bar, what made Upton, which appeared to have seen its best days, the best town on earth. The Cowboy Bar looked as if it had been closed for decades. "Been here near on ten years and I'm still tryin' to figger that out myself," she admitted, tapping the computer register. We were buying Gatorade and apple juice and a jug of spring water for Amos. Her smile was pleasant enough. "Reckon it could be that we haven't had no drive-by shootin's yet and the rivers round here are pretty clean. That's about all we got for charm."

We kept climbing, crossing Crazy Woman Creek and getting our first sight of the snowcapped Rockies eighty miles to the west. A hundred years before, this had been part of the Oregon Trail that first carried trappers and mountain men and later settlers and prospectors farther to the West after the gold fever subsided and the Black Hills became too danged crowded; the same route, a few years prior to that, was used by Sitting Bull and other remnants of the Indian force that wiped out Custer at the Little Bighorn and fled to the West and thence to Canada with the whole U.S. Cavalry on their heels. Now we were following a white Crown Victoria with Florida tags that had caromed past us doing about ninety, a dangerously swaying barge captained by a small elderly woman whose head barely reached above the wheel, occasionally wiping out ranks of wildflowers on the road's narrow shoulder and throwing up gritty dust whirls in her wake.

I slowed and tuned in to the late morning news. Fifteen midshipmen at the Naval Academy had been kicked out for cheating, the worst scandal in the school's history, and Jack Kevorkian had just presided over his thirty-fourth assisted suicide, the death of a Cincinnati woman who suffered from Lou Gehrig's disease. Out-of-work coal miners in Beckley, West Virginia, had come up with a novel way of making ends meet: They'd flooded the unused mine with spring water and begun commercially raising char and rainbow trout. For the second year in a row, the U.S. Postal Service had shown a decent profit, and a team of scientists examining part of a meteorite that fell to earth thirteen thousand years ago found evidence of microorganic life, perhaps indicating life-forms on Mars. The president, reportedly thrilled by this discovery and about to depart for his western vacation, was so pleased that he'd announced an upcoming summit on the subject, while down in Atlanta, coming soon to a Wheaties box near you, a gymnast named Kerri Strug had courageously completed a critical floor routine the night before on a strained right ankle, assuring the U.S. Olympic squad a gold medal.

The Crown Victoria became a dot on the horizon and, being one of those gifted individuals who can read and drive simultaneously, I browsed a geologic guide to the region. The hills we were passing through were striated with layers of umber, gold, and sulfurous yellow—dolomite hills, Mississippian in age and tawny with limestone, 580 million years old if a day. Now Paul Harvey had come on, fretting that the reason America was going to hell in a handbasket was because we no longer had front porches on houses. Porches taught people civilized behavior, he said, encouraged them to slow down. What that Crown Victoria really needs, I thought, is a nice front porch.

We stopped for lunch in Ten Sleep, a town no bigger than the hips on a snake. There were a dozen dusty cars and pickups in the gravel lot of the Flagstaff Cafe, whose menu engagingly read: *"Ten Sleep, Wyoming: West of worry. East of envy. South of sorrow. North of normal."* Elevation 4,206 feet, population 311. I asked our waitress how the town got its name and she explained that an Indian measured distances by the number of sleeps required to reach his destination. Ten Sleep was located at a water source exactly halfway between traditional Indian winter camps on the Platte River to the south and their summer quarters near Bridger Mountain to the north, ten sleeps in either direction. The desert valley where the town sat looked as desolate as a moonscape, but a good-sized creek rushed through it out of the Bighorns. She recommended the hot dog special to Maggie and was rewarded with a dazzling smile.

The cafe was full of men in sweat-stained straw hats, the usual lunchtime crowd of ranch hands save for a table of German tourists directly beside us, two shockingly skinny couples wearing short haircuts, short shorts, and sandals with dark socks. They looked profoundly unhappy, but then German tourists always look profoundly unhappy to me,

and one of the men, squinting over a pocket-sized road atlas, leaned over to me and said, in heavily accented English:
"You know about *me-rages*?"

Me-rages?

He nodded, a lean, sunburned face. "Ya. Das iss here,
ya?" He jabbed his finger at a yellowish patch on the map,
indicating high desert country north of Utah's Wasatch
Range.

"Is that the way you're headed?" I was leaning over to
look at his map.

"I think he's saying 'mirage,'" the waitress chipped in
helpfully. She'd just slung our lunches before us. "Do you
mean *mir-age*?" she said to the German slowly and loudly,
because shouting at foreigners always helps aid their understanding when they don't speak your language.

A brisk nod. "Ya. Loss Ve-goss."

"I think he *saw* a mirage," said one of the ranch hands at
an adjoining table. The table chuckled.

"Hell, I reckon I'd see one too if I was crazy enough to
try and ride a bike across this country," another one said,
and the table chuckled harder.

I remembered the four bicycles weighted down with
bulging travel packs we'd seen parked by the cafe's front
door. It then came to me what the man was asking.

"I think he wants to know if this is the best way to the
Mirage Hotel in Las Vegas."

"Ya, ya." A brisk bob. One of the women gave me a bleak
little smile.

"Holy shit." The heavyset ranch hand muttered beneath
his straw hat, poking his meat loaf with a fork and shaking
his head.

"Y'all tryin' to ride those bikes clean to Las Vegas?" The
waitress seemed equally astounded. Three of the four heads
bobbed, as if they were saying yes to the daily dessert pie
special. The other German woman was busy leafing through
a tabloid newspaper whose bold headlines announced that

Dolly Parton's chest had exploded and the "Secret Writings" of Gandhi had been unearthed, revealing the exact moment the end of the world would come. How terrible, I thought, to have your whole chest explode like that.

"Good luck," said the first ranch hand with a mild snort. "You folks'll sure need it."

I felt sorry for them and tried to show the guy who seemed to be in charge of the doomed expedition the best possible route to Las Vegas, tracing a line down U.S. 20 to the Wind River Indian Reservation, then across the Green River to Salt Lake; then, assuming they were still alive at that point, they could pedal the remaining three hundred miles or so straight down I-15 to Vegas, perhaps arriving at the Mirage Hotel sometime around Wayne Newton's annual holiday extravaganza.

I wondered what kind of deranged Düsseldorf tour operator had set this curious odyssey in motion and if I might be sending them to their deaths. The leader profusely thanked me nonetheless and I went outside to take Amos some ice water and a bit of my sandwich while Maggie finished her lunch.

As Amos slurped the water, I studied the main drag in Ten Sleep. A merciless sun was beating down and not a thing was moving. It's not fair to say Ten Sleep felt unfriendly, just remote as hell, the kind of place you could break down or throw a wheel and go frothing mad beneath the noonday sun. Thinking of a breakdown, I decided to be on the safe side and check Old Blue's oil. I opened the hood and found we were almost a quart low, which perhaps explained the mysterious ticking sound she'd been making since the Adirondacks. I fetched one of the spare quarts I was carrying in back, switched on the engine, and was standing on the bumper pouring oil into the chamber when I happened to glance over and see an empty pay phone. Speaking of madness, I had a phone call to make.

My friend Bobby sounded so small when he finally came

on the line. That's the only way I can think of describing him. *Small.* As in "reduced" or "diminished" or "fading away." I made my customary little joke about being an enlightened pacifist with a bloodthirsty bird killer for a friend who would stoop to any cheap stunt to try and persuade me to hunt with him again and he didn't laugh and then he told me he was going through something I couldn't understand because *he* didn't understand it, a sense of everything's falling apart, a fear he couldn't shake, a kind of living death. These were his exact words.

I listened with the hot Wyoming sun making beads of sweat on my neck, wishing there were something I could say that would fix what was breaking or broken in him. But the simple tone of his voice told me nothing I could say could fix him, any more than the things I'd said had fixed my broken marriage. Sometimes things, people, fall apart. It's not fair, doesn't make sense, doesn't add up. You wish it would stop but it won't. You wish it would go but it can't. I told Silent Sam I was thinking about him and then fell as silent as the landscape around me, helpless to help, fairly certain he would hang up if I suggested he listen to his wife and take the doctor's medication.

Perhaps it was good for him to talk. He went on a while, babbling about side effects of antidepressants and the social damage he'd done to his family and practice. His partners were being very understanding, he said, but that made him worry. He was pretty sure Maureen was thinking of leaving him. Even his golf game had gone to hell. Thank God for his daughters, though. Megan was still at camp but Julie, the oldest, had been up to see him twice. The hospital told him he was free to go anytime but he really wasn't. He had this god-awful rash on his back and neck and he couldn't sleep. His mind was churning like some demented answering machine he couldn't shut off.

"Look," I said to him. "You don't need to worry about

any of that. Nobody's leaving anybody and everything will be just the same when you get this sorted out."

"No it won't," he cut me off sharply. "You don't know what you're talking about."

Perhaps I didn't. Every man's madness looks different. "You're probably right," I said. "The point is, take it easy. Get some rest."

"I don't want to rest," he said with the first sign of life in his voice—cold exasperation. "Christ, this is not where I'm supposed to be. Six weeks ago I was happy as a clam. I can't believe it, man." He didn't really want my opinion so I didn't give it. We fell silent while I waited for him to speak again.

"Where are you?"

"Pay phone by a trout stream. Someplace in Wyoming. East of envy, I think." I certainly wasn't quite west of worry yet.

"No joking?"

"No joking. Maggie, Amos, and I are fishing and camping our way out to Yellowstone."

"I thought you gave up trout fishing."

"Did. Maggie lured me back."

"I'd like to meet her sometime."

Bobby had never met Maggie; he and Maureen often threatened to come visit Maine but they never had.

"You okay?" I said quietly, wiping my neck.

"No. This is hellish."

"I know. Stay cool. I'll call again."

I hung up as Maggie was coming out of the cafe.

"The German man said to say thank you," she said, opening a fresh grape Blow Pop for the afternoon ride.

"Mad dogs and Englishmen go out in the midday sun," I said. "The Japanese don't care to, the Chinese wouldn't dare to. But let's don't be beastly to the Germans."

"What's that?"

"About all the Noël Coward I can recall at the moment."

"Was that Mom?"

"Nope. Just an old friend who took a nasty fall."

"Is he okay?"

"Will be, if he takes his medicine."

Eighty miles later, we stopped in Greybull, where there was a large plastic horse standing on the main drag in front of Probst's Western Store: "Cowboy Clothier, Western Shirts, Stetson Hats."

We walked in to buy Jack a pair of real cowboy boots and while Maggie was nosing around the vast store, which smelled pleasantly of new leather and well-worn wooden floors, I fell into lively fish talk with Tyson Probst, the firm's heir apparent, a large, friendly, fair-haired young man who told me he'd attended the University of Montana principally for the excellent trout fishing. He said if we were headed into Cody, we should camp at Buffalo Bill State Park just west of town on the Shoshone River Reservoir. "Keep this under your hat," he said with a sly smile, "but at the back corner of the campground, on the North Fork, back where the river splits around a little rock island—you'll see lots of upturned trees from the spring floods—is the best trout fishing in the state right now. No joke. We're talking *major* hogs here—fifteen- to eighteen-inch rainbows and cutthroats. I've been drivin' up there every night after work and fishin' till dark. Man oh man, it's great. But don't tell anybody, all right?"

I promised him I'd keep it under my hat, even though I didn't have a hat and was tempted to buy one because Saul Bellow once advised men to wear hats so the world could never know what they're really thinking. Fishermen love to tell secrets and I was glad to have Tyson Probst's. We bought and mailed a pair of handsome cowboy boots to Jack that were made of nicely tooled cowhide leather, flamboyantly two-toned in beige and saddle brown, real Sunday-go-to-meetin' boots, and I admitted to Maggie that

I wouldn't have minded a pair of them myself, recalling how I'd spent the first two years of life wearing little more than jeans and cowboy boots, during the two years we lived next to a horse pasture outside Dallas. But that was another story and then she asked for a pair of boots of her own so we bought her some, too—black, pointy-toed jobs with elegant curlicued designs. Real sweetheart-of-the-rodeo numbers, I thought, and then Tyson's mother Nan wrapped them up for Maggie and said, as if she'd read my thoughts, "You could wear them to the rodeo in Cody tonight, sweetheart."

"There's a rodeo in Cody?" Maggie's antennae shot straight up.

"Every night." Nan Probst handed me the receipt, leaned over, and whispered, "Trust Tyson to know where to fish. That boy's been trout-crazy since he was two."

We drove into Cody an hour or so later, passing the famous landmark Irma Hotel, which Buffalo Bill named for his daughter. It was a couple hours before sundown and a big banner strung across Main Street informed us it was the 150th anniversary of Buffalo Bill's birth. A party seemed to be under way. The street was full of shoppers and traffic, throbbing with family attack vehicles—Eddie Bauer–edition Ford Explorers bearing mountain bikes, purring Chevy Suburbans with Dallas Cowboy window stickers. Cody looked like a swell place to have a week's pay in your Levi's.

We pulled in to the Buffalo Bill and Plains Indian Museum, parked beneath the shade of a large cottonwood tree, and cranked open the windows so Amos could snooze in peace; then we wandered into the air-conditioned museum, paid our admission, and walked around gawking at Buffalo Bill's actual Pony Express saddle, his actual buffalo-hide coat, actual knife, actual pearl-handled Colt revolvers, actual horse carriage, actual jewelry, and actual other stuff you can't imagine one man actually needing out there on the Great Plains.

I confess a complicated attraction to William F. Cody, a former army scout and Indian fighter turned flamboyant showman. His Wild West Shows toured America and much of western Europe for nearly three decades. At his death in 1917, Cody was arguably the most famous man in the world. Three thousand cars followed his coffin to its final resting place in a cemetery in the mountains above Denver. My father was two years old that year. With his death, the American Wild West was officially dead and ingenious new ways of exterminating ourselves as a race were being field-tested in the trenches of the First World War, but my father's earliest memories were of listening to his father talk about Bill Cody's Wild West Show, which he saw sometime around 1910 at the Raleigh Fairgrounds. Walter, my grandfather, was Aunt Emma's youngest son, the one who, in dim photographs, resembles her the most. A skilled carpenter and general handyman by trade who worked on crews raising the first electrical poles across the South and helped wire North Carolina's first "skyscrapper," the Jefferson Standard Building in Greensboro, Walter had retired and moved to central Florida by the time my brother and I knew him in the middle sixties.

He seemed to us then, smelling faintly of King Edward cigars and paint thinner, a preternaturally calm old gent with paint-flecked pants who lived to fish for bass in a black-water bayou. But he also had an eerily dignified bearing that belied his blue-collar work life, a contradiction that would chew at me for years, until I realized what it was he reminded me of—an aging Indian chief. And then one day my father told me about Aunt Emma, Walter's mother, the Cherokee foundling, and that explained so much about him—his great calm dignity and passion for nature, his seeming unconcern for the judgments and ambitions of the white man's world. My father said that even though his family was dirt-poor during the Depression, Walter treated every man who drifted by looking for a meal or a shed to sleep in with the same dignity—black, white, Indian. It didn't matter. He gave them a bed and something to eat and work if there was some to do. My father speculated that he'd gone to see Bill Cody's Wild West Show at the Raleigh Fairgrounds hoping to see Sitting Bull, the great holy man and Sioux chieftain who wiped out Custer but ended his days touring with Pashuka's Wild West Show until, fed up with the white man's ambitions, he returned to the plains to die, seeing his death at the hands of his own people in one of his celebrated visions. When I finally saw a photograph of the great chief, I was pleasantly surprised by the resemblance to my grandfather.

I told Maggie about this as we drifted from the Bill Cody part of the museum into the section devoted to the life of the plains Indians. This part of the museum was noticeably emptier and we walked slowly past life-sized displays of daily Indian life, looking at buffalo tepees, mothers with babes doing domestic chores, women weaving cloth, hunters crouching behind fake tumbleweeds. "They look so lifelike and real," commented an elderly woman to her husband, who was fussing with the earplug on his cassette narration device.

I told Maggie about her great-grandfather's passion for Buffalo Bill's Wild West Show and, pausing by an incredible black-and-white photograph of the show's re-creation of an Indian raid taken in Paris in the 1890s, she mused, "So he saw all this? Wow. Cool. Did you, like, like your grandfather?" It seemed an odd question—and I resisted the urge to ask her to drop the extra "like"—but I knew what she meant.

"Yes. Quite a lot. He took me fishing when I was about your age. He never said much but I still felt very close to him. I sometimes feel his spirit around me, though maybe that's just the Indian wanna-be in me."

"I feel Granddaddy's spirit," she said without the slightest doubt, meaning, of course, Opti the Mystic. Then she asked: "Do you, like, miss your father?"

"Every day. Same as, like, Black Elk." I smiled at her. She didn't have a clue that I was mocking her Valley Girl routine.

"Who was Black Elk?"

I explained to her about Black Elk—about his extraordinary vision at age nine; about the six grandfathers and how he left his people to try and find a way to save them but was unable to stem the juggernaut; about how he, too, had toured with Pashuka and then grown heartsick of travel and come home to die, having completed the hoop of his being. I told her, too, a Kiowa story about how the American bison, seeing the end of his days, decided to leave the earth. All religious peoples, I said, share the belief that something is made sacred by sacrifice.

A mountain opened and the last buffalo vanished from the plains, thereby making it sacred. In the myth, the last bison returned to a place of plentiful prairie grass and beautiful streams, where no buffalo hunters followed, and he found eternal peace—no less a vision, it sometimes seemed to me, than a Southern Baptist's view of Heaven. The year my father was born in the soft upland hills of Piedmont, North Carolina, there were less than 150 buffalo surviving on the North American continent. The animal was essentially extinct. Now, thanks to the revitalizing efforts of places like Custer State Park and Yellowstone, the bison herds numbered in the high thousands and were no longer an endangered species. It was the plains Indian who never came back, who became, in a sense, sacred by passing from the earth.

We pitched the small tent by a bend in the Shoshone River, below towering cliffs and across from the rock island Tyson

Probst had perfectly described, cooked and ate a quick macaroni supper, then drove back in to Cody to attend the Cody Night Stampede Rodeo.

The main grandstand was full of spectators and we sat up high, above the stock pens, between a Honolulu fireman and his wife and a large family from Turin, Italy. The fireman was a beefy guy wearing a T-shirt that said, *Beam me up, Scotty. There's no intelligent life down here!* He kept firing off flash pictures with a disposable camera over the heads in front of us and declaring, "I hope like hell these things come out." The Italians were beautifully dressed, a mother, father, and five incredibly handsome and well-behaved children, ranging from about age three to sixteen. They sat silently watching the steer-roping and barrel antics of the Cody Rodeo clowns, betraying little or no feelings about the performance. I wondered what they must be thinking and I tried to strike up a conversation with the mother, who turned out to speak only fragments of English. She seemed delighted that I was interested in their take on the rodeo and tried with visible frustration to understand my explanation of the origins of the spectacle—essentially a cowboy's way of breaking the monotony of life among the herds, a gaudy homegrown entertainment that began in Arizona in 1888, about the time the last buffalo herds began to vanish and the cow became the dominant creature of the West.

When the calf-roping segment began, she suddenly looked mortified and asked, "Do they, um, keel it?" I shook my head and said that the calf would be fine and probably only wish it were dead. Then the booming PA announcer's voice invited all children down to the arena floor to participate in the evening highlight, the celebrated "Calf Chase." None of the Italian children budged and, to my surprise, neither did Maggie. I suggested that she go, so she could tell Jack about it, but she shook her head resolutely, seemingly more offended by the idea than shy about participating. A short while later, a small calf with a flag attached to its tail loped frantically around the arena while a couple hundred children wildly stampeded after it, slapping, gouging, and kicking the terrified animal. Finally, the calf was cornered and a kind of gleeful pig pile of a hundred or so children developed. A boy emerged from the pile, ecstatically waving the blue flag. Rodeo hands descended and the calf wobbled off in a daze. The crowd cheered lustily. A cannon was fired, setting off several car alarms in the parking lot.

I sat there thinking what an entertaining show the Wild West had become thanks to the town's namesake, Bill Cody—but also what a living contradiction. Cody was awarded the Medal of Honor for fighting Indians in 1872. In 1913, the army withdrew the award, citing regulations that permitted the nation's highest military honor to be bestowed only on enlisted men and officers; Cody had been a mere scout. In 1916, after intense deliberations and the intervention of several members of Congress, the army decided to return the medal to Cody, noting that his service to America was "above and beyond the call of duty."

Cody's life was, in fact, a study in such ambiguity. Among other things, he claimed he'd been a Pony Express rider in 1859, but the Pony Express did not come into existence until a year later, and historians have learned he "borrowed" the name Buffalo Bill from a man named William Mathewson. *The great fascination and peril of Cody's life,* historian, poet, and artist N. Scott Momaday has written of him, *was the riddle of who he was. The thing that opposed him, and perhaps betrayed him, was above all else the mirage of his own identity.* As Momaday and others have pointed out, Buffalo Bill Cody was an undisputed marksman of the first rank, a horseman nonpareil, a legendary scout, and a buffalo hunter without peer—having slaughtered 4,280 bison in less than eighteen months, more buffalo than exist in Yellowstone Park and the Grand Tetons combined today.

It was only when his life drifted into the realm of fantasy

and he retooled himself in the splendor of fringed buckskins astride a great white horse, hat raised to the crowd as he cantered to the center of the arena to open the "spectacle of the American Wild West"—speeding Pony Express riders, a "real-life" Indian attack on the Deadwood stage, famous gunslingers in action, Annie Oakley and Wild Bill Hickok in person, a "faithful reenactment" of Custer's last stand, followed by a grand finale buffalo hunt featuring live buffalo, perhaps a chance to get Chief Sitting Bull's autograph for a dollar afterward—on the polo fields of New York or exhibition fields of London or Paris, that Buffalo Bill became something much larger than life itself. *What we have in this explosion of color and fanfare is an epic transformation of the American West into a traveling circus and of an American hero into an imitation of himself. We have seen this transformation take place numberless times on the stage, on television and movie screens, and on pages of comic books and dime novels and literary masterpieces. One function of the American imagination is to reduce the American landscape to size, to fit that great expanse to the confinement of the immigrant mind. It is a way to persist in our cultural being. We photograph ourselves on the rim of Monument Valley or against the wall of the Tetons, and we become our own frame of reference. As long as we can transform the landscape to accommodate our fragile presence, we can be saved. As long as we can see ourselves on the picture plane, we cannot be lost.*

Watching the Cody Rodeo finale, and thinking about the enigma of Buffalo Bill, a womanizing drunk who transformed himself from a frontier hero into a living parody of his own fame, it struck me that what was perhaps ailing my friend Silent Sam in his grass-cloth room in Savannah, what seemed to be troubling so many modern American men and probably me as well at times, was a sense of no longer being able to see ourselves in the picture frame of the landscape— a marriage we'd believed in, a job we thought could never vanish, a center we imagined would always hold. The hard truth was, the West had been tamed and the fascination and peril of our lives was trying to determine who we were—or should become—to avoid being lost.

Perhaps, on the other hand, I was simply reading too much into a night out at the rodeo. As we left the rodeo grounds, Maggie held my hand and pointed to a cowboy sitting astride a cutting pony in one of the cow holding pens. He was slumped in the saddle like a Frederic Remington original, hat tilted forward, backlit by the still-pinkish corona of the sunset, and I thought, that instant, that he looked almost perfect. Then I noticed he was speaking into a small cellular flip phone.

"Let's green light that one," I heard him drawl as we filtered slowly above him. "That's right. Sell when she reaches twenty-nine."

The Shoshone, at dawn, was surprisingly cold, the current strong in the lee of the rock island. I waded in to about my waist and was glad I'd bothered with the neoprene waders—it was cold. Maggie was still sleeping and the sun was not yet up. Amos had followed me to the river, peed on a bush, then stretched out to sleep for a while longer on the rocky bank. I made my first cast, using a #12 Sparkle Dun. Tyson Probst had said wet flies with a sinking line worked best, but a trout's diet is much more varied in rushing water than still and I hadn't packed any sinking line precisely to avoid the temptation to use it and was determined to stick to my declared objective of luring trout to the surface on a dry fly—I wanted to see the critters take the bait.

The allure of trout fishing is not about catching and eating fish; it's about seducing and fooling them, making them rise to your imitation of life. I made a couple overhead casts and then shot my line into the gray-tinted darkness. I felt the swift current take the line; I lifted the rod tip and made another backcast, sending an even longer cast upstream. It was maybe my best one of the trip. Either I was growing more adept at fly casting, I thought, or I should always practice my technique in the half-light, when casting becomes more a function of trusted body rhythm than the eyes. My eyes drifted up the canyon walls. Huge limestone cliffs rose around me and the sky was turning lighter above them by the minute. *Beautiful,* I thought. If only Silent Sam could see this. Just might cure whatever ailed him.

I felt a strong pull and thought it was the current, then realized I'd hooked a large fish. I pinched the line and held the fish against the current, slowly reeling in my excess line and trying to restrain my excitement. In the half-light, the fish felt immense—but then, they always do to me. I felt the line shift toward the center currents, then move back to the shore. I reeled slowly, watching the Scott rod double over.

It was a handsome cutthroat trout, maybe thirteen inches in length. I got him in the net, wet my hands, and lightly touched his side, the muddy orange flash on his side. Perhaps catching a trout helps. The sun was coming up and I suddenly felt an almost illicit pleasure at what we'd done and where we were and I saw the same star George Custer saw a hundred years before, a few mornings before he met his death at the Little Bighorn. The morning star was low on the rim of the Shoshone's canyon, glittering like a frozen tear. I let the trout go and went back to camp to wake my daughter, shivering with either excitement or cold, thirsty for coffee, and hoping to make Yellowstone Park by eight.

CHAPTER NINE

Oh, Yellowstone

THE FIRST WHITE men to set foot in Yellowstone, probably early French trappers searching for a mythical river cutting through towering golden bluffs they'd heard the Mandan Indians of the Dakotas speak of in the late 1700s, were undoubtedly astonished by the wonders they met.

Thermal geysers, hot springs and boiling fumaroles, towering lodgepole pines, a beautiful golden-bluffed river teeming with trout, forests thick with elk—a real American Eden. But it wasn't until Lewis and Clark passed this way in 1805 that anyone east of the Missouri knew this place of wonders even existed. Passing through the northern fringes of the present-day park, they encountered the river with towering bluffs and named it the Yellowstone, a name that stuck. On the return trip, the party split up and a member of the expedition named John Colter became the first white to cross the heart of the wilderness. His account of seething cauldrons and exploding geysers was widely ridiculed back East, but as more prospectors and trappers moved into the region over the next sixty years, confirming stories of an American Eden, Congress finally dispatched the first survey teams to the region in 1870. Two years later, after a rancorous debate on the Senate floor during which several participants allegedly traded punches, America's first national park came into creation.

The idea—virtually without precedent in human history—was to set aside an entire region for legal protection from development and business interests, a managed-care system aimed at preserving the pristine quality of the wilderness. But the park's first years proved a management nightmare. Congress provided lip service but no real funding for preserving Yellowstone and irresponsible tourists soon dumped laundry soap down geysers, ruining their intricate plumbing, and washed their clothes in hot springs. Bandits routinely preyed on stagecoaches bearing wealthy excursionists into the park, and the same peaceful Nez Percé Indians who'd saved the exhausted and disease-riddled Lewis and Clark expedition from certain death in 1805 killed two tourists during the uprising that resulted when the gold fever once again caused the U.S. government to renege on a signed treaty and the army was sent to round up the Nez Percé and move them to a reservation.

Under the leadership of Chief Joseph, a band of 250 warriors, protecting twice as many women, children, and elderly people, outmaneuvered an army many times its size for nearly four months, launching brilliant guerrilla attacks and eluding captors for nearly 1,700 miles before the insurrection ran out of steam and, just thirty miles from relative safety over the Canadian border, Chief Joseph gave his famous speech of surrender: *I am tired. My heart is sick and sad. From where the sun now stands I will fight no more forever.* The Nez Percé had been promised they would be sent to new

lands in Idaho. They were shipped instead to a cramped and
marshy reservation in Oklahoma, where an outbreak of ma-
laria killed nearly a third of the tribe.

I was telling Maggie these tales, gleaned from a handy
pocket guide on the park, as we sat in gridlocked traffic
outside Yellowstone's eastern gate. Having gotten an
earlier-than-expected jump from Cody, we'd arrived at the
park's eastern entry gate shortly after seven, only to find
fifty or so cars, motor homes, and recreational vehicles
parked in the middle of the road waiting for the park to
officially open. The delay was due to a repaving project up
ahead, we were informed, and a woman in the trading post
at Pashuka, where we rolled to a stop and got out to go try
and scout up pancakes, said it would probably be eleven
before we reached West Thumb and the Bay Bridge campground.

"Won't be a problem," she assured us with a big western
smile, "if you've got a camping reservation." I smiled back,
wondering if we were dead meat because when I'd phoned
from Minnesota a week or so ago, the Yellowstone reservation person had politely informed me all of the park's camp-
grounds were now operated on a "first-come, first served"
basis, due to heavy demand. She'd advised us to simply get
there early, "preferably on a weekday," but apparently
spoke with forked tongue because by the time I found myself standing in line at the Bay Bridge ranger station two
hours after pancakes, it was clear that everybody ahead of
me in line had a reservation of some sort.

The ranger smiled sympathetically and suggested we try
driving up to Mammoth Hot Springs; she heard there were
still a few campsites available there but we'd better hurry.
We could also try below Grant Village at Lewis Lake, she
added, though that park often filled up first with people
coming from the Tetons. I pointed out we were fly anglers
and asked which direction she, an expert on such matters,

would go, given such limited time and choices, and she smiled again. "I'd go north to Mammoth Hot Springs. That way, if it's full up, you can follow the Yellowstone up into Montana. There's a nice fish camp near Pine Creek you could probably get into. The crowds don't usually go that far." She wrote the name on a piece of paper and handed it to me, then apologized again that there was no room at Bay Bridge. "This is the crazy season."

I thanked her, put the paper in my breast pocket, and walked back to where Amos had attracted a small crowd of children. Maggie was holding court, as usual, and asked me where we were headed. "South to Lewis Lake," I said.

Clever me. Like Chief Joseph and his band, we would do what they least expected. We passed miles of blackened forest from the park's recent devastating wildfires and procured the last campsite at Lewis Lake. The campground was crammed full of tents and campers. Our campsite number was B-1, which Maggie optimistically insisted stood for "Best One," which might well have been true if not for the fact that it stood on a small dusty rise beneath some overhanging pines just behind one of the campground's main toilet facilities.

As I began unloading the gear and spreading out the ground tarp for the large Bean tent, Maggie, world-renowned expert on public bathrooms, went to inspect the facilities. She came back as I was pegging down the last corner pin and announced, "The toilets don't flush."

"Of course not. They're privies," I said with a ridiculously transparent enthusiasm, "just like the park's original explorers used. I wouldn't be surprised if Meriwether Lewis didn't use this very one."

"Yeah, well, he pooped on the seat."

I asked if she was joking.

"Come on, I'll show you." She sounded delighted to reveal the horror to me. "I mean, it's like, *totally* gross."

I thanked her and said I would take her word on it and that we could use the facilities up at Grant Village. That way, I said, we could have a shower as well.

The ranger came by in his truck to collect our six bucks per diem. I explained we might be staying two or three nights, thinking as I said it, given the sudden shift of the breeze, what a wildly optimistic scenario that was. The ranger looked as if he'd just graduated from the Explorer Scouts but I didn't fail to notice the .38 on his hip and the pump-action Remington bolted to his dash. His name was stitched on his shirt. Karl. Karl said we could just pay for the weekend and asked for $18. I handed him the money and asked if it was okay for us to move campsites if another site opened up, someplace a bit farther upwind of the johnny. Karl said that was fine but to please notify him if we made the switch. I said we would do that and, speaking of the johnny, wondered if he knew that someone had missed the designated drop zone in there.

"It's a problem, sir," he said, looking solemnly at the offending structure. "I'll report it." He looked at Amos and asked me if he was my dog. I didn't deny it.

"We ask that you keep him on a lead at all times, for his sake as well as that of the wildlife." Ranger Karl explained that there'd been reports of an active grizzly in the area and said we should also be sure and lock up our food materials in the truck each night.

"Will do," I assured him, then pointed at his Remington and asked if the shotgun was for any wildlife that got out of hand.

Ranger Karl smiled. He looked like a nice kid.

"The human wildlife, mostly," he said.

I felt my mood sinking fast. By the time I finished putting up the tent and arranging the camp, I was tired and hot and filthy and wanted a cold stream to fish in and a cold beer to drink and realized I should have taken the nice lady ranger's advice and driven us up the Yellowstone to a swell uncrowded fish camp in Montana. Then I told myself to snap the hell out of it because (a) we were *finally* in the heart of Yellowstone Park, the world's first national park and the place I'd dreamed of going as a kid, and (b) tomorrow we were actually going to see Old Faithful and maybe fish the Yellowstone or Madison. So what if some cretin had dumped on the seat and we were camped on the sorriest patch of campground in all of Yellowstone and possibly the entire continental United States. How much worse could it get than that?

Then, a few yards to starboard, Maggie casually remarked, "Gosh, Dad. Check out these red ants."

Actually, "these red ants" didn't quite cover it. Within minutes it became clear I'd pitched our camp on one of Yellowstone's legendary ant colonies, inciting the collective fury of a couple million ants who dutifully poured out of their holes to protest our arrival. To be honest, I couldn't tell if they were red ants or black ants, but I wasn't in any mood to whip out my *Complete Field Guide to American Wildlife* and properly identify them. If I'd had Ranger Karl's pump Remington, I probably would have emptied the chamber on them. Instead, I marched to the truck and fetched a jumbo can of wasp spray and spent the next quarter hour rendering the site biologically sterile until the year 2050. As the smoke settled and their little bodies twitched pathetically in the dust, I felt sort of bad about murdering so many bugs in cold blood and remembered reading about a sect of Buddhist monks who were so determined to avoid causing any suffering to the living world that they went to their evening prayers sweeping the path before them. Obviously they'd never tried to camp behind a privy in Yellowstone Park, though.

"I really wish you hadn't done that," a testy voice said. I looked around and saw a young woman glaring at me from the adjacent campsite. She and another young woman had been hanging wash on a line in their campsite, and I'd noticed them at one point pause and exchange a sisterly kiss over drying apparel that probably would have caused emotional distress to their pioneer grandmothers.

Maggie saw it, too, and I realized we'd never had any kind of discussion about lifestyle choices and gay people. I didn't have a clue if she even knew what it meant to be gay but it followed that she didn't because, as I say, we'd never had the Big Talk about sex. The Indians called gay people "two-spirited." "I'm sorry," I called over to the angry two-spirited woman, "but they had us outnumbered a million to one."

"That stuff is deadly poison. You should know better."

I gathered from her tone that we probably wouldn't be roasting marshmallows together and singing Woody Guthrie songs by the fire later on. The women slipped into their tent, where they probably meant to have a nice refreshing afternoon nap, and I suggested to Mugs that she give our traveling elder statesman a proper walk. A few minutes later, she and Amos disappeared down the road, and when they came back half an hour later they brought two new pals in the persons of an eleven-year-old boy and his little sister who were camping with their grandparents somewhere beyond the two-spirited ladies.

"That's a cool tent," said the boy, who said his name was Darrell Sablonski. Darrell was wearing a New Jersey Devils hockey shirt and a Packers cap and immediately began talking as if someone had pulled a string. "We only have my grandpa's trailer. It kinda smells. We're from Wisconsin. My grandpa works at the sausage factory in Sheboygan. I'm going into the sixth grade. Have you ever been whitewater rafting? We're supposed to go whitewater rafting on Monday. I just took my hunter's safety test back home. I'll be twelve in October. Back home I have an iguana, three cats, four hamsters, four dogs, one shitzapoo, and twelve fish. Have you seen the movie *Forrest Gump*? I did. It was really cool. I really like your tent."

I invited him to go in and have a look around, hoping to shut him up. Maggie showed our new neighbors around the tent like Ivana Trump squiring Barbara Walters through her penthouse suite and I heard her cooing, "My father will sleep here, you see, on this cot, and I'll sleep there, on that one. That's my bear Susie. . . ." Darrell's little sister wandered out of the tent and asked me for something to drink. She looked parched and I started to offer her a cold beer like the one I'd just opened but offered her a Pepsi instead. She thanked me. I smiled down at her and asked her name. Her name was Kelly Sablonski and she was five. "My grandpa drinks beer, too," she revealed sweetly. "He farts a lot at night."

"Ah, well. The winds of change come to every man."

"Dad," asked Maggie, "can Darrell and Kelly roast marshmallows with us later?"

"Of course," I said, not thinking of what that might lead to, thinking instead how Grandpa the Sheboygan sausage man might feel right at home in our smelly but ant-safe campsite.

We put the canoe in and fished Lewis Lake, catching absolutely nothing, paddling downwind for a while and trying our apparent lack of luck in a nice evergreen-embowered cove where black logs lay just beneath the crystal-clear surface. It looked like a can't-miss trout or bass hole but missed its objective of improving my sinking mood; then the wind came up strongly and I realized we had a real fight on our hands just paddling back to the boat landing. Norumbega Girl's bow kept turning in the wind and we would drift that way for a while until the deranged paddler at the rear of the canoe managed to flail the craft back on course. Maggie, bless her, heroically tried to help, slapping at the water with her junior-sized paddle, displacing a large percentage of the lake directly onto her father. It had taken us fifteen minutes to smoothly glide down the lake—and almost an hour to crazily paddle back. By the time we hauled the canoe out, I was soaked with sweat and Lewis Lake water and felt as if I'd gone three rounds with a Yellowstone grizzly. My aching shoulder muscles were ready for a hot shower, my stomach for a decent meal, my mind for a nice big friendly Highland Scotch.

"That was kinda fun," Maggie chirped, prompting me to give my beloved firstborn the kind of look Meriwether Lewis must have given his old Charlottesville buddy Tom Jefferson when Jefferson asked him to name the neatest part of the trip that had nearly killed him.

We chained the canoe to a tree and drove to the park store at Grant Village to buy groceries for our stay. The store was full of sunburned shoppers buying movie magazines and Yellowstone souvenirs. The grocery section was small but the souvenir department vast and full of German and Japanese tourists buying T-shirts with the Old Faithful and Yellowstone logos. I looked around, hoping to catch a glimpse of the Ten Sleep cyclists, but they weren't there. We bought a few groceries—two rib-eye steaks, a fresh tomato, a box of Kraft macaroni and cheese, a pint of fruit yogurt for dessert—then beat a retreat to the village showers, where a couple dozen equally beaten-looking vacationers waited in two lines with towels and little soap containers like the ones city kids carry to summer camp. I got in line behind a man who looked as if he had the weight of the world on his broad, hairy back. "The last time I did this," he groaned, without looking at me, "was in the army. At least I got paid."

Darrell Sablonski and his little sister were still sitting together on a log waiting for us at our campsite; perhaps they'd never left. They watched me get a fire going and the macaroni started and slice up the tomato onto a platter on the tailgate of Old Blue. I had five ears of sweet corn left from Blue Earth, Minnesota, and shucked that, too. I overheard Maggie explain to our visitors that we were mostly vegetarians who enjoyed a nice steak now and again, then she asked if Darrell and Kelly could stay for supper. I thought about it and said, "I guess so, but they better go ask permission," and she explained that they'd already done that while we were off taking showers.

The Sablonski clan was having S.O.S., for dinner, which Darrell explained he "really hated." I liked S.O.S., or creamed chipped beef on toast, which only a culinary philistine or veteran of WWII would dare call "shit on a shingle," and was sorely tempted to go ask the Sheboygan sausage baron if I could break bread, if not wind, with his people. Darrell insisted on cooking the steak he and Kelly would share, which he did, treating us to a detailed plot description of *Forrest Gump*, his views on Dennis Rodman and the recent National Hockey League draft, and how his grandpa had waited thirty years to finally get Packers season tickets and had a lot of gray hair growing in his ears. As he was lifting the steak off the fire with a fork, he dropped it on the ground. "Whoa. I'm not gonna eat *that*," he snorted, backing up. Both girls giggled. Darrell was such a riot.

My daughter and her dinner guests ate my steak split three ways and most of the macaroni and cheese, while I ate the tomato and five ears of sweet corn. Amos gratefully supped on the *filet au dirt* while Darrell filled us in on his new twenty-one-speed mountain bike back home, his *Star Wars* poster collection, and his views on space aliens. He believed people from other worlds were not only among us but sometimes abducted smart kids for all kinds of horrible tests. I couldn't be that lucky, I thought, smiling at him as I crunched my corn.

I suggested they all take Amos for an après-dinner stroll while I cleaned up the dishes and prepared the marshmallow skewers, and the happy trio hadn't been gone two minutes when the other two-spirited lady—the Large One, as I would fondly come to think of her—marched over and smartly informed me to "please keep your children from walking through other people's campsites."

I apologized once again, vaguely wondering if there might be a nice Hyatt Hotel with air-conditioning and room service somewhere in the vicinity. The Large One left me to scrub my pots in reproached silence and I gamely tried, as Opti no doubt would have, to look on the positive side of the situation. At least it wasn't pouring rain and, hey, there didn't seem to be any mimes wandering around. As a man ages, he should probably face up to his prejudices. The truth is, I loathe mimes. They give me the willies. I always feel an urge to punch them and make them recite the Gettysburg Address or something. Pantomime drama began in sixteenth-century Italy and I happen to wish it had stayed there.

The children came back a little while later, just as I was building up the fire and arranging the camp stools for a communal marshmallow roast. "Dad," Maggie said. "Can Darrell and Kelly sleep over?"

"You don't have sleepovers on camping trips," I explained, perhaps a bit more testily than I intended, as I speared the first marshmallow with a stick and presented it to little Kelly. "Besides, I don't think their grandfather would approve."

"He doesn't mind," the ever-helpful Darrell announced. "We asked him already. He said it's okay with him."

I wondered if I might be a decent candidate for alien abduction.

"Watch this, everybody!" Darrell suddenly barked, holding up a flaming marshmallow. "A meteorite!" He flicked his wrist, sending a flaming fireball soaring out of our campsite and down the hill toward the tent of our two-spirited neighbors, who mercifully had gotten in their car and left a short while after the Large One chewed me out.

This was the good news. The bad news was that the flaming ball quickly set a small patch of brush on fire mere feet from their tent. I sprang to my feet with surprising agility for an aging canoeist, filled a pot with water, and

rushed down the slope to slosh it on the ground and perform a little jig on the flames. Then I walked slowly back up
the hill wondering how I was going to explain the big
burned spot on the ground next to their tent. Perhaps I
could say I'd discovered another ant colony and wiped this
one out with a flamethrower.

I glowered gently at our camp guest. "Darrell, that was
pretty dumb. Please don't do that again."

"Jeez. *Sor-ree*," he said sullenly, as if I didn't know a good
time when I saw it.

We roasted marshmallows in silence for a few minutes
and, as things settled down a bit, I tried to think of what
book I might whip out of the Medicine Bag and casually
asked Darrell what his parents were doing while he and his
sister were palely loitering out West. I pictured them having
a wild party or perhaps quietly drinking Dom Pérignon and
enjoying the blessed sounds of Darrell-free silence.

"My dad lives with his new wife. My mom just died."

Maggie and I both stared at him. I was uncertain if I'd
heard him correctly. His face, though, told me I had.

"Really? I'm sorry. How long ago?"

He shrugged, balancing his roasting stick between two
fingers. "Three weeks ago. She'd been in the hospital in
Sheboygan for a long time. I think it was her blood or something. Her kidneys were bleeding. They moved her down to
the hospital in Madison and did some kind of operation. It
was supposed to save her life but it didn't. They told me to
come and see her on Friday and she died on Sunday."

"I'm very sorry. You must feel really sad."

"Yeah. I cried about it for a couple days, I guess. I really
miss her a lot. I didn't even get to say good-bye or nothing.
That's why my grandpa brought us out here. I didn't really
want to come but it's not as bad as I thought it would be. I
hope we see a wolf."

I nodded and decided not to tell him there was little
chance he'd see a wolf. Yellowstone's wolf reintroduction

program had recently been heralded as a success—there were believed to be dozens of breeding pairs now roaming the park—but wolves were possibly the most elusive mammals on earth. I glanced at Kelly. She was holding her marshmallow miles from the flame. It wasn't even slightly brown. "May I?" I said, taking her stick. I moved it closer to the flame and it started to get brown and she rewarded me with a tiny bow-shaped smile. "Maggie," I said, "why don't you let Kelly and Darrell sleep on the cots and I'll blow up the air mattress for you on the tent floor."

"That's okay," Darrell said, a small grin returning. "I'll sleep on the floor. I kinda like sleeping on the floor."

I watched them make shadow puppets on the tent wall for a while and then there was silence from the tent. I poked a couple more pieces of wood into the fire, opened another beer, and sat down on a log, turning on Maggie's boom box, hoping to get classical music or the weather; as I say, I love the weather. Instead, I got the news. The news was the same. The media had all but named security guard Richard Jewell as the official Olympic bomber, while the alleged "Unabomber" wasn't talking, even to his court-appointed lawyer. Meanwhile, Timothy McVeigh, the accused bomber of the federal building in Oklahoma City, was worried he couldn't get a fair trial because of all the negative publicity, and mechanical hands were still seining the ocean floor off Long Island for bits of wreckage that might indicate a bomb had brought down TWA flight 800. Bombs were the blue plate special that night in America.

I was starting to hate the news as much as I hated mimes. As I reached to turn it off, the news got a bit brighter: Mary Thompson of Orlando, America's oldest person, had died in her sleep at the ripe old age of 120, having outlived eight of her ten children and her husband and attributing her long and productive life to good food, the Gospels, and lots of yard work. I found a public station playing an aria from Puccini's *La Fanciulla del West* and watched the headlights of a small car pull into the adjacent campsite. A flashlight bobbed and the two-spirited ladies went into their tent.

The older I got, the more I fancied opera. Why was that? Perhaps it was because, as Mencken was supposed to have quipped, opera is to music what a bawdy house is to a cathedral. Everything went wrong in opera on a lush and grandiose scale, rather like life itself. I'd recently started buying opera CDs and had even worked my way through most of a biography of Puccini. On his first visit to the United States in 1905, Giacomo Puccini saw a horse opera called *The Girl of the Golden West* and was so enamored with the cheap stage theatrics of a fake snowstorm and the simpleminded western melodrama that he went home to Italy and wrote his own opera about a saloon owner named Minnie and her outlaw boyfriend Dick. Dick is a villain with a good heart, as Minnie discovers, and after several barroom brawls and de rigueur shoot-outs with pursuing vigilantes, Minnie saves Dick's skin from a ruthless gambler/bounty hunter by cleverly substituting aces from her garters in a poker match. The opera's grand finale comes when Dick is about to be lynched by the mob and he sings the opera's most famous piece, *"Ch'ella mi creda libero"* ("Let her believe me free"), hoping his beloved will never learn of his unhappy fate. Just in the nick of time, though, Minnie the barkeep, the girl of the Golden West, gallops in and pleads for Dick's life. The vigilantes know true love when they see it and agree to let the lovers live in peace.

Puccini believed, upon the opera's debut, that his *Girl of the Golden West* was one of his finest efforts, reflecting, he insisted, not only the values of the American people but the vigorous spirit of the West. The opera was initially a smashing success but coincided with the arrival of a wagonload of personal woe when, during the production, Puccini's wife became hysterically jealous of a housemaid and publicly accused the girl of being her husband's mistress. The house-maid committed suicide and a sensational trial followed, proving life really does resemble a disordered cathedral or at least a cheap horse drama.

As the famous aria played itself out, I snapped off the boom box and glanced around the camp to see if Amos was ready to have his evening aspirins. He wasn't lying any-where within the ring of firelight so I got up and walked around the camp, but failed to see him. I called his name, realizing how pointless that was. I walked around behind the tent, checked out Old Blue. No dog. He was gone.

"Jesus *Christ*," I heard myself say softly, not exactly prayerfully.

I wondered, for a moment, if perhaps he'd taken himself off to sleep with the sausage baron of Sheboygan or maybe just for an evening stroll in the woods. He often did that back home, disappearing for an hour at a time. Recently I'd followed him on one of these sorties and he'd led me to a perfectly shaped rock bowl in the side of a hill, a secret place filled with ferns. He'd immediately flopped down and wallowed shamelessly, growling with delight and even bark-ing with sensual pleasure. Watching him roll in private ec-stasy had reminded me of the secret place the elephants go to die in *King Solomon's Mines*. Then he'd looked up from his fern bowl, seen me, and struggled to his feet, appearing almost embarrassed.

But wandering around our cozy six-hundred-acre wood and this twenty-thousand-acre preserve primeval were en-tirely different matters. If Ranger Karl and the reverential guidebooks could be believed, Yellowstone was full of griz-zly bears—which once fed off tourist garbage but had now reverted to their natural predatory ways—and other dan-gerous critters an old amiable retriever from Maine had never seen the likes of. I mentally kicked myself for not heeding Karl's warning to keep the old fella on a lead.

I walked down the road and said his name louder, and a bossy voice I recognized came floating back at me from you-know-where, sternly advising me to please pipe down and be considerate of others. I stood in the darkness trying to think what to do. I honestly felt my heart racing, my blood pumping, my panic rising. The thought of losing Amos was simply unimaginable. He'd always been with me and I'd always been with him. We were best friends, old allies, lifelong partners in crime. I half considered marching up to the Tent of the Two Spirits and shouting through cupped hands that people who were so politically sensitive about other people's minding their own business really should *mind their own fucking business!*

But that would be no solution—just me confirming their view that men like me were really hysterical intolerant jerks. I wasn't a hysterical jerk and I had nothing against two-spirited people and I walked down the campground road a way feeling really at loose ends, walked as far from our camp as I felt I could go, then turned around and walked back. I tried to kill time doing normal prebed chores, hoping against hope for the sudden sound of a dog walking up. I boxed up the rest of the foodstuffs and stowed them in Old Blue, closed the rear hatch, picked up a few things in camp.

We were getting the hell out of Dodge in the morning, I told myself—me, my girl of the Golden West, *and* my dog. I turned on the radio again and tuned it to another station where a country music singer, yet another Lonesome Shorty, was moaning that his wife had it all—good looks, great personality, and, thanks to her lawyer, most of his weekly paycheck, the house, and his bass boat. I was reminded of a joke Silent Sam had once told me: If you played a country music record backward, your wife, job, and dog all came back.

Someone got up in the tent, I heard the zipper door open,

and Maggie came out, sleepily rubbing her eyes. She walked over to where I'd resumed my existence as a knot on a log, this time with a tin tumbler of Scotch in hand. She bent and kissed me on the cheek. "I forgot to kiss you good night," she said sleepily. "Thank you for letting them sleep over."

"Thank you for the kiss. I really needed it."

She yawned. "Where will you sleep?"

"In the truck. No problem. Scoot back to bed."

"Okay." She paused. "Dad, I heard you calling Amos. Where is he?"

I explained that Amos had taken himself for a walk but would probably be back any moment, that I wasn't worried and she shouldn't be. *Liar, Liar. Neighbors' tent on fire . . .*

"He's real smart," she assured me. "He'll come back."

"I know. You're right." How nice to have her faith, I thought.

"Dad, don't *worry.*"

"It's my job, remember?" I reminded her.

"Then get a new job," she said, and smiled.

She went back to bed and I poked more wood into the fire and turned off the radio and slipped down to rest my head on the log and finished the Scotch and pulled a small wool blanket over my legs and lay there thinking that maybe I should say a prayer. I tried to avoid praying for *things* because I didn't think of God as some kind of QVC operator in the sky who would send you swell items if you were prepared to pay the price and your spiritual credit rating was good enough. Someone once said praying doesn't do a thing for God—it just works wonders for the person praying.

I lay there and reminded God, though he probably didn't need it, that "dog" was his own name spelled backward and said that if he saw fit to help this man's best friend find his way back through the darkness I would be profoundly grateful and would try extra hard to avoid saying mean things about mimes or thinking bad thoughts about the way life often really does resemble a sorry horse opera.

I don't know how long I lay there talking to God, wherever he was, but I began to feel a bit better and soon dozed off and must have been asleep at least a couple hours when I suddenly awoke, imagining that I heard the snap of a twig. I opened my eyes and sat up and was a little confused by how dark it had become and how stiff and cold I was. I shoved a couple smaller pieces of wood in the fire's embers and tugged the blanket back over my bare legs and sat blinking at the darkness for a few minutes until what appeared to be a shape began to come slowly toward me out of the night, a large white shaggy face that became more familiar as it approached. Amos slowly ambled into the camp, circled twice, and flopped down beside me. I reached over and touched his head.

He'd been out for an evening walk, perhaps a nice wallow in a fern bowl somewhere. He'd known where he was all along even if I hadn't, and he knew he would be back even if I didn't. *See? Here I am. Relax. Have faith.* I told him he was a smart dog and I was glad he'd come home but he shouldn't feel too smug because, let's face it, only one of us thought it was okay to drink from the toilet.

Amos inhaled and exhaled calmly, as if he'd heard it all before.

In the morning, on the road to Old Faithful, we saw a wolf.

She was standing in the middle of the road, having paused as we suddenly rounded a corner in Old Blue. We'd gotten an early jump on Old Faithful. It was Sunday morning just after seven. Maggie saw her first.

"Dad, look. A *wolf* . . ."

At first, I thought it was a dog. But the closer we got, the more I realized Maggie was right. It was a female wolf, a she wolf—silvery gray, rather thin in the haunch, but unmistakably a wolf. I came to a complete halt on the road and we sat there staring at each other for a few seconds before she turned and loped into the woods, disappearing like a shadow.

"Wow," Maggie said. "I wish Darrell could have seen him." Darrell's grandfather had come to fetch him and his little sister just after sunup. He was a nice big rosy-cheeked midwesterner who had, as reported, impressive tufts of gray hair growing from his ears and a soiled Packers cap on his head and homemade sausage links already sizzling on the griddle, which he invited us over to sample. We took him up on it and went over for the full Yellowstone camp breakfast experience, including a full rundown on the Packers' rookies and free agents and some excellent hotcakes. Nobody, so far as I know, broke wind, and on the walk back to break down our camp, the smaller two-spirited lady asked me if I'd found my dog and seemed pleased when I explained that he had come home. I thanked her for asking after him. The world was back on its axis.

Old Faithful had just erupted when we got there, pulling into a space near the main reception lodge. A large clock in the reception center's main lobby indicated the next eruption would be around 8:08. We had most of an hour to kill. Maggie wandered into a gift shop that was just opening while I chatted up a blue-haired uniformed park volunteer. I asked her if Old Faithful really was faithful and she explained that contrary to the broad popular notion Old Faithful did not erupt on the hour, every hour, but varied somewhat depending on how long or short the previous eruption was. Historically, she said, the geyser spouted anywhere from 150 to 175 feet in the air, lasting approximately five minutes. She admitted that in recent times the height of the eruption had been slightly less. The geyser was faithful only in the sense that of all the park's geysers, Old Faithful is the one that never disappoints the visitor by refusing to perform. Theories varied as to why the spout was typically smaller than ever before. Some geologists believed it was due to overdevelopment in other parts of the West and a shrinking water table that was vulnerable to fluctuations; others maintained that subtle shifts in the earth's geologic crust meant that hot water funneled off to nearby geysers.

The volunteer's name was Betty. Betty was a no-nonsense retired bank executive from Missouri and grandmother of six, a human geyser of useful geyser data. She told me most visitors had no clue that they were standing on a massive volcanic basin that could essentially "blow to high heaven at any moment," and she pointed out, on a distinctly more encouraging note, that a fifth of the world's geysers—totaling 140—lay within a mile of Old Faithful in the Upper Geyser Basin. There were only three other places in the world, she said, that even remotely compared with Yellowstone's awesome geyser basins—and they were in Iceland, New Zealand, and someplace way out on the steppes of the old Soviet Union.

I thanked her for this helpful information and she demanded to know, in a tone once reserved for discussion of a customer's credit history, if I had the slightest idea who named Old Faithful. I admitted I was stumped. I guessed John Colter or maybe Jim Bridger, the famous mountain man who ventured through the region in the late 1800s.

"Wrong," she said triumphantly. "It was General Henry Washburn, surveyor general of the Montana Territory." Washburn, she explained, was a former Union army general who came West to try and restore his health after the Civil War ruined it. I asked Betty if Washburn's strategy had proved successful, thinking what a recurring theme this seemed to be. "I reckon *so*," she fired at me with a brisk Mizzou smile. "They named a durned mountain range after him."

Outside, Old Faithful's big show was about to commence. People were drifting toward the large platform amphitheater around the geyser and I was surprised, though probably shouldn't have been, to see the handsome Italian family from Cody pass in the flow of the crowd, still immaculately dressed, the kids still beautifully behaved, all five of them, the papa smiling as ever, the mama still looking slightly mortified. She saw us and waved vigorously and I waved back. We found spots near them on one of the front benches—why come this far, I thought, not to have a view at least as good as General Washburn got. Maggie was eating a corn muffin and as the geyser began to make its first tentative rumbling and hissing sounds, a couple large striped squirrels showed up to beg food.

"Aw, Dad. Look. Aren't they *cute*?"

"Yep. Adorable. Hey, check it out, babe. I think the old girl's about to blow."

Maggie didn't appear to hear me. She was over the platform onto the graveled ground in front, feeding the squirrels pieces of her muffin. A particularly portly one waddled right up to her hand and allowed her to feed him.

An elderly woman seated next to me commented, "Your little girl is the adorable one."

"Thanks. We drove three thousand miles just so she could feed these squirrels. How far did you come?"

"From Fresno," she said. "My husband Orville and I came here on our honeymoon. That was in 1946. You could walk out there almost to the geyser itself back then."

"Life before lawyers, I guess." I was busy getting my camera ready. "Has the geyser itself changed much?"

"Not much. I find that rather comforting." She explained that Orville had been dead two years. Her grandson David had brought her to Yellowstone to see Old Faithful, perhaps for the last time. He was sleeping in this morning at the inn. David was twenty and about to go into the marines. He hoped to be an officer. She hoped he wouldn't get sent to Bosnia. Orville had been a navy cook. "Oh, look," she said with gentle urgency.

I turned my head and looked. Old Faithful was spouting hot water, slow gurgles that quickly became pulses and grew rapidly in strength and intensity. I nearly couldn't believe what I was seeing, a sight millions of people have witnessed over the past century but that still felt, unaccountably, almost intimately personal. The veil of water made a hissing noise as it rose, like silk rustling in the wind.

"Maggie, look," I said. "Isn't that *fantastic*?"

My daughter turned her head casually, still feeding the portly squirrel from the palm of her hand.

"Yeah. Cool."

"Move out a bit," I said, opening my camera lens. "I want to get a photo of you both. You and Old Faithful, I mean. Not the squirrel."

She gave me an embarrassed look, as if to say I *must* be kidding; like, what a *totally tourist* thing to do. I was reduced to shamelessly begging her and she finally obliged me by moving out a few feet more into the lens of my camera where the geyser was erupting. The squirrels followed her. She was much more interested in them.

I snapped a photograph of her kneeling on the gravel, with the geyser fully erupting in the background. Her back was arched, her palm lifted, her eyes shut. She was making an exaggerated pose, perhaps even a gentle mockery of her father's embarrassing excitement. I'll never know for sure and that's really fine with me. The camera caught something extraordinary. She looked like a smiling girl of the Golden West. A girl laughing in prayer. When I turned back to the old woman beside me on the bench, she was smiling, too. Dabbing her eyes with a Kleenex.

Later that day we followed the Firehole River to the Madison, then followed the Madison River through the commercial clutter of West Yellowstone to the Gallatin, then moseyed up the Gallatin River into breathtaking open country, angling toward Big Sky, where we found a place to camp for two more nights.

The campsite was yards from the rushing river's edge, set in a place that resembled a postcard of the great pioneer West. Framed by small rugged mountains where the evergreens abruptly gave way to rock and grasslands at the higher timberline elevations, the sky was blue and the water was clean and fast with plenty of shallows that were easy to navigate on foot and had plenty of pools to investigate. We were listening to beautiful Trout Music and soon catching beautiful trout, too. Maggie caught a couple nice-sized rainbows and I took her picture with them before we released them back into the river. Then she asked if she could swim for a while. I said I didn't mind, and I really didn't. We'd pretty much accomplished what I'd hoped we would — found our way to Yellowstone, then found a place that was maybe even a little more like Heaven. Whatever she wanted to do from this point on was fine by me. I was going to relax and let the river of life just *take* us.

I sensed a subtle shift in my fishergirl's interests. She wasn't fishing with the same avid curiosity as she had been at the start. She would fish for a half hour, catch a trout, then start to lose interest, tangle her line or hook it on a log. It occurred to me that perhaps she was tired of fishing and maybe even a little homesick. When I asked her about this, though, she merely smiled and shook her head and wondered if we might take a hike or drive in to see what Big Sky was like.

"You know," I said, "I was wondering that very same thing."

We drove into Big Sky, which turned out to be an attractive ski resort town where everybody looked like a model from the L. L. Bean catalog. We ate dinner at a nice cafe and took in a movie, which happened to be *Forrest Gump*.

Maggie loved the movie and I liked it well enough, though thanks to Darrell Sablonski I knew the plot inside out.

The two men in the adjoining camp were serious fishermen, a father-and-son tandem named Bill and Greg Greer. They were from Chicago. Bill, an airline executive, knew a great deal about Yellowstone region trout. It was surprising to learn that none of the trout we'd caught were native to the region but had been introduced to local waters by Europeans at the end of the last century. Like other newcomers, browns and rainbows thrived in western waters, Bill explained, and generally stood up better than some of the native species like west slope cutthroats and golden trout to changing environmental conditions and, of more recent threat, invasive parasitic tapeworms and infectious metabolic disorders like whirling disease, a protozoan parasite infection that disrupted a fish's central nervous system by damaging cartilage tissues surrounding the brain, causing skeletal deformities that made the fish twist, or "whirl," in the water. The disease, an accidental European import, was already present in twenty-two states and had decimated many trout species. Fearing the massive economic consequences, he said, state fish and game departments were hesitant to come out and say it but whirling disease was running like a medieval plague through western trout and if it wasn't checked soon it would wipe out most of the region's native species—nothing short of a trout apocalypse.

We were sitting around the Greers' campfire on the second evening when Bill Greer told me this. Maggie was very still, holding a marshmallow over the flame. I asked Bill where he got his trout knowledge.

"My father used to bring me out here when I was a kid." He glanced at his son Greg, a lanky youth sprawled in a beach chair. "I did the same with Greg but I'm about to lose my fishing buddy." Bill smiled a little bit. "Ole Greg just graduated from college and is about to get married."

This caught Maggie's attention. She looked at Greg with new interest.

"Naw," mumbled Greg beneath his Ohio State cap. "We'll still fish."

"When's the date?" I asked. The groom seemed almost too relaxed.

"Next week," his father answered for him, winking at me. "I'm giving them two weeks on the Williamson for a wedding present."

"Yeah, right," Greg grunted. "Not unless Martha says so."

The groom explained, with a laugh I feared he might someday come to rue, that the bride did nothing without first consulting her Martha Stewart wedding book.

I'd heard of the Williamson, though I couldn't place it. I asked Bill and he explained that the Williamson was a fabulous trout river in southeast Idaho. This got us talking about great trout streams they'd fished and I hadn't. The conversation reminded me of golfers talking about the world's best golf courses, places they intended to make sacred pilgrimages to someday. Bill and Greg, it turned out, had fished many great rivers together, from the Williamson to New York's Beaver Kill.

Bill wanted to know if being from Maine meant I'd fished Grand Lake Stream, which was supposed to have the best rainbow and landlocked salmon fishing in eastern America. I admitted I hadn't but knew another Bill—my accountant, the guy whose wife calculated his trout cost $375 a pound to catch—who had, and that Bill verified everything I'd heard about the place. I said it was my ambition to get up to Grand Lake Stream soon, possibly in the early autumn.

The trout talk was losing Maggie. She finished a roasted marshmallow and then asked to go back to our camp to bed. Our camp was only a few yards through woods. I asked if she would mind feeding Amos his cheese and aspirin and she nodded, politely said good night, then led her dog off to bed.

"How old is she?" Bill asked after she'd gone.

"Seven." I decided to skip the rest of the weary joke and to keep the divorce business under my hat as well.

"Amazing girl. Bet you're proud."

I said I was and explained to the Greers that Maggie had been a real trouper on this trip but I feared her interest in fly angling was beginning to wane a bit. We'd been away from home over three weeks; she'd never before been away from home more than five days.

"That's okay," Bill said, waving his hand. "It'll come back—her fishing interest, I mean. Maybe she just needs to do a few other kinds of things, like riding a horse or something. Does she ride?"

I said no; she'd never ridden a horse.

"You ought to take her to a dude ranch we know up near Great Falls. It's in the Lewis and Clark National Forest. Incredible place. Very low-key. Great trout streams. Beautiful scenery. They also have a terrific riding program for kids. If they're not booked up you could let her do her thing on a horse while you go off and fish till you fall over."

I told him that sounded good, perhaps just what we needed. We agreed that in the morning he would give me the ranch's phone number.

"If they can't take you," Bill added, tossing another log on the fire, "I know another place down in Durango, Colorado, that's even better with kids. Their riding program is actually famous. Are you thinking of heading south?"

I said I wasn't sure which way we'd planned to go, but since I'd heard on the radio that afternoon that there were thirty-eight separate wildfires blazing in Oregon and Idaho, going farther west seemed pointless and we would indeed probably go south a bit before turning for home. Jack's birthday was in exactly two weeks.

"Good. I'll give you the number of Colorado Trails Ranch. Maggie'll love it. And you'll love the San Juan."

"The San Juan, eh?"

I couldn't believe he'd said the San Juan. That was the place Saint Cecil had described as a cathedral of trout. I told the Greers about Saint Cecil and described how he described the San Juan River near the dam.

"He's right," Bill said. "Wait till you see it."

"Awesome," Greg Greer agreed with an amiable grunt from beneath his ballcap.

Later that night, I called my friend Silent Sam from Old Blue.

It had been five days since we last spoke. He was still in the grass-cloth room and wanted to know where we were.

"Montana. Some God-ugly river." I held the cell phone out the window, hoping he could hear the Gallatin gurgling in the darkness.

I asked him how he was feeling.

"Not as bad as yesterday. Yesterday I was climbing the walls of this place. They're going to let me go home tomorrow. I've been talking to a shrink." He gave a bitter little laugh.

"What's he say?"

"Not much. Getting a shrink to open up is damn hard."

This was a good sign, I thought; Silent Sam was getting his sense of humor back.

"Let me ask you something," he said before I could ask him if he still felt the sky was falling.

"No. I won't come kill ducks with you this fall."

"You've always been religious. . . ."

"I guess so. Religions start wars, though. The older I get, the more I think I'm just plain old spiritual. A no-name brand at that."

"Well, what I mean is, you believe in God."

I didn't deny the charge, but I pointed out that it often felt more like God believed in me, though I probably didn't deserve such good luck.

He chose his words carefully. "The thing is, I keep thinking none of this would have happened if I believed in God. We quit going to church ten years ago."

I said I didn't think God zapped people for not going to church, otherwise most of England would be toast. Recently I'd seen a poll that showed there were more psychologists than priests in Great Britain and that less than 10 percent of the population fessed up to going to church on a regular basis. I said that a life of faith had nothing to do with going to church.

"Why do you believe in God?" he asked, sounding every bit like the skilled cross-examiner I knew he was in the courtroom.

I replied that I believed because I'd spent years trying *not* to believe but hadn't quite managed to pull off the feat. He thought I was joking. I assured him I wasn't.

"Who do you think God is?" he tried next.

I admitted I didn't have a clue as to who or what God really was; I simply *felt* God. I couldn't prove He was there—I couldn't even prove "He" was a *he*. For all I knew, God might be a woman, because God was different things to different people. There was the God of wrath and the God of love, the brimstone-chucking God of the Old Testament and the error-forgiving God of the Gospels. One was the bearer of a sword, the other an olive branch. But that was just our choices of a creator. The Hopi Indians believed God was music. The Shakers found divine presence in the workings of a simple well-made table. A Sufi Muslim said God was "breath within the breath." Personally, I added, if God was a woman I sure hoped like hell She didn't turn out to be my long-lost fourth-grade teacher Miss Wettington or else we would all wind up getting grilled in the janitor's closet someday.

Bobby laughed a little bit. It still wasn't a real laugh. He asked me to suggest something he could read on the subject, and I warned him that religious faith wasn't like auto maintenance—you couldn't just pick up a manual and "learn" it. I gave him a couple titles, books of essays he might wish to browse through, but nothing too deep. I also suggested the writings of a couple poets I fancied.

"I forgot how you dig poetry," he said. "Personally I hate the stuff."

"Maybe you're not crazy enough."

I pushed the off button on the phone and was somewhat startled to discover Maggie standing beside the truck in her sleep shirt.

"I thought you were asleep, Mugs."

"Can we call Jack and Mommy?" she asked. "I want to say good night to them."

"Of course."

She climbed onto my lap and I dialed the house by the salt marsh three thousand miles away, figuring they would be home by now. Her mother picked up on the second ring. We chatted pleasantly for a moment and then I put Maggie on. She filled her mother in on seeing a wolf and Old Faithful and the cute fat squirrels who ate crumbs from her hand. She made no mention of the great trout fishing we'd finally encountered but repeated the stories for her brother's benefit, then handed the phone to me.

"Dad," Jack said. "I found bumps growing on the back of my tongue."

I assured him finding bumps on the back of your tongue was perfectly normal. Those bumps had a point, I said, though I wasn't exactly sure what it was.

"Dad," he said, "will you be home for my birthday?"

I assured him there was no chance we'd miss his birthday.

"Oh yeah," he said, almost as an afterthought, "one more thing. I learned to swim yesterday."

"No kidding?"

I felt a small lump rise in my throat. I told my son I was very proud of him for learning to swim, as I knew his mother was. It was one of life's great accomplishments, I said. I told him I loved him and said good night. He told me he loved me and said good night.

"Dad?"

"Yes, Rocket?" He refused to hang up just yet.

"Where are you?"

"Somewhere in Montana. A forest by a river. If you listen you may hear it in the background. Can you hear it?" I held the receiver out the window, aimed at the river.

"I think so."

"I'll bring you out here someday soon."

"Is it dark there?"

"Yes. Incredible stars. They're the same ones shining over you. Jack?" I thought I knew what was chewing at him.

"What?"

"Don't worry about those bumps on your tongue. They're supposed to be there. Okay? Believe me."

"Okay." Another stalling pause. "Dad?"

"Yes, Rocket?"

"Where are you and Maggie going tomorrow?"

I thought for a moment, then answered: "To the Grand Tetons. We're headed home."

"What are the Grand Tetons?"

I explained that the Grand Tetons were a very high mountain range in Wyoming and told him what the French name meant in English. He laughed on his end and Maggie laughed on our end and I thought how nice it was to hear my children laughing across a darkened continent.

CHAPTER TEN

....

Song of the Snake

Dear Pocahontus,
This was so cool. We went down the Sneak river in a driff boat
and had a guyed named Tom who liked to ski and said we
should go see Jacksons hole and showd us some baby trout
who were like the oldest fish on earth. I could tell Dad loved it
and a big raft came by but the president wasn't on it but we
waved anyway. I left him a letter at Jackson lake Logge to
say we could do something if he wanted to but Dad said he
prorobly didn't get the letter. We left there and drove old blue
to Jacksons hole and saw some cowboys shoot in the stret.
Then we drove threw the montins to Salt lake Utaw and saw
the church where the mormens lived and thot about going
across the salt lake but it was verry verry hot and we drove to
colorotto insted and stayed at a cool ranch called coloratto
trials and I rode a horse named Luke all week with some
frrends named Lucy and Becca and we saw a very funny show
and laughed alot on the last night. Dad rode some two but
mossly fished in the san won rivver. Then we went to the new

mexxico and camped on a desert mountin and looked at stars. I boght a dream catcher at the indian festival. When the truk blew up in oclahomea we stoped at a gass staison and I got a gatorade and these men towed the truck to ther workshop and took us in their jazzy guys truk to a nice air condission motel to wait in hinton until the truk was ready. We met a verry nice lady who new jessy james. When the truk was ready we left early in the morning and drove to see the oclahomea city bombing but it was dark and I dont remember much but dad said I saw it. It makes me sad to think about. But it made me happy agan to go to gammy's house.

Love, Maggie Dodson

P.S. That is all for now, Love, Maggie.

Our guide was named Tom Hruska. He had been guiding down the Snake River for five years. In the winter he taught skiing above Jackson Hole. He looked like a skier, lean-faced and good-looking, agile on his feet. We'd booked him for half a day's trip. He had already made one trip down the river in his drift boat and said the cutthroat were hard to scare up — the late summer blahs.

"Do you think we'll see the president?" Maggie asked him.

He smiled at her. "You never know. I read he's rafting the Snake today."

"We left him a note," she explained, and Tom glanced at me to see if that was true. I confirmed it. Checking into Jackson Lake Lodge the previous afternoon, we'd learned the Clintons were there on vacation and Maggie had promptly asked the assistant manager for a piece of paper, upon which she printed a note — beautifully, I might add, with two thirds of the words spelled correctly — to "the President of the United Stats."

"What did you tell him?" Tom was clearly impressed.

"That my dad could play golf with him if he wanted to. He's probably going to call us or something."

"I don't see how he could pass up an invitation like that," Tom agreed, winking at me.

We added extra tippet to our lines and pinched our barbs because this portion of the Snake was all catch-and-release. With a little luck, we'd be replacing flies right and left and the spare tippet would be necessary. Tom suggested we try #12 Hopper Flies because they were easier to see in the swiftly moving water and then explained about the uniqueness of the Snake River fine-spotted cutthroats we were after. They were technically considered part of the general cutthroat genus, with no formal Latin name of their own, he said, but anybody who fished the river knew that the Snake's cutthroats were one of the last wild, pure, native trout species of the West, unique as the river they came from, with a fine spot pattern running from head to tail fin, a distinctive rosy-red cheek patch, and a muddy-orange slash under the throat. He had a gut feeling the afternoon fishing was going to be good because this morning's run hadn't been.

"These are some of the oldest fish on earth, perhaps even some of the oldest living *things* on earth," Tom explained as he maneuvered his rugged drift boat into the Snake's swift currents. Drift boats, or "Mackenzie boats," as they're sometimes called, after the Oregon river of the same name, are an engineering marvel and something of a unique species unto themselves—wide in the beam, shallow-drafting, ruggedly constructed with multiple oarlocks so a pilot can shift positions quickly as the river dictates. Their design recalled to me some of the seaworthy wooden dinghies Maine lobstermen traditionally used to row out to their boats. Both craft were meant to take a pounding and handle anything the elements and currents could throw at them.

The boat began to gently buck and I saw the excitement come into my daughter's eyes. She was clutching her fly rod, wearing a purple life vest that looked three sizes too big, seated behind Tom in the rear of the boat. I was standing in the boat's front leg braces in the bow, thinking how the rearing Tetons looked almost unreal, as perfect as a painted stage drop. Tom explained that the thrill of drift fishing was the "hit-and-go" technique of working pools and shallows of the river as we went down, searching for holes where the trout were lazing beneath submerged logs and overhangs or feeding in the swifter current. "These trout have college degrees," he said with a quick grin before his attention went back to the river. He rowed aggressively for a minute and then, as we suddenly caught a swift patch of current, we accelerated along and he held his oars up, explaining that the Snake River changed shape almost every season due to factors like the size of the spring runoff from the mountains or the summer rains. "The river, as a result, is always changing shape. And I mean radically, too—new oxbows and channels, pools you've never seen before. This river can seem so tame at times, like now, in a drought. But turn around and it's raging like a storm."

As he said this, we were bucking through some pretty lively rapids, appearing to just miss several large submerged boulders. I knew from canoeing swift waters that submerged rocks can be bad business—snagging a craft just long enough for the currents to flip it. But a drift boat is designed to draft in less than two feet of water and its width makes turning over a virtual impossibility. Tom told us he was heading us to a pool where he'd had a bit of luck that morning and thought several choice cutthroats might be loitering for an afternoon feed.

From a side channel, a big black rubber raft suddenly appeared, emerging like a truckload of cantaloupes on a busy interstate, bouncing right into our path on small white-capped rapids. Tom used his oars to slow the boat and steer us sharply to starboard. A dozen people were seated on the large raft, wearing bright red safety helmets. Some of them appeared utterly terrified; a few were grinning. Several people waved, and Maggie waved back.

"Is that the president?"

"I don't think so," Tom said, and explained to me that guided-raft traffic had doubled on the Snake during the time he'd been working on the river, which was only five or six years. It was becoming something of a nuisance to fishermen, he admitted, though he quickly added that perhaps the rafters felt the same way about the fishermen.

We made our first casts near a rock island where the heavy spring floods had cranked over some large cottonwoods. The river turned sharply right there and a side channel had several deep and promising pools where the current entered through narrow shallows—just the kind of place, in theory, a trout would lie and wait for his lunch to be served. Tom was impressed with Maggie's basic casting skills and showed her a technique of backcasting her line over an imaginary "brick wall," making an economical forward movement—or "chopping off the chicken's head"—then finishing, as her fly presented itself on the water's surface, with her hands in the attitude of "folded prayer." "Over the wall, chop the chicken's head, and pray. That's my theory of fly casting. If you're lucky, a big cutthroat is waiting there to snack on it."

A big one wasn't waiting, but a small one was. On her fourth or fifth cast, Maggie reeled in a small cutthroat no longer than a school pencil. Tom rowed us onto the shore of the rock island and we all got out and examined the baby fish before releasing him in the shallows. I snapped a photo of the guide and the girl with the baby fish on her line. Another raft bucked past with its occupants whooping and hollering and waving arms like people on a theme park ride. After the fish had been released, Tom offered to take a photo of Maggie and her father backdropped by the Grand Tetons.

We shoved off, then bucked and slashed our way down the Snake through another impressive set of churning rapids, turning out every so often to fish in the lee of rock islands or slower channels. I was surprised each time at how shallow the boat could go without scraping bottom, and Tom explained that a trout was less of a predator than an opportunist who would hang around narrow shallows conserving energy and waiting for his lunch to come to him.

"They'll feed in as little as six inches of water," he said, scanning the breaking water ahead. "Of course, that makes them vulnerable to ospreys and eagles. I once had an eagle swoop down and take a trout right off the line before I knew what happened. Unbelievable. You gotta admire skill and speed like that." Our own theme park ride soon became part birding expedition as we scanned the shore for eagles and ospreys. We spotted several nests and finally saw a small male golden eagle circling way up high, floating on thermals.

Banking into a pool where the river made an abrupt switchback, I made a long roll cast to shallows under overhanging limbs and suddenly saw a flash as a trout took my hopper and ran with it. He felt large but turned out to be only slightly bigger than Maggie's pencil fish. While Tom doped up a new fly for Maggie with silicone, he talked about how the Snake was born in the waters of the Yellowstone and wandered all the way west to the Columbia. Our boat's bow was pulled onto another narrow rock island beach and I was wading bare-legged in the icy shallows, making short casts into a promising pool, wanting a bigger trout, seeking something to remember the Snake by besides its photogenic setting and hypnotic song. Changing strategies, I put on a fresh stone fly, a stimulator whose silhouette in the bright sun just might lure a greedy hog to the surface, and aggressively stripped line and worked my way back up the river. I could sense a trophy trout about to sip my fly and run. Carefully studying the river, I moved a few yards every time I cast, allowing my fly to drift with the current for only a minute or so each time. A hundred yards behind me, Maggie and Tom landed another cutthroat, a fine ten-incher.

I fished alone up the river for perhaps half an hour, certain a strike would happen at any second. But none happened. I finally turned around and walked back to the boat, dragging my bare legs through the beautiful water as I went, remembering a Chinese proverb that says something about water that's too pure holding no fish. Tom and Maggie caught another trout and were now up to fourteen inches.

"This girl can fish," Tom said, and invited me to share their hole.

I thanked him and said it was a joy just to watch them fish. I asked him if we were typical of his paying customers, greenhorn fishermen anxious to experience the song of the Snake, prompting him to smile a bit lopsidedly. "It's funny," he said, adjusting his cap a bit, "you really get all kinds of people out here these days. You get the serious fishermen who just want steady action and no conversation and you get people more interested in the gorgeous country. A few just want to ride down the river. Every client is different. They come with their own set of expectations and every kind of skill. Some want help, some don't. That's why I love this job. I love teaching skiing, but this is really something else."

I asked him if customers were ever disappointed by a day on the Snake.

"Yeah. You get them every so often, some hotshot who blames you if the fish don't bite. I find those guys really aren't here to experience the beauty and grandeur of this place, the joy of being on such an incredible river. To them, it's just about catching fish, an ego thing really. They could be fishing in the Detroit River for all they notice. Some days the trout are biting, some days they aren't. That's really the attraction of trout fishing. It's always a mystery what will happen. You never know if what you do will work but, hey, check out what you get. . . ." He waved at the Tetons with a broad sweep of his arm.

"Too bad it's not real," I agreed, smiling at the panorama.

"Is *that* the president?" Maggie said as another big raft suddenly rounded the corner into view. It sloshed within yards of us and a tubby gent seated at the front did indeed rather resemble our president, though I doubted Bill Clinton would be wearing a T-shirt that jauntily read, *Who says white men are confused? I have the brain of a horse and am hung like a Harvard graduate.*

We finished our run down the Snake two hours later, fishing a pool mere yards from the take-out spot where Tom's assistant had left his truck and boat trailer. The pool was fairly deep and green, the water fairly sluggish, and suddenly we couldn't unhook the cutthroats fast enough. I caught a pair of fifteen-inchers in less than five minutes and Maggie snagged an even bigger one that she worked diligently toward the net without any assistance from Tom until the trout got within a foot of the net, spit the fly, and threw up a contemptuous fantail of river water as he sped away. It was a terrific way to finish the afternoon and I sensed it had been the fishing highlight thus far for Maggie, the thing she needed to revive her sagging angling interests.

Tom asked where we were headed next and I replied that we were probably going to mosey into tony Jackson Hole, wet clothes and all, to see if we could scour up supper and maybe a place that had live music. He told us a place that specialized in good steaks and western line dancing and I thanked him sincerely, adding another twenty to the tip.

"Did you like us?" Maggie asked him.

"What?" Both of us glanced puzzledly down at her.

"I mean, were we, like, good clients or something?"

Tom laughed, folding the money into his shirt pocket. He

ruffled her hair and said, "You were awesome, Maggie. I'll never forget you."

Nice man. Smart dude. Thanks, Tom.

Jackson Hole was packed with shopping tourists and there was gunplay in the street. Spectators lined the wooden boardwalk to watch the sheriff face off with a couple desperados who'd come to town looking for more than a good buy on Gap jeans. *This is how it once was on the streets of old Jackson Hole,* boomed an amplified voice. *When men settled their disputes with six-guns and frontier justice came from the point of a gun. See how far we've come as a civilization?* Amos tugged impatiently at his lead and I was sorry to spot a mime working his way toward us in front of the crowd. With a little luck, the desperados would miss the sheriff and shoot the mime before he reached us.

Closer and closer the bandy-legged cowboys edged, hands hovering over six-shooters. In 1965, a UCLA historian wrote a provocative essay in which he pointed out that most of the technology that tamed the Wild West evolved from the Middle Ages, proving 1850s America was really closer to King Arthur's England than to modern Britain. Archaeological evidence indicated, for example, that spurs and log cabins had really first appeared in Spain and Sweden and that the three principal items believed to be responsible for taming the American frontier—barbed wire, the revolver, and windmills—all had their origins in medieval Europe between 1100 and 1500. Ditto the Conestoga wagon, which brought thousands West, and the stagecoach: first depicted in an Anglo-Saxon manuscript of the eleventh century. The parallels between Merrie Olde England and the Wild Wild West, believed to owe their existence to waves of European working-class immigrants, were almost uncanny. Both societies were broken down into small independent fiefdoms (or territories) traditionally ruled by the shire reeve (or sheriff)

who collected the king's (or president's) taxes and who
served as justice of the peace, chased outlaws, and meted
out swift and often corrupt social justice. Shoot-outs and
hangings were commonplace—often considered a crude
form of public entertainment—and powerful popular my-
thologies grew up around the roguish outlaws who refused
to be tamed (Robin Hood, Jesse James). Saloons and
brothels of the Old West served whiskey, a Celtic invention
of the fourteenth century, and cardplaying, which featured
face cards of kings, queens, and so forth, was really a porta-
ble form of chess.

*The restraints of law could not make themselves felt in the rar-
efied population,* western chronicler Walter Prescott Webb
mused in 1931. *Each man had to make his own law because there
was no other to make it. He had to defend himself and protect his
rights by his force of personality, courage, and skill at arms. All
men went armed and moved over vast areas among other armed
men. The six-shooter was the final arbiter, a court of last resort,
and an executioner.* The knight vanished from Europe around
1400, the theory goes, only to appear again four hundred
years later in the American West.

Across the street, a homeless man was moving through
the well-dressed crowd, pausing to check rubbish bins. Mythology seemed to be everywhere afoot on the prosperous
streets of Jackson Hole. He made me think of Odysseus
finally returning to Ithaca in the disguise of a beggar, moving invisibly among the godless party crowd. Unable to con-
tain his rage at the way his homeland has been spoiled,
Odysseus finally throws off his disguise and slaughters his
grieving wife's suitors, and given the choice of sparing a
wealthy priest or an impoverished poet, he spares the poet,
ensuring that his saga will be told for ages to come.

The sheriff of Jackson Hole was telling the cowboys he
wanted them to clear out of his town, and one of the cowboys hooted derisively. I had difficulty seeing what happened next because the mime had paused directly in front of

me and was making cute happy-sad faces. He was pretending to be terrified of Amos, who appeared almost as annoyed as I was by his presence. There should be a federal
law prohibiting left turns in traffic and public miming, I
often think, and had this been the Middle Ages—or even
just twenty years ago—I might have punched this pale-
faced jester for being such an unwelcome nuisance. See how
civilized I have become? I merely asked him if he wouldn't
mind moving along so I could see the show. He made a
rubbery sad face and moved but it was too late to see the
sudden exchange of gunfire that sent both desperados
sprawling theatrically to the pavement of Jackson Hole.
The crowd applauded enthusiastically and when the smoke
had cleared the public-address announcer was thanking
people for stopping in town and reminding them most stores
stayed open late. In the new mythology of the West, men
came armed with plastic gold cards and swaggered after
their wives into Eddie Bauer.

We found our way to the lively saloon Tom recommended, where people were dining in one room and two-
stepping in a line in another to loud country and western
tunes. Troubadours and country music singers—was this
another link to the doomed Middle Ages? After supper,
Maggie and I found our way to vacant bar stools in the
crowded dance hall, ordered shot glasses of straight Cherry
Coke, and watched groups of middle-aged tourists trying to
learn the Cotton-Eyed Joe, shuffling to a Patty Loveless
torch song. Observing the men stiffly stumbling past in
their brand-new Levi's reminded me of why white guys
really shouldn't dance, so I concentrated my attention instead on a sharp-looking redhead whose jeans looked as if
they might have been helpfully sprayed on by Earl Scheib.
As she sashayed by, the redhead gave me a smile I could
feel in my hip pocket and the guy she was with frowned as
if to say he was fully prepared to climb a water tower armed
with a can of spray paint to defend his sister's honor. I

remembered that every time he saw a pretty girl, Mormon founder Joseph Smith admitted, he prayed for grace.

"Dad," Maggie said, nudging me. I realized she'd seen me watching the red-haired lady. "Can I ask you something?"

I nodded and leaned over to hear her question better. Basically I go deaf in honky-tonks.

"Do you think you'll get married again?"

I straightened up and smiled, then drained my Cherry Coke. I motioned to the barkeep for another one, almost asking him to make this one a double. It wasn't a question I was prepared to answer, not least of all because I wasn't even legally divorced yet. Would she be happy if I admitted I would eventually like a new woman in my life, or sad that somebody else might try and fill the void her mother's departure was going to leave in my life? We were traveling through uncharted territory here, a Wild West of unexpected dangers and ambushing emotions. I chose what I hoped was a suitably obscure response, taking the high road over the dangerous gulch.

"Not unless Patty Loveless is looking for a rhythm guitarist."

Maggie nodded and smiled. I didn't know if she thought I was just trying to be funny or telling the truth. The truth is, I didn't know, either. It was an uncomfortable evasion on my part—she must have felt that as much as I did. How a child processes the events of her life is really a mystery, but from my perspective I was beginning to feel she was either doing a heroic job of suppressing her anger and disappointment with her mother and me, the inevitable sense of betrayal, or else was somehow working through the sadness with an almost eerie composure and levelheadedness. Perhaps the constantly shifting landscape helped, giving her something new in front to look at rather than something painful in back to figure out. It was certainly helping me that way.

First the wedding ring. Now this. It must have startled her to see her old man being a man and admiring a woman other than her mother. I wanted to answer her question honestly—*Yes, babe. I'd like to get married again someday. You see, I loved being married. I need a good woman in my life. When the right woman comes along . . .* —but it just wasn't the right place and time for such revelations. I was still mad at her mother and still madder at myself for somehow ruining Paradise, and I *still* hadn't figured out how we'd managed to do that and was largely unable or unwilling to forgive either of us at this particular moment. Any conversation with Maggie beyond what we might do and see tomorrow seemed grossly premature—and potentially scarring. As a family, we already had enough scars to last a lifetime.

So I did something that surprised even me: I asked my daughter to dance. We joined hands and wandered out in fish clothes to join the fancy line dancers in all their western-style fringed and sequined glory, a couple trout among the rainbow fish. It was quickly another case of a child leading the man, the man feeling faintly absurd on his two left feet, a laughing girl somehow getting them through the ordeal. Trisha Yearwood was tenderly wailing that maybe it was love that she'd run away from. And that maybe it was love that would bring her home again. *Sing it, girl,* I thought.

A little while later, Maggie yawned and said she'd had enough of Jackson Hole and line dancing. It was a half-hour drive back to bed and I wound up carrying her sleeping in my arms through the lobby at Jackson Lake Lodge, wondering how my firstborn lamb could have become so long and heavy or else how I'd become so elderly and weak. She suddenly opened her eyes as we passed by the reception desk.

"Has the president left us any messages?" she sleepily asked the clerk on duty. I paused and gave him our room number and he checked our box and told us, barely suppressing a smile, that he hadn't. "Would you tell him we have to leave real early if he wants to have breakfast or something?" Maggie said, dropping her head back on my shoulder.

"Certainly, miss. Who shall I say?"

"Maggie," she answered, leaving it at that.

The clerk raised his eyebrows, waiting for me to supply a last name. My date was already gone.

"Just say a fishergirl named Maggie," I said.

We followed the Snake River and Route 26 to the Idaho state line, then angled due south on U.S. 89 through the Salt River Range, going through towns with names like Smoot and Cokeville, passing beneath the "World's Largest Elkhorn Arch" before reaching the Salt River Pass and sliding into the right-hand corner of Idaho. A road sign informed us Idaho was "too great to litter!" and another told us it was celebrating its centennial that month. We reached Montpelier—"Settled on the Oregon Trail by Mormon Pioneers in 1864"—and pushed on past Bear Lake to Fish Haven, pulling over at Gladys's Place to reprovision Gatorades and ice down the cooler. The radio reported that the intense heat wave had caused a nine-state power outage and much of Utah was affected. Salt Lake was our destination.

Gladys herself was there, running the counter. I asked her why Bear Lake was so incredibly blue—it looked almost unnaturally blue set against the evergreen forests in the hazy distance.

"Limestone," she answered curtly.

"What kind of fish?"

"Kind that swim."

Maybe Gladys didn't care for hayseeds from Maine, or maybe she was just too dad-blamed hot. It was barely ten o'clock, and the mercury on a tree thermometer outside read ninety-two. Salt Lake was projected to top one hundred. I asked the gregarious Gladys how far it was to Salt Lake.

"Two hours if you know the canyon. Four if you don't."

We didn't know the canyon; it took us five. When we reached Logan, the Miss Cash Valley Pageant was going on and "Twister" was playing at the Utah Theater and the marquee read "All seats $150," a misprint, I hoped. Then a bank's time-temp sign announced it was 3:41 and 97 degrees. We passed a golf course where several people were out pursuing golf balls and heat stroke, then saw a weathered barn pitching "Dr. Pierce's Favorite Prescription— Women's Tonic!" At Brigham City we picked up Interstate 15 and the temperature rose another eight notches to 105.

"Dad," Maggie suggested, "could we turn on the air conditioner?"

I reminded her we'd left the air conditioner at home in Maine and assured her things would cool down in Salt Lake. I suggested she have Cool Blue Gatorade and that she wet down our elderly occupant with ice water while she was at it.

An hour or so later on the fringes of Salt Lake, we passed a Buick on fire and came to a halt in dense rush-hour traffic. The radio was warning motorists to avoid the main thoroughfares, if possible, due to numerous overheating vehicles. Old Blue must have heard this because she immediately began to run hot, too. As we sat there broiling, a boy about seven or eight in the luxurious Jeep Grand Wagoneer next to us began making puke faces at me. The windows of his mother's vehicle were rolled up and he was obviously enjoying an air-conditioned ride.

I tried my best to avoid his rude gestures but he kept making faces and I realized he was beginning to really get under my skin. True, our truck was ten years old and we were covered with the dust of five states and sweating like sinners on Judgment Day—but was that any reason to be so darned unfriendly? We were all in this traffic jam from hell together, weren't we? I glanced at the kid again. The second he caught my eye, his face contorted into a pig face; then, to my even greater surprise, he gave me the universal anti-sign of motoring brotherhood, a smug singly raised middle digit. I smiled in amused disbelief and then did something I hadn't done in probably forty years: I stuck my tongue out at the pint-sized creep. It felt strangely . . . liberating. In some eastern tribal cultures, sticking your tongue out at a stranger is simply a safeguard meant to keep his infectious evil spirits at bay. That's all I was *really* attempting to do but the boy looked stunned and turned abruptly to his mother, evidently squealing about some child-hating pervert in the ugly rust bucket beside them. The mother turned and looked at me in horror and I immediately steered Old Blue onto an exit ramp because a sign to the tabernacle had given me a good idea how we might kill time until the heat backed off.

A few minutes later, we parked off the square and staggered up to the front doors of the mother church of Mormonism. The church rose above us like a mighty rampart, an American Vatican. What better place to cool off and plot our next move than a *huge* stone church. I opened a large door and we felt a refreshing gust of cool air. A suited man immediately materialized, smoothing his hair with a palm, and softly informed me our dog was not permitted in the church. I asked if we might just stand unobtrusively in the entrance foyer and cool down for five minutes and take in the splendor of the church and he repeated, with quiet urgency, that dogs were not permitted in the church and we would have to leave. At least he didn't stick his tongue out at us.

"Dad," Maggie wondered right on cue as we left, "do you think dogs go to Heaven?"

I said of course dogs went to Heaven, the place was probably crawling with mutts of all shapes and sizes. If and when I got to Heaven someday, I grumbled as we hoofed

back through the heat of the square to Old Blue, I fully
expected to find every dog I ever owned faithfully waiting
to say howdy. Brigham Young was so busy collecting wives,
I almost added, it was too bad he didn't take time out to
own a dog. A dog would have done him a world of spiritual
good. Dogs are walking seminars in loyalty and blind faith.

"What exactly *is* Heaven?" she asked next, and I should
have seen it coming.

"Everyone has a different idea and no one knows for sure
exactly what it is," I said. "One place in the Bible says it's a
place in the clouds filled with sapphire streets. A guy named
Plato said it was the most beautiful star you can imagine.
The people who built this church, the Mormons that is, say
Heaven is a place with lots of swell lakes and beautiful cities
where everybody is happily hard at work—sort of Heaven
for Republicans. Your grandfather once told me that the
way to Heaven is Heaven, but that may have been the Indian influence in him. My own thought is that Heaven is
where your dreams finally come true, it's the place of your
best hopes, your heart's desire, the place you really want
to be."

Was this sufficiently vague?

"Cool."

"*Definitely* cool," I added.

Speaking of cool, Salt Lake felt like Hades, no place I
particularly wanted to be, so we drove on to Provo and
found a motel with industrial-strength air-conditioning next
to the Brigham Young University stadium and ate dinner at
a joint filled with BYU freshmen and their parents—all of
whom, I noticed, were intensely blond and entirely dogless.

At dinner, Maggie said she wouldn't mind seeing Las
Vegas because she'd heard Elvis was born and lived there. I
explained, over ice cream pie, that Elvis was born in Mississippi and died in Memphis, both of which we might catch a
glimpse of on the way home, time permitting, but actually
we might be dead, too, if we attempted to reach Las Vegas

across a desert where the reported temperature was 120 degrees.

I suggested we make a beeline straight for the dude ranch in Durango, Colorado, where I'd been fortunate enough to snag somebody else's canceled reservation. The famous riding ranch was expecting us tomorrow or the next day, I said, and we faced a hard ten-hour drive over the southern Rockies. That also meant we were less than a day's drive from a legendary river I couldn't wait to fish. We shook hands on the plan, ordered extra ice cream pies for strength, and decided to turn in early.

CHAPTER ELEVEN

....

The Oldest Thing on Earth

TWO AFTERNOONS LATER, I drove into Durango to a fly-fishing shop to purchase dry flies for a planned excursion to the San Juan with three guys named Ted, Chris, and Michael. They were fellow dads from Colorado Trails, the splendid dude ranch spread over five hundred acres of a narrow canyon rising above the banks of the Florida (pronounced "Flo-reeda") River east of town. There, less than five minutes after our arrival, Maggie had fallen enthusiastically in step with a gaggle of little girls in the "Buckeroo" riding group and fallen for a large chestnut gelding named Luke. After her first afternoon ride, the Buckeroo group leader, a young woman named Wendy, pulled me aside and asked how long Maggie had been riding, and seemed genuinely surprised when I replied, "Never, if you don't count this afternoon." Because we were late arrivals, we'd missed the ranch's rigorous introduction program, which every guest, regardless of horse skills, must go through.

Colorado Trails' ninety-eight horses are widely considered to be some of the most expertly trained animals in the West, and egos must be parked at the gate in order to ride them. George, the head wrangler, had given me my own indoctrination on a mustard-colored mount called Poncho. But, once again, my rudimentary skills were nowhere close to my daughter's apparent aptitude for horses. She was cantering fearlessly by the end of the first day, and all I could do was marvel. She asked me to buy her a real cowboy hat, black preferred, and that's why I went to town.

A fellow in the shop said the local trout were taking some small dry flies like midges and duns but because of the drought if I really wanted to catch trout I should use wet nymphs with a sinking line. I thanked him, bought several beautiful elk-hair midges, and skipped giving him my speech about dry flies and free-will salvation.

Besides, the theology debate was waiting for me out on the street twenty minutes later when I returned to Old Blue with the flies, *two* cowboy hats—one black, one white—and one brand-new pair of men's size 11 Tony Lama cowboy boots. A curious little man with a tense red face and rawly barbered white hair peeking from under a sweat-stained straw hat was standing beside my truck, more or less glaring at Old Blue.

"That your dog?" he demanded as I unlocked the truck and dumped my shopping bonanza in the back. The windows were down and Amos had been peacefully dozing on the rear seat. I said yes and he snapped, "Here. You better read this." He handed me a printed piece of paper.

I thought he might be an angry pet activist, stalking the streets of Durango to ferret out dog abusers. I was about to explain to him that the windows were wide open and Amos was perfectly fine—about to do a nice restful stretch, as a matter of fact, at an attractive, fully air-conditioned kennel on the edge of town—when I read his leaflet.

The paper warned me that I wasn't saved. I nodded and looked up at his truck, which was parked beside mine. It was a weather-beaten camper van with Texas tags and a large hand-painted sign of doom on the side. How could I have missed it? An orbiting satellite couldn't have missed it. The lettering was the bloodred of a martyr wanna-be. *Wicked baby burning thugs and sinners please listen! 86 dead in Waco and suicide not likely. We don't want a wicked sex perverted color blind drug addicted baby burning society! I am not color blind, spiritually dead, spiritually blind, not a queer loving Satan worshipping sinner! Start reading the Bible and awake ye hipocrites, I speak to you of your shame. Your wickedness perverts drugs, abortion, Waco, AIDS, Ruby Ridge, Dr. Death's euthanasia, burning babies in the USA! Don't blame me. I voted for Bush. Time is short Eternity is long. Hell is horrible. This is America's holocaust.*

And this was just for starters. There was more but I forgot to take it down.

"Let me ask you, stranger. Are you a born-again?"

I smiled at my inquisitor, whom I'll wildly guess appeared a wee bit stranger to the citizens of Durango than I did. Would it ease his worry to know I was a practicing Episcopalian who loved transcendental poets and had slightly Buddhist sympathies?

"As a matter of fact, I am. A born-again fly fisherman."

Emerson said we wear the gods we believe in on our faces. I could tell from his face that his god was most displeased with my response and he thought I was a total smart-ass, perhaps even mocking him. On the contrary, I was really telling him the gospel truth. Thanks to a little girl in love with a horse named Luke, I'd been reminded how much I loved fly-fishing—learned, too, perhaps for the first time or at least since my own childhood, how turning my cares loose in a beautiful winding river could pull my thoughts a lot closer to God than being grilled by some angry pulpiteer of the pavement.

"You can joke if you like. But your government is pure evil and salvation's no joking matter."

Neither is fishing, I said, and reminded him that Jesus lived in a difficult time and chose fishermen for his closest field associates. Man's gotta have faith to fish, I countered. You cast your net wide and haul it in, never knowing what kind of crazy fish you'll get. We could have gone on like this for a while, I suppose—him fuming righteously, me gently baiting him, one of the oldest games on earth—but time really was short and a dinner ride was about to happen out at Colorado Trails and I had a date with a little girl who dearly wanted a black hat. I put on my own white cowboy hat—proof I was a Good Guy after all—apologized for having to run, thanked him sincerely for his interest in my soul, wished him luck, and said good-bye. I backed Old Blue out into Main Street and waved and he stood there glaring at me as if I'd just plastered a Clinton-Gore '96 bumper sticker on his holy war wagon.

I felt sorry for him, he felt sorry for me. Perhaps we were both poor salesmen for our faiths. Or maybe one man's Hell is simply another man's Heaven. In any case, I couldn't wait to see Saint Cecil's cathedral of trout on the river San Juan.

I rose and dressed before dawn, then sat with my gear on the darkened porch of our A-frame cabin waiting for my ride. The cabin was called Mountain View and perched dramatically on the edge of a high ridge in a forest of silver spruce, overlooking the narrow valley. The air was chilly and to take my mind off that fact I sat there thinking about my conversation a few hours before with Silent Sam. I'd called him from the pay phone at the ranch's trading post after supper, while the kids were off on a hayride.

I learned he had checked out of the hospital and gone home and I found him there on my next call. He'd been out changing the filter on his swimming pool's self-cleaning system and said something about all the jobs he'd been able to get done around the house. Maybe going nuts had a silver lining; at least his pool was now cleaner. Maybe he'd give up marine law and become a pool man.

"How's the fish safari?" he asked. "I'm living vicariously through your trip, by the way."

I said it was good but about to get a whole lot better because I was waiting for some fellas to drive down to the San Juan River in New Mexico. The trout there, I said, were something to write home about. He asked how Maggie liked being out West. I said she liked it fine but that fly-fishing had suddenly taken a backseat to a big brown-eyed lug named Luke. Luke was twelve, I said. All legs and whiskers.

"I sure hope Luke is a horse. My daughter went out with a kid just like that. I'm beginning to think he caused this whole thing, in fact."

I asked what he meant.

"She started seeing this kid from the day school. Your basic metalhead who lives out at the mall. We know his parents. Watching television is about the height of this kid's life ambition. Maureen tells me it's just a phase all girls go through, seeking out the biggest losers. Anyway, one after-noon after golf one of the guys I was playing with turns and asks me if I minded my daughter's tattoo. His daughter is thinking of getting one and he can't decide whether to say yes or put her little fanny in a nunnery. I told him he must have the wrong kid, my daughter didn't have a tattoo be-cause she's not that kind of kid. If she had a tattoo, by God, I'd know it. He just gave me this sick little smile, like he let something big out of the bag."

"I assume she had a tattoo."

"Yeah. A nice little swastika with ivy on it. She claimed it was some kind of Celtic fertility symbol. It was on her ass. I tried to imagine what my father would have said and done. That's when I lost it. I realized I had no control of anything. It was all a joke. Things sort of steamrolled after that."

I asked how he was feeling now.

"Better. Still up and down. I'm serious about becoming a pool man. The work suits me. It still involves water." He chuckled and explained he was still talking to the head-shrinker—his word, not mine—and was finding it "sort of interesting" to roam around in his own head. God, there was so much in there . . . "junk" you could stumble over, feelings you never knew you had, fears and anger that just sat around gathering dust. He was surprised how good it made him feel to talk to somebody who understood what he was saying. He suggested I give it a try sometime, too; I didn't bother telling him I had spent months talking to a family sociologist after my father's death and when my marriage began to crumble. I hadn't told Sam about the demise of my marriage. Considering all the stuff he was trying to sort through, he probably didn't need or wish to hear my problems. Maybe a bit more accurately, I didn't want to tell him yet. Telling the Mormon couple had been hard enough; at least I'd never see them again.

"I've been reading," Sam said, "how many people go through this sort of thing. You wouldn't believe it." He ticked off a list of famous names—presidents, movie stars, captains of industry, artists. "This only seems to happen to bright people." The idea seemed to comfort him. "By the way, I read some of those books you suggested. I liked the essays but I have to say I hated the poetry. Knew I would. Those guys sound *really* depressed."

I admitted poetry wasn't everybody's cup of tea and decided not to ask how his search for God was going, though I did let it slip that I'd met a man on the street in Durango who said The End was near. "See?" I joked. "You can always find somebody who feels worse than you."

"Maybe his daughter has a tattoo on her ass," Sam said, sounding a bit like his old self. I didn't know whether that was a good sign or a worrisome one. "You don't believe that garbage, do you?" he asked.

"What?"

"About the end being here." He laughed nervously. "The jig being up."

I considered for a moment and said I thought the end was always near at hand for somebody. Just ask somebody in a cancer ward or a homeless shelter or a parent whose child has died. I didn't say it to Sam but the night my marriage came apart felt a little like Armageddon, or at least the end of civilization as we knew it. I did admit to him that I wasn't entirely sure what the Scriptures had in mind when they said it would all end in tribulation and fire, followed by the Second Coming. Was it something we should regard as advice on personal growth or was it a dire warning for the species? The jury was still out but if it helped, I said, one of my favorite poets, Edwin Robinson, a man who hailed from just up the road from me in Maine and who was Teddy Roosevelt's personal poet laureate, wrote, *We've each a darkening hill to climb; / and this is why from time to time / In Tilbury Town, we look beyond / Horizons for the man Flammonde.* Some scholars thought Flammonde was Jesus. Did it really matter? The human race probably needed all the help it could get to save itself—saviors without and within. Then I remembered I was speaking to a man who was depressed enough without having more poetry thrown at him.

I laughed and said: "It may be the end but I try and convince myself it's really just a beginning in disguise."

"You sound like your old man."

I hadn't considered that possibility. I'd forgotten he'd known Opti the Mystic. Perhaps, good or bad, we become our fathers after all. I thanked him.

"If you get bored," he said, "call again."

A car horn tooted softly in the darkness. My new fishing buddies were ready to roll. I went back in the cabin and kissed Maggie, who woke briefly enough to ask where I was going. I reminded her I was going fishing on the San Juan with several other papas and suggested she sleep for a while until the dining hall opened at seven. I said I hoped she had a nice day with Luke and she nodded sleepily, then dropped her head to the pillow again.

It was just over two hours to the Navajo Dam. The sun crept up slowly through low desert hills and stone canyons, painting the scrubland lavender and then pink and then gold. Ted, who was driving, was a civil engineer from St. Louis, a quiet older man who'd been fly-fishing for thirty years. He didn't have much gear but I got the impression he knew a great deal about fly-fishing. Chris was a New York adman. He had beautiful clothes and handsome equipment and no shortage of opinions about the morning news. He was certain Muslim fundamentalists had brought down the TWA jet with a Stinger missile and knew that was possible because he knew Long Island Sound like the back of his hand—there were plenty of places to launch a rocket from. Clinton was going to "smoke Bob Dole's ass" in the general election and that would probably kill the bull market once and for all. He thought they ought to publicly hang the guy or guys who blew up the building in Oklahoma City. "Christ, the news never gets better. We've become Tabloid Nation. What would the media do if they didn't have O. J. or some murdered cheerleader to exploit to pieces? Cronkite was lucky to get out when he did," he said as if he'd personally known the anchorman, sipping his coffee, glancing at me as if it were all my fault.

As someone who'd once made a living writing the very kinds of news stories he was so worked up about, perhaps I did share some of the blame for Tabloid Nation. News reporting, having evolved from the humble village pump gossip of the Middle Ages, is by nature selectively invasive, and he was right that standards of modern reporting had woefully declined since Walter Cronkite had abandoned his anchor chair while airing his concern that the news was in the

hands of ratings-hungry accountants and was rapidly becoming a dangerous hybrid he called *infotainment.*

On the other hand, we were a nation that worshipped
NBA basketball players and MTV stars who beat their girl-
friends. So what did Chris really expect? I was tempted to
say these things to him, perhaps mix it up a bit in defense of
my journalism colleagues, but then I remembered I was out
of the reporting business, and weary of the news myself,
and decided instead to be a proper guest and keep my
mouth shut and think about trout.

Michael ran a candy store in New Jersey. He asked why
I'd only brought one rod, a light one at that, my old friend
Pat's four-weight Scott. Michael had three rods and four
reels, a full neoprene wading ensemble, a vest jammed with
various reels and types of line, and a small arsenal of wet
nymphs and sinkers. For all I knew he had a loran fish
finder and a couple depth charges in his bulging pockets.
He was a new and enthusiastic fly angler, full of all sorts of
arcane fly lingo I either had forgotten or never knew. I
explained that I had a second reel in my vest and a nice
batch of dry flies to try but that my overall strategy was to
keep it simple because Saint Cecil would have wanted it
that way.

"Who's Saint Cecil?"

"Patron saint of worriers."

It was almost ten by the time we reached the river, which
was wide at the base of the dam and narrowed as it wound
down the limestone canyon through a series of scrub-
crowned islands. A dozen trucks and cars were already
parked in the gravel lot off the state road and I counted no
fewer than a dozen fly fishermen already in the water,
fanned out across the valley.

"Looks like a fishing convention," Michael grumbled, already wiggling into his chest waders. He wished me luck
with my dry flies and I wished him luck with his sinkers. I
draped my waders over my arm and set off down a steep,

narrow trail toward the valley floor, wishing Amos and my favorite fishergirl were with me.

I wandered along through the tall willows for a while and finally came to the river's edge, where two men were standing waist-deep in the currents, thirty or so yards apart, studiously making casts. They both glanced over and gave me looks that said *Do Not Enter*, so I moved on downstream, walking perhaps half a mile farther, passing several more anglers until I saw no one else and found a small shrub-covered island where the river split and there was what amounted to a large protected pool with three or four entry channels overhung by brush. It looked like a trout cathedral to me so I set up shop. I placed my bag lunch on a nice large rock and then put on my waders. I checked my gear, released the drag on my reel, started stripping line, and stepped into the river. The water was beautiful and cold and the cobblestone rocks underfoot were silky with algae. Taking a confident step, I suddenly slipped and fell on my bottom, cold water flooding into my waders. For a moment I sort of floated and flailed my arms, cursing myself for not buying waders with felt bottoms instead of the cheaper rubber ones. This was the way fly fishermen often drowned, of course, dragged down by their own stupidity and water-filled britches. I swore softly and hauled myself out of the river, flopping down on the large rock to peel off my waders and start the whole process again.

This time I took more care stepping into the river, feeling the rocks with my feet as I went. I waded across to the island and unhooked my fly and once more stripped several yards of line into the water running past my waist. I made a few overhead casts, lengthening the cast with each pass of the fly overhead, making a long lazy S and finally sending my fly shooting to a promising spot beneath some willows. My Hairwing Caddis snagged on an overhanging branch. I reeled in the excess line and tugged it gently, unable to make the fly shake free. I sighed with disgust and gave the fly a firmer yank. It popped free and flew toward me, nearly hooking my cheek. A moment later, I realized I'd hopelessly tangled my line in a mess of casting knots.

I might have been embarrassed if I hadn't been so damned annoyed with myself. Haste had made waste. Around me, middle-aged pilgrims were dispatching flawless casts into one of America's most sacred trout streams, no doubt hauling in hogs they would remember on their death-beds. And I couldn't even manage to get my first cast in the water without knocking myself out of the game. I slogged out of the water again, stumbling and nearly pitching under a second time, and sat down on the rock to try and sort out the nightmare I'd created.

I worked on the line for over an hour, snipping, twisting, retying tippet that proved to be a Gordian knot of hopeless-ness. I finally gave up and cut off the whole mess and took out my other reel and lengthened the tippet on it and tied on one of the new elk-hair midges. The air was still cool and my fingers were stiff from my premature dip; they refused to make a proper Duncan knot. Where was Maggie when I needed her? I finally resorted to a simple granny knot and hoped that would suffice. During this time, the wind picked up, turning the surface silver with wind wrinkles, making my tiny fly even more difficult to see.

I fished the pool for at least an hour, working my way along the edges, drifting my fly for a rise that never oc-curred, poised for a strike that never came. I presented that pretty little midge decently over several promising sub-merged logs, holding spots where a big rainbow surely lay pondering the meaning of life. But no trout rose to my bait. I took to imagining I was fishing with Saint Cecil and tried to think what he would advise me to do—keep patiently working the same piece of water, no doubt, *work* being the prelude to salvation. Most anglers would have given up on the spot and moved on to find something more promising but I felt certain Cecil would have stayed put. Perhaps he'd even fished this very spot. Thinking of Cecil made me think of Haig-Brown and I remembered an essay in which he says few fishermen can recall a day when everything they did went right. Everything on a river has its purpose. A smart fisherman remembers the good things, learns from the bad.

I felt hungry and went and sat on my rock to eat my lunch. I took off my waders and dangled my feet off the rock. The sun was almost at its highest point now; I'd been fishing for three hours and the canyon floor and the surface of my rock had grown intensely warm. Much of the land-scape around the river looked dry and unforgiving, a virtual mountain desert, yet the vegetation around the river was green and lush—like one of those Renaissance paintings of the Garden of Eden. I took a bite of the sandwich. It was delicious. The water felt wonderful sliding silkily between my bare toes. I saw a large bird flying over the river but it was too distant to identify. I would remember these things.

I would also remember what Sondra, the woman who ran the ranch's trading post and made the sandwiches, had told me the evening before after my conversation with Silent Sam. I'd ordered one of her famous vanilla malts and we began chatting about how she enjoyed seeing the same fami-lies come back to the ranch year after year, watching the children grow older and more independent, wiser about horses and life. Ranch life was good for that, keeping fami-lies close and teaching kids good values. "I reckon that's what makes this past year or so so difficult for me," she confided, suddenly turning solemn. "It's really shaken my faith." I'd asked her what had shaken her faith.

"Oklahoma City," she said.

Slowly wiping the counter with her sponge, she explained that she had a close friend who knew someone who had died in the bomb blast that brought down the Alfred P. Murrah Building in Oklahoma City, killing 168 people, in-cluding 19 children. She knew another man from her church whose wife had been standing in the building when an entire wall just *disappeared*. She'd barely survived but couldn't seem to put her life back together. Nobody touched by the tragedy could. The families torn asunder, the innocent blood spilt, the press swarming like vultures, the overwhelming grief just wouldn't go away. "People can't seem to accept that something that terrible could happen out here. If it didn't make me so heartsick I reckon I would spit, it makes me so mad."

I hadn't known what to say to her so I simply drank my malt and listened while she quietly articulated her personal struggle to overcome the tragedy, vacillating between a desire for vengeance and her knowledge that she needed to forgive those who'd planted the bomb. A few minutes later, several children from the hayride burst through the door, demanding milk shakes for nightcaps. My daughter was among them, beaming and smacking the dust off her new black hat. Oklahoma City was the first news event she'd ever shown a continuing interest in, perhaps because prior to the tragedy she was simply too young to comprehend the meaning of such things, perhaps because the tragedy involved the incomprehensible murder of children and now unfortunately she was old enough to grasp that.

Now, as I ate my sandwich and let my feet float in the San Juan, I pictured Maggie in her dusty black hat, climbing a trail somewhere on Luke. Tomorrow was the weekly kids' rodeo. She was thrilled about competing in it, perhaps winning a ribbon to take home and show Jack. These nice thoughts were interrupted by the sound of someone shouting, giving out a real rebel yell. A trophy had been landed somewhere up the lazy river. The legend had given up a trout.

It was then I realized I was also looking at a trout, one of the biggest I'd ever seen, in fact, hovering almost motionless in the slow currents, mere inches from the toes of my right foot. I swallowed my bite of sandwich and sat immobile, staring at the fish. I'd heard the trout in this part of the San

Juan were so big and brassy they'd been known to actually bump your leg, secure in the knowledge that if you caught them, by law you'd have to toss them back. They had a kind of guaranteed immortality. Still, I couldn't believe such a monster would swim right up and almost buss my pinkies.

I was tempted to slowly reach for my fly rod and try and drop an enticing fly in the water without scaring off the prey. Instead, I just sat there watching him, perhaps slightly mesmerized by his presence. He permitted me a good long look at him—a brown trout with flecks of gold who seemed to know exactly what he was doing and displayed no trace of concern. The water was almost up to my knees and I calculated he was maybe two feet below the surface and over two feet in length. The trout is an efficient eater who holds his wiggling prey with a series of small teeth until he can swallow the victim whole. Perhaps he was about to try and swallow my little toe. The thought gave me a small thrill. Could he do it? Would it hurt? A moment later, the big trout gave my baby toe the faintest investigative nip, apparently found it to be poor-quality fish food, and nonchalantly swam away.

I sprang out of the water and hauled on my waders, anxious to give chase. A few moments later, I was waist-deep in the stream again, angling off to where I thought my trophy had gone. I floated my fly all over the pool for the next hour but once again no trout rose to take the bait. I worked my way back toward one of the channels and fished some promising riffles that produced nothing to write home about. I went through my repertoire of fancy new dry flies and then sat down on the bank to try and decide if I should give up the pool and move on.

There was movement in the willows near the rock where I'd eaten my lunch; probably, I figured, another fly angler searching for the mother of all trout holes. Instead, the willows parted and a large doe warily stepped through, scenting the air. I sat dead still but couldn't believe she didn't see or smell me. After a few seconds, she dropped her head and began to drink from the river.

Seeing a deer in the wild always gives me pleasure. No animal moves as gracefully through the forest or seems more at home. No creature lives more by its wits and senses — God's cattle, a neighbor lady friend of mine calls them. She's a native Mainer who grew up hunting deer each autumn until she realized she really liked seeing them alive more than killing them. So far as I know she's never been in a church in her life, yet she thinks of them as God's cattle, and I know exactly what she means. Perhaps I moved or the wind carried my scent. The doe raised her head and stared at me. Her ears lifted delicately and she turned and hopped almost without a sound back into the brush.

Michael appeared around dusk. He'd followed the river past me and was looping back to join the others; we'd agreed to meet at the car come sunset. He was surprised to learn I'd been working the same pool the entire day. He was even more surprised when I said I hadn't landed any trout but had seen some beauties. The pool at that moment seemed to be full of them, cruising along indifferently like the big "tame" trout you find in L. L. Bean's indoor trout pond. The wind had died and there were rises all over the surface of the pool. Michael saw this, too, and must have thought only a fool couldn't catch a trout here.

"How'd you do?" I asked conversationally — wanting him to keep his greedy behind on the bank and out of my hole.

"Awesome. Stopped counting at eleven. Want to try one of my sinkers?"

"No thanks. I'll give this a last shot."

I made another long cast, dropping a large homemade woolybugger on the water. It was the last unused fly in my vest, the gaudy Liberace number Maggie had tied at Bean. It actually plopped on the water and a moment later a large trout flashed up and took it to the bottom. My rod doubled over and I began to strip line and then realized I'd stripped too much because, minus the proper tension, the fish could easily spit the debarbed hook. I pinched the line with my left hand and began reeling in, finally achieving the proper tension and getting the fish under control. Michael was anxious to help. "Get your net ready," he called over. "Keep your line firm." I worked the trout to within a few yards and reached a hand back to unhook my net and realized it was floating in the water behind me. To complicate matters, I'd moved too far into the river and was losing footing in the deeper water. For a moment I comically scrambled backward, slithering on the slippery rocks, fighting to avoid going under and trying to hold the rod aloft. I could see Michael smiling. I backpedaled into shallower water and continued reeling in the fish and was finally able to work him to the edge of my net. I got him into the net and lifted triumphantly.

The trout flipped out of my net and splashed into the river.

As we walked back to meet the others, Michael said: "That was a really nice fish. I wish you could have landed him. I missed a couple big ones like that today, too."

It was decent of him to say. But I didn't feel as bad as he probably thought. True, it was possibly the biggest trout I'd ever hooked, and I would have loved to hold him in my hands and try to guess his weight, but I'd fought him to the net and managed a good inspection of him before his strength outmatched my skill and he returned himself to the river. You learn something every time out, Haig-Brown says—sometimes more on days when the fish don't bite. You learn to see the river for its beauty, to absorb pleasure from the unexpected sight of a doe leaning to drink or a trout drifting up to smooch your toe. Next time I would come to this shrine of trout more prepared, or at least bearing fewer expectations that probably couldn't be met. This was the lesson I seemed destined to have to repeatedly learn in every aspect of my life.

The others had done well for themselves. On the drive home, they talked giddily about their day's adventures, reciting tales of straining gut that miraculously held and big ones that got away. They sounded like weekend footballers who'd been invited to play in the Super Bowl and caught the winning touchdown pass. I sat there idly wondering if I was the only angler in the San Juan who hadn't landed a trout that day.

Chris asked me if I was up for another crack at the river in the morning and I said I would love nothing better. Then I remembered that the kids' rodeo was in the morning and I'd promised Maggie I would take an afternoon ride up the mountain to see something she wanted me to see. It was called the Cathedral of Aspens. I thanked Chris and said I would have to catch the San Juan another time.

Before breakfast the next morning, I slipped down to Durango and parked in the Kmart parking lot and waded into the Animas River directly behind the store and landed three brown trout and a nice-sized rainbow in less than an hour — a small redemption for yesterday's performance. George, the ranch's head wrangler, had told me it was the area's best-kept secret, home to some of the hottest trout action in the valley and right smack in the middle of town, ten minutes from the ranch. The local guides kept this info to themselves, he said, safely tucked under their hats.

After breakfast, putting on my own new cowboy hat and boots, I sat on the corral bleachers and watched Maggie and Luke perform in the kids' rodeo; they claimed a blue ribbon in the egg trot and tied for second in the apple bob race. As she went off for an afternoon swim with her riding group, Maggie was glowing like the golden girl of the West and visibly pleased that I would be spending the afternoon with Wendy, her favorite counselor, riding up to the aspens. "Be sure and keep your hands low and relaxed on the saddle horn," she helpfully coached before agreeing to let me go off on my own. "Let your horse do the work, Dad. All right? Also, keep the reins loose and never use your heels."

"Anything else?"

"Well . . ." She hesitated, then smiled shyly. "You could, like, ask Wendy or something if she, like, you know, really thinks I'm a good rider or something."

I winked and promised I would get it straight from the horse instructor's mouth.

Due to the drought, the trail up to the Cathedral of Aspens was very dusty. But the slow ascent on Poncho suited me just fine and a surprisingly intimate chat evolved with the three women on the ride. Sharon was a social worker from Seattle, a divorcée with two teenage sons, one of whom was dyslexic. Diane was from somewhere back East, a lapsed Catholic who'd discovered she was half Hopi Indian and had been on a three-week pilgrimage to find her roots. She'd already been to Arizona and looked up a distant cousin who introduced her to an elderly tribal medicine man who spent several days speaking to her about the "old ways" of her relatives. Her children were grown and thought she was flaking out and her husband repeatedly made jokes about her "going native" on him. But her little "vision quest," she said, had been the closest thing she ever expected to have in the way of a true religious experience. She understood so much more about herself and the world.

Sharon told a bit of her story next. Her father had been one of the founders of the CIA. "Remember those photos of Ike boarding an airplane to South America, waving to groups of schoolchildren? Well, I was one of those children. My father was never around, which I guess was good. He was so angry—you could feel his anger. He drank a lot, too." She smiled. "I must have loved him, though, because I grew up and married a man just like him." Being a single parent was tough and trying to figure out how to raise boys these days, she said, was even tougher. "There's so many

conflicting images of what men are or are supposed to be.
Our schools say one thing, our popular culture another. We
want boys to be strong but not macho, sensitive but not
wimps. The old rules are dead but the new rules haven't
been established. I see so many boys in the schools who
seem to be just lost. No wonder they gravitate to gangs."
Recently, she added, she'd begun seeing a nice man who
treated her and her sons very well. He had strength of character and an appealing openness but it was too early to tell
if something good was evolving. In any case, she'd brought
her sons to Colorado to have some time together before they
decided they were too old to travel with their mother.

Someone asked Wendy about her family. I could see why
Maggie had taken a shine to her. Wendy was a lovely
honey-haired girl of eighteen, poised beyond her years—
Maggie in another ten years, I thought hopefully. Her story
was maybe the most surprising of all.

"My father and mother divorced when I was very
young," she began. "I had five older brothers. My mother
was a waitress who gambled. I grew up learning to spit and
cuss pretty good." At thirteen, she'd found a job at a ranch
and a woman who knew of her desperate situation took her
in. "They were a large Mormon family. This woman took in
a wild, swearing girl with painted toenails and called me her
princess." Ranch work and this fairy godmother had saved
her, she felt certain, from a deeply unhappy life. Instead,
she was about to begin studying drama at a community
college and had a boyfriend doing missionary work for the
Church of Latter-day Saints in Central America. Her dream
was to own a ranch for troubled teens someday, to teach
them to sing and dance and ride.

"When I saw how confidently Maggie rides," she told me,
"I totally thought of myself. She's smart, she listens, but she
definitely wants to do it herself. That was me to a tee." I was
pleased to hear this character assessment and knew a little
girl who would be even more pleased to hear it.

A little bit later, Wendy gently reined her horse to a halt. "Well," she said, "we're here."

We were high up, probably close to seven thousand feet above sea level, sitting on our horses in a dense outcropping of quaking aspen trees that rose another hundred or so feet above us. The trees looked old, scarred by time. Sunlight filtered through the canopy and you could see why someone might think the trees recalled stained-glass windows. "There's a belief that these trees are the oldest living things on earth," Wendy explained, making me think of what Tom Hruska had said about Snake River cutthroats. "Their roots go extremely deep and intertwine. Most of the growth, they say, is beneath the surface."

Diane smiled. "That's sort of like what the medicine man said about people. Most of what we really are is invisible to the eye. He said the reason human beings have such difficulty in life is because we're all essentially spirits trying to become human. The spirit state is our natural state; the human one a folly. We spend our lives forgetting that." We sat gazing up at the trees for a few minutes and then I realized that the three women were looking at me.

I was the only one in our horseback encounter group who hadn't shared his story, and to tell the truth I still wasn't in any rush to blab my personal problems to a group of Muses on horseback. On the other hand, what better place to bare your soul and get used to the public consequences than a church of trees? I told them Maggie's mother and I had decided to get an amicable divorce and I was a bit worried about the world we would soon return to back East; actually, I admitted, "a bit worried" didn't quite cover it. Our story, I said, wasn't terribly unique. We were two people who'd built a nice life and thought they were in love but turned out to be more in love with the nice life and their progeny than each other. At least that was the best explanation I could come up with.

"I think these things are always a mystery until one day it

just becomes clear why it happened," Sharon said. "The important thing is, you're showing your daughter how much you care about her by taking the time to make this trip. You can't imagine the impact that will have with her and, if she's at all like me, you'll never know how much she looks up to you. I tell you this from personal experience—you'll be the yardstick she measures every man against till the day she dies. You have lots to teach your children."

I thanked her but said it felt like I had more to learn from them.

"One of the problems with marriage these days," Diane said, "is we were all raised to put our children's interests first. For a lot of working couples, especially women, that involves a lot of guilt, and we become so child-centered in our family life we forget about the original point of the marriage: two people making a lifetime commitment."

The wind had suddenly come up; she tightened the leather thong that held her hat on her head. "My husband and I went through an awful time when our girls were about your daughter's age. It really is the most dangerous time of life for a family, I'm convinced. Everyone is rushing here and there and basically you stay in a state of exhaustion. We were probably headed for divorce ourselves but luckily realized the reason our marriage had lost its spark was because we gave everything we had, too much probably, to the children. It may sound selfish but the best thing you can do for your children is make sure the person you married comes first."

It didn't sound selfish, I said. I told her my father had given me the same advice a few months before he died, but that maybe it had come a bit too late to save my marriage, that I hadn't exactly dismissed his advice but that I hadn't given it the consideration it probably deserved, either. His marriage was so different from mine, and his wife so different from mine, that I'd mistakenly decided his advice wasn't particularly relevant. Then again, I admitted, I preferred to learn things the difficult way.

Diane smiled sympathetically and said, "The medicine man said to me that the answer to the riddle of who we are resides in our history, our personal trail into the past—seeing how those who preceded us dealt with the same trials. I hate to sound so corny but I think he was right. To go forward we have to remember where we've been, which includes honestly facing up to our mistakes."

"You're talking about getting rid of guilt and grief," Sharon put in. "Two of the toughest stains on earth to get rid of."

There was a distant rumble of thunder from beyond the mountain. Dry thunderstorms had been in the forecast but the one approaching us didn't feel as if it would be dry. Wendy suggested that we start back and so we turned our mounts and started after her down the trail.

It struck me as odd that Wendy hadn't made any comment on my story—the conflict that would define Maggie's life, to some unknown extent, for the rest of her days. Perhaps Wendy was too young to have an opinion on marriage or was simply too busy calculating whether we could make it back to the ranch before the storm broke. A few minutes later, though, she turned in the saddle and thoughtfully said to me: "I think the important thing is for your children to always know how much you both love them and for neither you nor Maggie's mother to try and use the children against the other. My mother was so angry at my father she tried to use my brother against him, and it really screwed him up for a while."

I smiled at her and thanked her for the advice; she was obviously wise beyond her years. She gave me a nice smile and added, "If you wouldn't be offended, I'd like to say a prayer for you all."

I said I wouldn't be offended in the least to be included in her prayers and that I thought I could speak for Maggie in that regard: We would be pleased to be prayed for. Then I leaned back as Poncho went down a steep slope over wind-fallen aspens and I tugged my cowboy hat down to keep it from blowing away.

The rain drenched us to the bone before we reached the corral. Lightning bolts bleached the evergreens almost white. I ran up the hill to our cabin feeling almost light-headed from the unexpected pleasure of my ride into the mountains with the three Muses and anxious to convey to Maggie Wendy's comments about her riding skills. This was our final night at Colorado Trails and the farewell dinner was about to begin, followed by the weekly staff variety show. I'd laid out Maggie's best dress on her bed for the occasion.

I found her sitting in the darkened cabin watching the storm, still wearing her damp bathing suit, wrapped in a towel and shivering slightly. I flipped on the lights and asked why she hadn't showered yet. I reminded her the farewell dinner started in just a few minutes.

"I don't want to go," she said.

As I peeled off my soaked duds, I paused to look closer and realized she'd been crying. I sat down beside her on her bed and asked what was wrong. It took a few minutes to coax the story out of her. The girl cousins she'd been pals with all week had for some reason turned "mean and bossy" at the pool and informed her they didn't wish to sit with her at the farewell dinner. I asked if perhaps she'd been bossy to them first and she gave me a look of almost pure fury and vigorously shook her head.

"Well," I suggested, water dripping from the end of my nose, "let's talk about it, can we?"

She nodded but didn't want to talk, so I did. I said some-thing about kids being kids and having notoriously short

tempers but also famously short memories and tried to assure her that all fences would be mended by the time we
pushed ourselves to the grub table. If not, well, she could
make a new friend for the variety show or just sit with me in
the Old Fogy section.

"I don't *want* a new friend," she snapped at me.

"There's no reason to bite my head off," I said calmly,
then tried to explain why making new friends was so important.

"Dad," she said, "you just don't get it."

I smiled and kissed her forehead. The smile was intended
to reassure her that everything would sort itself out with
time and a nice hot shower, but she took it to mean I
thought she was making a mountain out of a molehill. Lightning blasted a tree somewhere on our ridge and we both
flinched.

"Guess the drought's over," I said.

"Dad, Jessica said I must be a baby or something because I still have Susie Bear and she said there's no such
thing as the tooth fairy or Santa Claus and how would *you*
like it if she said that to you because she said only babies
believed in Santa and the tooth fairy and even angels aren't
real . . . they're just, like, like, made up or something and
I said, yeah, well, what about Jesus and God I bet you
believe in them and she said no they weren't real either, *Dad*.
How about *that*? How would you feel if somebody said that
to *you*?"

I nodded, suppressing a smile at her impressive run-on
sentence and trying to remember who Jessica was in this
little drama. I thought a moment and said there was always
somebody around who wanted to challenge what you believed in and no shortage of rude people in the world with
whom you would sometimes have to share a swimming pool.
That was part of growing up, I told her. You had to learn
to ignore the jerks, because life was full of them. You had to
learn to defend your beliefs.

"But, Dad, I *can't.*"

I sighed. "Oh, Maggie. When *are* you going to grow up?"

I regretted uttering this bromide of parenthood the instant it came out of my mouth. The truth was, I didn't want her to grow up and it wasn't really what I meant to say.

"Oh, *Daddy.*"

She burst out crying and blew straight out the cabin's screen door into the storm. I kicked off my wet jeans and gave chase and was fifty yards from the cabin when I finally caught up to her. I caught her arm and spun her around. She was sobbing almost inconsolably. The rain was hammering down. I kneeled and put my arms around her and pulled her close but she tried to shove me away. I squeezed tighter.

"Maggie," I said firmly in her ear, "please stop. This is . . . silly."

Once again, another poor choice of words for a man who makes his living finding the right words. Who was calling whom silly: I was the one kneeling in the middle of the ranch's main road in my boxer shorts and a soaked polo shirt, trying to repair the unintentional damage I'd done.

"No it's not," she said with a small hiccup. "You broke your promise."

"*What* promise, darling?" My mind groped for some Gatorade or tourist trinket I'd neglected to buy, some tourist haunt we'd failed to see.

Out of the corner of my eye, as she collapsed on my shoulder and sobbed anew, I saw an entire family assembled at the front door and screened windows of their cabin and realized that one of them was the strange potato-shaped man I'd seen wandering around the ranch all week with a Sony video camera plugged to his eyeball. If he's videotaping this, I thought, I'll throw that camera off a cliff and maybe him with it.

I picked up my daughter and began walking slowly with

her in my arms back to our cabin. "Maggie," I said quietly. "What promise did I break? I just can't seem to remember."

She hiccuped into my chest, refusing to look at me. Her voice was slightly muffled by my wet shirt.

"You swore to me that you and Mommy would never get a divorce. Don't you *remember* that?"

I heard the words but it took a moment for their meaning to sink in. When they did, I was stunned. Stunned by the power of her accusation and stunned by the accuracy of her incredible memory. I did remember this promise, given with tremendous overconfidence one night several years ago when Maggie came home from her day-care center talking not about the adventures of Barney or the latest intrigues from the sandbox but about a pint-sized chum whose parents were divorcing. She'd asked me what divorce meant and I told her with that slightly smug reassuring tone grown-ups employ to dispel the terror of unknown shapes in a darkened room that it was what happened when two married people fell out of love and realized they were better off living apart than together, but it was certainly nothing she or her brother needed to worry about.

Pinkie promise? she'd asked.

Pinkie promise, I'd promised.

And now I'd broken that promise. That wasn't my interpretation, of course, but it was hers and that was all that really mattered at this moment. A pinkie promise was the ultimate promise and I'd broken one, pure and simple. That's what this was really about and this was clearly what had been churning around in her head and eating her insides up for weeks as she put on such a brave face to the world and to me. The questions about the ring, the questions in the bar . . . they all added up now. Foolish, stupid, unseeing me. We were surrounded by happy, two-parent family units on vacation, recounting tales of their day's adventures over cookhouse grub, laughing and squabbling with the easy immunity of people who simply couldn't imagine their well-made lives suddenly falling apart. No wonder having her belief in Santa Claus and the tooth fairy and the existence of angels teased and challenged was such a moral affront, such an earth-shattering thing. They were simply too much, the final straw, and this was her last good defense against the unknown shapes that terrorized her room and her life. She'd finally dug in her heels and made a stand against the chaos.

I was speechless. As I thought all this, tears began to come to my own eyes. I couldn't think what to say and I remember thinking how matters weren't helped much by having this flood of raw emotions come pouring out so publicly amid a rollicking thunderstorm—a backdrop straight from a cheap stage melodrama or some shameless movie director who was stooping to use an unmistakable metaphor from nature.

On the other hand, it could have been snowing and we could have been stark naked for all I really cared about Mr. Potato Head and his family. Their curiosity wasn't my concern. This was my daughter who was crying her eyes and heart out, wondering if her world would ever feel as safe again. And I damn sure had to somehow find the words to help her believe it would.

I hugged her to me as I walked, feeling the rain on my face. She clung to me like ivy on a post.

"Maggie," I said, "here's your milk shake."

This was an hour later. The thunderstorm had blown over and I'd walked up to the trading post to fetch us both chocolate milk shakes while she showered and put on new jeans instead of her dress. Passing the dining hall, I could see that the farewell dinner was almost over. A knot of little girls, including Becca and her cousin Lillian, tumbled out the door and Becca asked me in a chirpy voice if Maggie was coming to sit with the Buckeroos at the variety show. Such sweet faces and short memories. At least I'd been right about that.

"Yep. She'll be right along," I assured her. "Save her a seat in the front row."

Maggie came out to the front porch, where I was sitting on the wet steps waiting for her to finish dressing. She was combing out her hair. The storm had scoured out the awful heat and left a tinge of coolness in the air. There were a few stars reemerging to the south. She sat down beside me and I handed her the chocolate shake.

"Dinner is served."

"Thank you."

I didn't know where to begin, so I began by saying I was sorry I'd told her to grow up. The last thing I really wanted was for her to grow up anytime soon. I wanted her to be my beautiful firstborn baby girl for as long as possible.

"I know."

I knew she knew. Furthermore, I said, she'd been right— I had promised her that her mother and I would never get a divorce. "When I made that promise to you," I said, "I genuinely believed there was nothing that could tear apart our family like this. I think it's safe to say neither your mother nor I envisioned anything like this happening un- til . . . it did. But sometimes things happen we can't ex- plain. Something changes. Worlds come and go. It may take us years to begin to understand it. The one thing that doesn't change, though, is the love your mom and I feel for you and Jack. That's like a star." I pointed to a star glim- mering in the silver spruce trees. "You may not always be able to see it but it's always there shining."

She sipped her shake and said nothing, looking up.

"Yesterday," I kept going, "I went with some of the other fathers down to the San Juan River. As you know, the San Juan is one of the greatest trout rivers in the world. Fly anglers come from everywhere to experience catching a fish there. I was so incredibly prepared for a wonderful fishing experience, for catching the trout of my dreams, and guess what?"

"What?"

"I didn't catch one. I saw a bunch of huge trout in the water and I saw a beautiful lady deer. But I didn't catch a trout."

"Were you sad?"

"Not sad exactly. Just disappointed. Especially since the other fathers seemed to catch their weight in big fish."

"Is that why you didn't go back with them today?"

"No. I didn't go back to the San Juan with them today because I hadn't taken a good trail ride and I knew you wanted me to see those aspens and get to know Wendy, who, by the way, says you're one of the most special girls she's ever met. I think she sees herself in you—the way you handle a horse, the way you jump right into things."

"You really liked her?"

"Wonderful girl." *Shame Wendy's not thirty,* I thought, and immediately asked for God's grace.

"We can go fish the San Juan tomorrow if you want," Maggie said.

"Well, we'll see. We've only got eight days to make it home before Jack's birthday."

"I miss Jack."

"I know."

"And Mom, too."

"I know."

"And Amos."

"Well, the good news is you'll see him tomorrow."

"Do you think he misses us?"

"He's probably asleep."

"Can I ask you something?" she said.

"Sure." I said I hoped she would want to ask me stuff until the day she died—or at least the day I died.

"Dad," she said, "that's not funny."

"Sorry. Ask away."

"Do you believe in Santa Claus and the tooth fairy?"

I smiled. "Of course. If you don't believe in Santa Claus or the tooth fairy they can't possibly exist. Belief keeps everything alive, like rain on roses. Some call it faith. I have faith that Santa will come every Christmas Eve, and guess what. The old geezer has never let me down. I have faith in the tooth fairy, too. I mean, she's never failed to leave you money for a tooth, has she?"

"Just once when she didn't come and then left too much."

Once again, her memory was dead on target. The night Maggie lost *two* teeth at once, her mother and I slipped up and thought the other had already played tooth fairy; it took some fast talking to convince Maggie that the TF had been so busy that night she'd run slap out of pocket change and that under Section Three, Rule 2F of the Tooth Fairy Procedures Manual she would have to pay double for her mistake. Unfortunately, we hadn't yet established the standard per-tooth rate and her mom and I, determined to make amends but performing a scene from the Keystone Kops, each made nocturnal trips to her room to make the necessary deposit. Not having the proper change, I slipped a ten under one corner of her pillow, failing to find the four bucks already waiting there. In the morning Maggie wondered why the tooth fairy left her fourteen bucks and we had to explain to Jack, who was evidently short of funds and suddenly pulling on his teeth, that the tooth fairy's math skills were somewhat lacking.

I could just picture Maggie's agnostic Scottish grandmother shaking her head at my predicament, amused that I'd painted myself into a theological corner where I'd more or less equated God with the tooth fairy—nice, polite fairy tales, she would argue, that we eventually outgrow the need to believe in. At the other end of the spectrum, my Southern Baptist grandmother would be spinning in her grave that I'd reduced God to an image of a generous, jolly fat man in a bright red suit. Well, they had their beliefs and I had mine. Maggie would someday have hers, too, independent of what we all thought, and there was probably precious little or nothing the three of us could do about it at this point.

"Well," I said. "That just goes to show. Not even the tooth fairy is perfect."

"I know. Do you, like, believe in Jesus and God?"

She knew I believed in them. She simply wanted or needed me to say I believed in them. I was tempted to try and say something funny but I couldn't think of anything funny to say, so I resorted to the simplest answer.

"Yes."

She nodded, as if thinking it over, and drank her shake.

"Dad," she said a minute or two later.

"What?"

"Do you think we'll be, you know, going home soon?" She looked at me and managed, at last, a smile. She quickly added: "Not that I'm homesick or anything."

I slipped my arm around her. "Well, to tell you the truth, I'm kind of homesick," I admitted. "I've been worrying about my roses. I think they may need watering. Would you mind very much if we went home?"

CHAPTER TWELVE

....

Letter from a Hill

Deer Dad,

I am sory to make you madd last night and miss the fairwell dinner. If you want to go catch trowt in the san won river today its okay with me. Thank you for taking me to the veriety show and to the ranch. It was very funny and I liked it alot. This has been a grate trip and I'm not really home sick.

> *Love, Maggie.*
>
> *P.S. would you please write me a leter sometime too.*
>
> *It would be nice to have one. Love, Maggie.*

The note was lying on my seat in Old Blue, waiting for me when I opened the door to crank up the truck. I'd just tossed the last of our bags into the back and used the atlas to calculate that it was 2,300 miles home, give or take a state.

I drove up to the dining hall, where Maggie had just finished her pancakes and was saying lengthy good-byes to Becca and Lillian. The Sabbath morning air was crisp with a hint of autumn and a man on the radio was reading the Book of John in his native Navajo tongue. Maggie started to walk toward the truck but then saw Wendy standing on the steps of the trading post and suddenly sprinted that way. They embraced and Wendy walked her back to the truck.

"Where's your next stop?" she asked me.

I said we'd discussed driving to Mesa Verde on our way down to Albuquerque but that wildfires had temporarily closed the ancient cave dwellings to the public so we might drive through some of Chaco Canyon instead to see what we could see there. Chaco Canyon is home to the extensive ruins of what's believed to be the largest pre-Columbian city in North America, the greatest architectural achievement of the Anasazi people, a true lost civilization that baffled the European mind when a U.S. Army surveyor stumbled on the site in 1838: thirty-five square miles of circular kivas and abandoned Great Houses, scattered villages and formal planned cities made of sandstone and mortar, joined by extensive roadworks. I'd first heard about Chaco from an astronomer who annually camped on a mesa there to look at stars, and I'd picked up a bit more information about it from a guidebook on the region I'd been noodling.

Part of Chaco's powerful allure was its mystery—archaeologists had mapped, photographed, and excavated the canyon extensively for more than a century but found themselves forever debating such unanswered riddles as why towns that were obviously wealthy and home to people of advanced engineering capabilities contained so few traces of the people themselves, including burial sites. Where had the people gone? The canyon's remoteness was another part of its allure. Even today you reached it over arrow-straight dirt roads built on the remains of an extensive network of ancient highways radiating from the heart of the canyon. It might be biting off more than we cared to chew to try and see the canyon, but maybe not. The annual Indian Festival was going on in Santa Fe. That might be worth a look, too.

"Definitely," Wendy said, when I mentioned all this. "Will you stay in touch?"

"Definitely," Maggie answered for both of us.

A little while later, after following the Animas River out of Colorado into New Mexico, and passing the Aztec Ruins National Monument, I felt a small pang of regret as we crossed over the San Juan River and turned south toward Angel Peak. I spotted a lone fly angler working the river and briefly envied him but remembered the river wasn't going anywhere soon and I could always come back. Amos hung his head out the window to let his jowls flap pleasantly in the wind.

The geology of the San Juan Basin, as it's called, is harsh and generally forbidding to the green-loving eastern eye, a lonely place of spiny scrub brush and yellow limestone rock that abruptly buckles and dips and changes hues as the relentless sun moves over the earth. Out here, I realized as we drove, it's easy to see why these ancient peoples based their secret religious rites on and set the rhythms of their lives to the movement of the sun. Among other things, they built ingenious spiral clocks in the face of rocks that dictated the best times for planting and harvesting, described animal migrations and the rising and falling river. The Southwest, according to one famous Indian song, was a House Made of Dawn.

Pueblo was the name given by the conquering Spanish to the various native peoples who descended from the prehistoric Anasazi and occupied more than eighty villages made of stone and adobe scattered around the Four Corners area of the American Southwest. They were perhaps the first people on earth to raise and cultivate corn, in fact, and 60 percent of the foods eaten all over the world today, it's estimated, was first domesticated by Native Americans.

Corn was the staff of life and the Pueblo people knew where it came from—from the Corn Mothers who climbed up from their secret kivas to the surface of the earth at the dawn of time. At birth, every Indian child was given a corn fetish, a doll made of corn husks designed to remind them that every plant, animal, and human was sacred and came from the earth. Women did most of the planting and harvesting but also directed the agricultural rituals, often praying while irrigating crops, generally managing the direction of village life.

I told Maggie this story as we rumbled down a dirt road, throwing up an impressive fantail of dust behind Old Blue. It had taken us a couple hours to reach Nageezi and turn off onto an unpaved road to the Chaco Canyon reception center. "Mom would have been a nice Corn Mother," she said, thoughtfully regarding the ancient landscape. "She's an excellent boss."

I smiled, unable to disagree. My wife was an excellent boss, a good worker, a nurturing mother, a natural-born organizer of life, a crack vegetable grower, a strong woman who would have survived nicely out here. She liked sun, thrived in warmth. Glancing around, I realized I probably wouldn't have fared nearly as well here. My soul needed evergreens and running waters, changing *weather*, rain and snow, dark soil, growing flowers. Perhaps this explained a lot about what happened to our marriage—right people, wrong weather—or maybe I was just being sun-mused by the House of Dawn.

We reached a paved road and suddenly, almost before we noticed, began to see ancient stone structures. It was nearly lunchtime, and observing the structures with their finely dressed walls and beautifully intact curving stoneworks flooded me with a powerful feeling of this place's remote antiquity. I'd had this feeling only one other time in my life—standing amid a prehistoric stone ring on a windswept ridge in the Orkney Islands. Ruins whisper. At its apogee of

life around the mid-tenth century, the Chaco Canyon area
was home to maybe five thousand people and was believed
to serve as a trading center and commercial storehouse for
the entire Southwest. Turquoise had been the principal coin
of currency.

"Where did the people go?" Maggie asked as we slowly
drove along the park's eight-mile ring road past several impressive kivas and Great Houses.

"God only knows," I said, but explained that according to
my guide, archaeological evidence indicated the towns were
evacuated in an orderly fashion. There was no warfare or
evidence of physical destruction. There were no mass
graves. The best theory was that a decade-long drought
shriveled up the Chaco Canyon River and forced the inhabitants to simply pack up and move, disperse through the
West. You couldn't eat turquoise. Their civilization vanished with them.

At the reception center, a ranger on duty explained there
were rudimentary camping facilities about a mile down the
road, back on the unpaved road that led out the south end
of Chaco. I was tempted to suggest that we camp and look
at the stars from a mesa but it was still the heat of the day
and the ranger said Santa Fe was only a few more hours
away, steady driving. We decided to push on and try to
catch a bit of the Indian Festival ending there. Seeing
Chaco had eaten up nearly three hours but I was glad we'd
seen this haunting place and Maggie seemed to agree,
though she was already busy writing a postcard to her
buddy Aileen.

We stopped in White Horse for gas and cold drinks.
Amos got out and stretched, yawned, and stiffly approached
a man gassing up his truck. The man had buckets of bright
blue paint in his truck, the blue of a blind man's eye. He
scratched Amos's head and asked where we were headed. I
said Santa Fe and asked what he was painting. Whatever it
was, it was sure going to be blue.

"My house. I bought way too much paint, though. Don't have a clue what to do with it. Shame to dump it out."

"If this was Maine," I suggested helpfully, "you could just slap a coat on your truck, too."

The man smiled. His face was brown as a saddle and deeply creased by the sun. The face of an aging Aztec prince or a Tuscan farmer.

"They do that here, too," he said with a grin.

We pulled out and Maggie, tugging the plastic off a fresh Wild Blue Raspberry Gatorade, said: "Dad, let me ask you something. What did you mean by 'God only knows'?"

I glanced at her, a little confused. I couldn't remember when I'd said that.

"You said that God only knows where those Indian people went."

"Oh."

I explained that it was simply an expression, meaning that perhaps only God was capable of knowing what happened to the Anasazi people, why they vanished and where they went.

"Do you think God sees everything?"

"I had a Sunday school teacher who told me Jesus did. She said that's why you had to watch everything you did. Jesus would tell God and then you'd be in hot water. She said Jesus knew your thoughts before you did, good and bad, and would show you the list someday. She made Jesus sound like a snitch and God a bit like Miss Wettington. I used to lie in bed composing secret lists of things Jesus couldn't possibly know."

She smiled. "Like what?"

"How many people in the world were yawning or farting right this instant. How many blades of grass were in our front yard. How much it would hurt if Randy Farmer beat me up. That sort of thing."

"Is that true?"

"About Randy Farmer? Absolutely. He was this tough

mill kid who terrorized every little kid in the neighborhood until I decided to go ahead and let him kill me and get it over with. One day he picked on us and I surprised myself by giving him a bloody nose. He left me alone after that. I kind of felt sorry for him. He was never quite the same. A lucky punch ruined his life—at least that portion of it. My guess is he's somewhere this very instant politely asking a customer if they prefer plastic or paper bags."

"No. I mean about Jesus and God seeing everything you do?"

"I don't know. But you see everything you do and I think God is in you."

Touché, Dad, I thought; brilliant theological segue. Then my eagle-eyed daughter pointed out I'd just missed the turn to Santa Fe. I might see the Big Picture but I often failed to see what was right in front of me, including road signs.

We parked Old Blue between a dust-covered Cadillac and a swank green Land Rover in a lot near Santa Fe's Plaza District and Palace of Governors, where hundreds of Indian vendors were selling their crafts under tents with fluttering white canopies. A thunderstorm had just swept through and the crowds appeared to be thinning a bit. The festival was about over and some of the vendors were packing up their wares. We paused to look at turquoise jewelry and at Hopi kachina dolls, which I thought were a steal at $7.50 apiece until I learned they were really $750, at which point we moved on to an early supper of blue corn burritos and sat down to eat them. Amos was not overjoyed to be back on the leash. Across the park, an overweight male Indian comic wearing a woman's dress was explaining how you could tell the difference between a reservation dog and a Bureau of Indian Affairs dog. The reservation dog chased every junk car that came along and I couldn't hear what he said the BIA dog did, but the crowd laughed and Amos looked slightly amused as well.

"Where do you think those Indian people went?" Maggie

asked. Obviously the mystery of Chaco was still weighing on her mind.

I chewed my gourmet mesquite-smoked bean burrito, which was delicious, or maybe I was just reluctant to have to eat my own humble cooking again, and watched a beautifully dressed white couple with packages come strolling out of a pricey jewelry boutique called the Turquoise Trail. They paused and looked around as if trying to decide what to go buy next.

"I don't know," I reflected, "but by the looks of this place they came to Old Santa Fe. Much better foot traffic."

"Why didn't God want to help them? Like tell them what to do or something?"

"Maybe he did. Maybe he sent the drought to tell them it was time to move on. Everything has a cycle, a time to live, a time to die. A time to open a jewelry store elsewhere. My personal view is that's why God made parents, for precisely this reason. It's the parents' job to protect their children and pass along stuff they've learned about life. Good stuff that will help later."

"You and Mom never did that," she said.

"Really?" I looked at my daughter and smiled, thinking how I'd tried to do nothing else but gently shape and protect her world since the moment on a snowy day in January I carried her pink and wriggling form in my hands from her mother's birthing room to the weighing scale, marveling at the true mystery of the universe. Perhaps I'd not done my job well enough or perhaps I—we—had done it a bit too well. For all our differences I knew her mother felt exactly this way about both our children.

"Speaking of good stuff, are you planning to eat the rest of that splendid burrito?" I said, pointing with my plastic fork.

She shook her head and pushed her paper plate across to me. I explained I wasn't thinking of myself but of our elderly dog-faced companion.

He'd been awfully patient this afternoon, I said, as we'd dawdled through New Mexican desert backcountry; he probably deserved a nice gourmet meal in Santa Fe before we hit the road again to God knows where, though it might give him the kind of gas we'd regret later.

"Can I get that doll?" Maggie asked.

My smile faded. I knew she would want the doll and tried to explain how insanely overpriced it was, pointing out that outside of town it probably really did sell for $7.50. I felt more like Randy Farmer than a wise parent firmly in control of the family purse strings, and wondered if she might settle for the $30 Navajo dream catcher instead. She nodded but you could see her disappointment.

"Do you think it really works?"

"I guess we'll find out."

"Can I get an ice cream, too?" Ever the skillful negotiator, she pointed to the Emack and Bolios across the square.

"Done."

"Two scoops?"

"Fine." Anything, Lord, but that kachina doll.

"Did you write me a letter yet?"

"Not yet. I'm still thinking what to say."

We made camp on a small mesa in the darkness at a state park near the Pecos River. Stars were swimming overhead and I pointed out the snout of Sagittarius on the southern rim, kissed Maggie good night, and went back to the small fire I'd made. Unfortunately, I didn't have a good pad of paper or even a decent piece of paper to write on, but I scrounged up the brown paper bag her dream catcher had come in, hoping that would suffice.

I sat for a while looking at the stars, trying to think what on earth to say. The brilliance of the stars reminded me of the night view from our hill in Maine, where light pollution is also at a minimum. It was funny, almost inexplicable really, to think I'd chosen to build the second part of my life on the thin soil of a rocky hill in Maine—a place you had to work like the dickens just to make things grow, a place where the growing season was so painfully brief you noticed how extraordinary your roses looked one day and covered them up for the winter the next. There were friends and even a few family members down South who, I suspected, thought I'd gone what my grandmother would have termed "funny in the head" to have such blind devotion to a forested hill in Maine.

But there was really nothing blind about it. *I live among a population, extraordinary in our culture,* New Hampshire poet Donald Hall wrote, *that lives where it lives because it loves the place. We are self-selected place-lovers. There's no reason to live here except for love.* The older I got the more I was convinced the ancient hill I'd cleared for a house and was grooming for a garden had chosen me as much as I'd chosen it. The abbreviated growing season was a perpetual source of frustration, to be sure, a time of seemingly endless *waiting* for the faintest green shoots to appear while the rest of the world snipped April bouquets, followed by an intense and short-lived burst of summer blooms, followed by too-soon rituals of mulching and pruning and early frosts that often led to snow before Thanksgiving. Life on a hill has peculiar joys and hardships, fresh air but constant exposure to wind and weather, long views but vulnerability to drought or eroding rains. Paltry reward, as one of my elderly rose-rearing southern aunts once sniffed over her sherry, for all that work and bother. Curiously, though, I was as drawn to the idea of making my hill bloom, my garden in the woods flourish, as anything I could name save seeing my children grow. The brief days somehow deepened my awareness, made me see more, perhaps were an unexpected payback for all those years spent cursing and turning and coaxing this thin Yankee soil to accept more life. Was it simple coincidence that on the day Maggie was baptized by a rector friend, that same friend and his family came to the house afterward and blessed the grounds and occupants, the two- and four-legged residents alike, a consecration seldom done much these days but one that felt not only spiritually refreshing but almost like a covenant. Two baptisms, we joked, for the price of one.

The world, I suppose, no matter where you are, always looks better from a hill.

New Mexico calls itself the Land of Enchantment and this vast glittering view of the cosmos supported that claim. Navajo and Pueblo traditions say the stars were scattered about by a mischievous coyote called the Great Trickster who played pranks on peoples across the Americas. The Pawnee watched the stars for signs of swimming ducks that would indicate returning migrations of game birds, and the Pomo used the position of the Big Dipper, also known as the Bear, to schedule fishing expeditions. My Cherokee great-grandmother's people believed the Milky Way was scattered flour, the bread of Heaven.

Enchanting stories all. No doubt true. What fool could say they weren't?

"Dad?" a small voice called from the tent.

"Yeah, babe?"

There was a pause. She was fighting sleep. Had the homesickness intensified? "What's your favorite Beatle song?"

I smiled and poked a stick into our signal fire, sending a few sparks up to the old gods. I said I liked "All You Need Is Love" and "We Can Work It Out" but sometimes thought McCartney and Lennon had me in mind when they wrote "Fool on the Hill." I thought she might laugh but she didn't. At least a coyote was howling with laughter a few miles away every so often.

"Dad?"

"Yes ma'am?"

"Are there, like, any snakes out there?"

We'd been talking about desert creatures during supper and I'd explained how citizens of the desert usually came out at night to hunt and feed. That was nature's way, I said, compensating for life in such a difficult place.

"Not anywhere around us, sweetheart. Besides, Amos and I are both keeping a sharp watch." Well, at least I was; Amos was sound asleep by the fire. The air force could have detonated an atomic bomb nearby and he wouldn't have noticed.

"Are you coming to bed?"

"Soon. Got something important to do first. Your job is to try out that new dream catcher."

She was finally silent and I sat gazing at the desert sky, wondering what this fool on a hill could possibly write to his daughter that would mean something. Did it really have to mean something? In ancient times fools were believed to be compensated by the gods, granted immunity from divine retribution by roaming the earth to dispense harsh wisdom and plant seeds of revelation. Their job was to challenge faith in the visible and turn logic upside down. In medieval courts, the only person the king couldn't kill for speaking his mind was the fool, and in many primitive cultures murdering a fool was tantamount to killing a holy man. Proverbs said a fool who had found peace was counted wise in the eyes of God. Napoleon said a fool had the advantage over ordinary men because he was always satisfied with himself.

I was no fool—unfortunately. My failings were far too ordinary, my dissatisfactions too deep, my vanities far too visible for that. But being with Norumbega Girl and her beast like this had brought me a most unexpected peace of mind, and surely that counted for something. Tossing another log on the signal fire, I finally started to write.

Dear Maggie,

I'm sorry I've never written you a letter before. Guess I goofed. Parents do that from time to time. I know you're sad about the divorce. Your mom and I are sad, too. But I have faith that with God's help and a little patience and understanding on our parts, we'll all come through this just fine. Being with you like this has helped me laugh again and figure out some important things. That's what families do, you know—help each other laugh and figure out problems that sometimes seem to have no answer.

Perhaps I should give you some free advice. That's what fathers are supposed to do in letters to their children. Always remember that free advice is usually worth about as much as the paper it's written on and this is written on a used paper bag. Even so, I thought I would tell you a few things I've learned since I was about your age. Some food for thought, as your grandfather would say.

Anyway, Mugs, here goes:

Always be kind to your brother and never hit. The good news is, he'll always be younger and look up to you. The bad news is, he'll probably be bigger.

Travel a lot. Some wise person said travel broadens the mind. Someone wiser said TV broadens the butt.

Listen to your head but follow your heart. Trust your own judgment. Vote early. Change your oil regularly. Always say thank you. Look both ways before crossing. When in doubt, wash your hands.

Remember you are what you eat, say, think, do. Put good things in your mind and your stomach and you won't have to worry what comes out.

Learn to love weeding, waiting in line, ignoring jerks like Randy Farmer.

Always take the scenic route. You'll get there soon enough. You'll get old soon enough, too. Enjoy being a kid. Learn patience, which comes in handy when you're weeding, waiting in line, or trying to ignore a jerk.

Play hard but fair. When you fall, get up and brush your-self off. When you fail, and you will, don't blame anybody else. When you succeed, and you will, don't take all the credit. On both counts, you'll be wiser.

By the way, do other things that make you happy as well. You'll know what they are. Take pleasure in small things. Keep writing letters—the world needs more letters. Smile a lot. Your smile makes angels dance.

Memorize the lyrics to as many Beatles songs as possible in case life's one big Beatle challenge. Be flexible. Your favorite Beatle song will probably always change.

Never stop believing in Santa or the tooth fairy. They really do exist. God does, too. A poet I like says God is always waiting for us in the darkness and you'll find God when it's time. Or God will find you.

Pray. I can't tell you why praying works any more than I can tell you why breathing works. Praying won't make God feel any better, but you will. Trust me. Better yet, trust God. Breathe and pray.

Always leave your campsite better than you found it. Mea-sure twice, cut once. If all else fails, put duct tape on it.

Don't lie. Your memory isn't good enough. Don't cheat. Because you'll remember.

Save the world if you want to. At least turn it upside down a bit if you can't. While you're at it, save the penny, too. Skip dessert.

When you get to college, call your mother every Sunday night.

Realize it's okay to cry but better to laugh. Especially at yourself. If and when you get married, realize it's okay if I cry.

Read everything you can get your hands on and listen to what people tell you. Count on having to figure it out for yourself, though.

Never bungee-jump. If you do, don't tell your father.

Make a major fool of yourself at least once in life, prefera-

bly several times. Being a fool is good for what ails you. We live in a serious time. Don't take yourself too seriously.

Always wear your seat belt even if I don't.

Remember that what you choose to forget may be at least as important as what you choose to remember. Someone very wise once said this to me—but I can't remember who it was or exactly what it means.

Admit your mistakes. Forgive everybody else's.

Notice the stars but don't try to be one. Always paint the underside first. Be kind to old people and creatures great and small. Learn to fight but don't fight unless the other guy throws the first punch.

Don't tell your mother about this last piece of advice.

Learn when it's time to open your mind and close your mouth. (I'm still working on this one.)

Lose your heart. But keep your wits.

Be at least as grateful for your life as I am.

Despite what you hear, no mistake is permanent and nothing goes unforgiven. God grades on a curve.

One more thing: Take care of your teeth and don't worry about how you look. You look just fine. That's two things, I guess.

Finally, there's a story I like about an Indian boy at his time of initiation. As you climb to the mountaintop, the old chief tells his son, you'll come to a great chasm—a deep split in the earth. It will frighten you. Your heart will pause.

Jump, says the chief. It's not as far as you think.

This is excellent advice for girls, too. Life is wonderful but it will frighten you deeply at times.

Jump, my love.

You'll make it.

Love, Dad

CHAPTER THIRTEEN

....

Stones in the Passway

THERE WAS A crack forming in Old Blue's dash, working its way north to the windshield. I regretted seeing this: the beginning of the end. It meant my beloved old truck was splitting apart. I would soon have to get out the duct tape, and God only knew where that would lead. Soon everything I owned would have duct tape on it, whether it needed it or not.

We'd had music from a Ukrainian polka festival and a lovely Chopin sonata through the Texas Panhandle followed by the Oklahoma Ag Report (soybeans up, corn steady, hogs down), followed by the noon news, which led with the report of another suicide bombing in the Gaza Strip and the mother of the Palestinian youth suspected of taking thirteen innocent people with him to kingdom come proudly saying: "My son is in Heaven now. He is drinking with his friends and has eleven virgin brides to please him. He is very happy." Hold the casseroles for that grieving mother, I thought. On the plus side of the aisle it was the fiftieth anniversary of Tide laundry detergent, named by a company executive who was vacationing by the ocean in Maine.

"Dad," Maggie asked, combing out the hair of one of her Barbies, "what did she mean that he is happy to be dead now?"

I tried to explain how ancient religious hatreds, fueled by politics and fear, invariably meant innocent people got caught in the cross fire between madmen. On a happier note, I said, it also meant it was time to jump off the interstate for a cool afternoon drink and quick gas-up. We'd just passed over the Canadian River (low from the drought) and a weathered sign with an American flag on it read: WELCOME TO HINTON. WHERE WE STILL WAVE. I spotted a Texaco sign rising like a lonely beacon at the top of an exit ramp. The vast brown emptiness of west Oklahoma was almost overwhelming and I was actually beginning to doze off. The break would do us all good.

As we rolled up the exit ramp, I was thinking about the irony of the news report and our destination—the Oklahoma City bombing site, Middle East meets Middle America— when a stray heat-seeking missile suddenly struck the front end of Old Blue. That's what it seemed like, at any rate. There was a muffled explosion in the engine compartment followed by a large blast, and then the hood suddenly flew up. Black smoke enveloped the front of the truck and the engine lost all power. I pulled hard on the steering wheel and we swerved into the Texaco station, spewing gravel. I jammed on the brakes and grabbed Maggie's arm, unhooked her shoulder harness, and yanked her across my seat. I carried her well away from the burning truck and ran back to get Amos, who had moved up to my seat but seemed in no particular rush to evacuate ship. Despite his grumbles, I scooped him up like a sheep and carried him over to Maggie.

"Dad," Maggie shrieked. "Susie!"

"Oh damn. Right." I ran back and got Susie. The flames in the engine were a foot high. I rushed back and said to my daughter, "Go inside the station and have them call for a fire truck. Don't come out till I tell you."

Then I ran and fetched a rubber hose, cranked on the spigot, and hauled the drooling hose back to my burning truck. A few minutes later, the fire was out and my face and arms were covered by a film of fire grime and flecks of black soot. I dropped the hose and walked slowly into the air-conditioned convenience market, where I found a young woman sitting placidly at the counter with her chin resting in her hand. She didn't appear to have moved since lunchtime.

"Reckon you don't need the fire department," she drawled pleasantly.

"Apparently not," I said, wiping some grit from my left eye. "By any chance is there a Chevrolet place in town?"

"Naw. They's a Chevy place in Oklahoma City, though."

I nodded, the enormity of what had just happened beginning to land on me like a house. It would take more than duct tape to get Old Blue rolling again.

"How about a good truck mechanic?"

"They's Jerry."

"Jerry?"

"Yeah. He works on big rigs, mostly. I reckon I could call him to come take a look."

I thought for a moment. I was half tempted to rent a Ryder truck, shove everything we had inside it, and head straight home, leaving Old Blue to the people of Hinton. Plant a few zinnias in her and she'd make a half-decent municipal flowerpot.

"Would you do that, please?"

She nodded; her chin reluctantly parted company with her hand and she picked up a phone book and began slowly thumbing for a number.

I walked over to where Maggie was staring into the depths of the drink cooler. She selected a Gatorade and asked if it would take long to fix Old Blue. I explained that we'd just blown an engine and might have to simply leave Old Blue and rent another truck in order to get home on time.

"I'm not leaving Old Blue," she said defiantly. "She's our truck."

"Then I'll put you on a flight home to Mom and I'll stay with Old Blue till she gets fixed. The last thing I want to do is argue about it."

"I'm staying too." There would be no argument.

She asked if she could go outside and look at Old Blue and I said she could but to keep a safe distance. The engine compartment was a charred canyon of exposed wires and sizzling metal.

I stood there myself for a moment staring into the depths of the drink cooler after she was gone, wondering what the hell we should really do. This was my worst fear come to life, I thought: stranded in the middle of God knows where with an old dog and a little girl. WELCOME TO MOTORIST HELL. HAVE A NICE DAY, the sign should have read. Just when you think you've got life on the run, life runs you down like a dog.

Behind me, the clerk helpfully drawled: "Jerry says he'll be up directly." I turned and smiled at her, said thank you, then studied the cooler again in case emergency instructions had been left there by the last fool who'd broken down in Hinton. I mentally kicked myself because I remembered that I'd been meaning to check the oil for the past couple thousand miles. *Do as I write, Love,* I should have added to my letter to Maggie, *not as I do.*

"Yonnacappychino?"

I glanced at the clerk again. She looked seventeen and probably had three kids living in a trailer on the edge of town.

"Beg your pardon?"

"I said yonnacappychino? We got a new machine that makes it."

It took a moment for me to realize what she was asking—pretty odd when you consider I'm a dumb southerner, too.

I smiled at her. What an age of miracles this was. I'd never bought cappuccino from a machine at a convenience market, but travel, as I always say, broadens the mind. So I ordered one.

Jerry hitched a ride to see us in his buddy Billy Paul Hughes's Chevy conversion van. Jerry was a slight white guy with shivery cowboy legs and a two-day growth of beard and Billy Paul was a handsome black guy with an impressive amount of gold jewelry hanging around his neck. Jerry took one glance at Old Blue's engine, shook his head ruefully, and pronounced her dead. He suggested that Billy Paul take us into town and he'd haul Old Blue down to his shop and make a few phone calls and see what he could figure out. I asked if anybody in town rented cars and he said he thought Rick England Ford might; that was up on the left past the school yard and before you reached the square.

Billy Paul dropped Jerry off at his shop and gave us a lift two miles into town to the Hinton Motel. His air-conditioned van had gold shag carpeting from the floor to the ceiling and a box on the floor was spilling dozens of blues tapes. Robert Johnson was moaning about stones in the passway to a slide guitar and we learned that Billy Paul was a blues singer, too, presently doing a gig at the Plum Tree Lounge on 36th Street in Oklahoma City.

"You mean where they blew up that building?" Maggie asked him.

"That's right, sweetheart," Billy Paul said to her softly. "That was some turble, I want to tell you. People still picking up the pieces. Tryin' to figure how something like that could happen out here in God's Country."

Billy Paul had come out to Hinton for a little bass fishing with Jerry because Jerry knew all the best spots. Due to the drought, he said, the bass fishing was poor so mostly they were hanging around the garage shooting the breeze. Jerry was a heck of a mechanic, Billy Paul wanted us to know, and if anybody could get that truck rollin' again quick, it was ole Jerry. I turned around and looked at my companions in back. They were sitting side by side, thoroughly enjoying the air-conditioning and slide guitar blues and the nice shag-carpeted ride.

Billy Paul dropped us off at the only motel in town. Beneath a blistering three o'clock sun, the parking lot of the Hinton Motel was empty and I went into the office, which turned out to be the owners' private home. A Chihuahua was raising hell and an elderly man was lying on the floor. His legs were shriveled sticks and he was grunting unintelligibly. My first thought was that he'd had a stroke or something. Ignoring the dog, I lifted him up and returned him to his recliner chair. *Wheel of Fortune* was playing on his TV. He nodded and tried to smile, then turned his skull-like head back to Vanna White. Maggie came in and quieted the dog. A moment later, a large Ford swung into the carport and a woman carrying a grocery bag came into the office, flushed and apologetic. "I had to run out and get him a prescription," she explained, looking at the man. Her name was Dixie Snow and the man with the shriveled legs was her husband. He'd had Parkinson's disease, she explained, for nearly thirty years and never sat in one place for long. "Worries me half to death at times. We've had him everywhere, even down to Dallas," she said with a sigh, looking at her husband, who was watching Vanna like a hawk. "Not a whole lot, I suppose, they can do for us now."

Mrs. Snow gave us room number nine, which had a joining door to room ten—two rooms for the price of one, a suite for twenty-six bucks a night. The rooms were plain and simple and had no phones but were spotlessly clean and featured a pair of window air conditioners that could have chilled a supermarket meat locker. There were also a couple color television sets with forty-two cable channels and a fresh indoor drinking toilet that one member of our expedition made a beeline for. Dog and girl then assumed comfy viewing positions on the beds and I walked down the road to call on Rick England Ford to see about rental wheels.

It was only a quarter-mile hoof to the dealership, past Jim Seurer Field, where the Hinton High Comets played, the Sooner Superette, and a farm implement lot. I walked past a yellow road sign politely advising me that "Hitchhikers may be escaping prisoners" and wondered vaguely if people might think I was a guy making a mad dash for freedom at a slow walk. A Dodge truck rolled leisurely past and a man and woman both waved. I remembered I was in a place where people still waved so I waved back.

While waiting for Rick England to appear, I asked his secretary how many people resided in Hinton. It seemed a tad *quiet*, the kind of town where nothing but weather much happened and old men like Mr. Snow waited for it to be yesterday. "Not countin' prisoners," she said, gently popping her gum, "I reckon about sixteen hundred."

Rick England didn't rent cars, he said, and then he remembered he might have something I could use while we were here. I followed him outside to a mustard-colored, vinyl-roofed Lincoln Town Car, a true relic from the high-rolling Ronnie Reagan years of wretched personal excess. Her grillwork looked as impressive as the seal of the U.S. Supreme Court and after Rick England gave her a neat jump start, she ran surprisingly well. "She's loaded," Rick said, slipping into salesman persona. "Velour seats, air, power everything, nice radio." He agreed to rent her to me for $29. "A day?" I said. He smiled. "Well, for however long you need it." What a deal, I thought, and what a neighborly guy. I borrowed his secretary's phone to call Jerry the mechanic.

"I was just fixin' to come find you," Jerry said. "I got some bad news and some good news. Which you want first?" I suggested he get the bad news over with. "They want twenty-eight hunnerd dollars to haul your truck to Oklahoma City and pop a new engine in her." Feeling my pain, he didn't wait for me to ask for the good news. "But I got this friend named Bill whose son is waitin' for a kidney transplant and's got a nice rebuilt three-fifty in his truck. Motor's got less than eight thousand on her and she runs like new. He wanted seven hunnerd for it but I talked him down to five. Said he'd pull the engine for me this afternoon and have it here in the mornin'. Everything goes right, I figger I could have her up and runnin' for you by this time tomorrow evenin'. I get five to put in an engine. So I figger with oil and filters and fluids it'll come out to about eleven hunnerd."

"Do it," I said. I was making deals from one end of Hinton, Oklahoma, to the other.

I drove back to the motel and bribed my daughter off the bed and into the Ronniemobile with the promise of soft-serve ice cream from the Sooner Superette. Amos came along for the ride and fell in love with the spacious velour backseat. Several people waved to us on our short drive to the bank on the square and we waved back.

There we found Elbert Isley at his clerk's window, a smiling grandfather who used my Visa card to debit eleven hundred dollars from my account. He counted out eleven mint-new hundred-dollar bills and showed us the clever anticounterfeit features on the new Franklin bill. He said some people didn't care for them because they looked like Monopoly money.

"Say," he said, "y'all are the folks broke down from New England, aren't you?" Word clearly traveled at the speed of an elderly Town Car in quiet Hinton, I thought, not denying it. "I love New England," he went ahead. "Particularly Boston. My grandson Kevin is going to Harvard this year. He's a wrestler, quite a young man. We're very proud of him. I wish I could go with him. My wife and I were in Boston last year and met the nicest people. They say people in Boston are, you know, kind of rude. But we didn't find that to be the case at all. In fact, we got lost tryin' to get to Fenway Park and these nice people showed us not only where to park for free but also helped us get across the freeway."

"You need help to survive freeways in Boston," I agreed with him.

He stopped counting and leaned forward to whisper. "I really do love Boston but I have to say some of the drivers there leave a bit to be desired. If you know what I mean."

I nodded sympathetically and explained that we were really from Maine and told him how people from Maine sometimes called drivers from Boston "Massholes" due to their aggressive driving habits. Elbert smiled and blushed. "Having said that," I added, "I love Boston, too. It's my favorite big city in the world. Beautiful. Cultured. A regular shining city on a hill." But put the mildest-mannered Bostonian brahmin behind the wheel of a car or in the cheap outfield seats at Fenway Park, I said, and he turns into a leather-lunged roadie for Sweaty Nipples.

Elbert smiled. I realized he'd probably never heard of Sweaty Nipples, but at least he'd heard of Maine.

As we had time to kill, I asked Elbert what sights we shouldn't miss in Hinton and he said we really ought to see Red Rocks Canyon and the Hinton Historical Museum. There was a man who raised miniature ponies and if we were around till the weekend, he said, we could come visit the Pentecostal church Elbert pastored on Portland Avenue in Oklahoma City. I thanked him and said we just might do that. I congratulated him on his grandson's success and thanked him for the new Ben Franklins.

"Dad," Maggie hissed as we left the bank, "I can't believe you used a swearword in front of a minister."

We tooled out to see Red Rocks Canyon, which turned out to be a marvelous mini–Grand Canyon with fifty-foot-high red rock walls, several attractive campsites, a community swimming pool, and a fishing pond woefully low from the drought. The pool was already closed for the summer but we swung on the nearby swings for a while and played Beatle Challenge lying on our backs in the grass beneath the shade of a large oak tree.

"Thanks for writing me that letter," Maggie said.

"My pleasure. What did you think?" I suppose I was trolling for a compliment about the pearls of wisdom I'd laid at her feet. She'd asked for a letter and I'd given her the Magna Carta of fatherhood. Suitable for framing.

"Well, it's kinda long. Do I have to read the whole thing?"

"Nah."

"I want to," she said, using her fingers to bracket a cloud floating overhead. "One thing I wondered, though. . . ."

"Hmm?" I felt a nap coming on.

"You said life is frightening."

Ah, I thought. So she read the whole sucker.

"I think I said it will sometimes frighten you."

"Is that true? Does it frighten you?"

I thought about what she was asking. If I said yes she might think her old man wasn't the fearless warrior every child hopes his or her father is; if I said no she might get the wrong impression that it was important to repress your fears rather than face them. In fact, a host of stuff scared me—cheap carnival rides, baby-sitters driving small cars, a fat letter from the IRS. It scared me to see an animal walking along the interstate or a bunch of nuns getting on the same airplane.

The list of rational and irrational fears, if I thought about it, could probably roll like the credits of a Freddy Krueger slasher film or at least keep a good Portland shrink safely employed for the summer: Phone calls after midnight. Manhattan cabdrivers who didn't speak English. My temper. Rupert Murdoch. The idea of something bringing harm to my children. Global warming. Chat rooms. Baseball salaries. That inexplicable numbness in my right middle toe. The coming death of Amos. Tall buildings. El Niño. My mother being alone. The popularity of Yanni. Freight elevators. Bosnia. Lost phone messages. Trent Lott. People who use "impact" as a verb. Hitchhikers who might be escaping prisoners. Fenway's bleacher seats. Africa's famines. I was a bit frightened—"anxious" was probably a better word— about the new kind of expanded family unit we were supposed to be upon our return to Maine, and worried about the number of droughts and what Japanese beetles back home might be doing on my roses. She probably didn't need or wish to hear all this mind clutter, though.

"Sure," I said, "but you know what? A curious thing. The older I get the less I'm afraid of stuff I used to be afraid of—like being alone in the dark or getting old and dying. Maybe that's because you and Jack worry about those things for me and I now worry about the stuff that frightened my father."

She turned her head in the grass and I could see she was surprised. I also saw she'd picked a wildflower and was holding it in her teeth. For a moment I was afraid it might be poisonous but then realized it was nothing to be frightened of. Just a wee Oklahoma dandelion.

"What scared him?" she wondered.

"Not much," I said. "At least by the time you knew him."

We ate supper at the Family Restaurant and chatted with several friendly people from Hinton, all of whom knew of our plight. A woman told us we ought to drive over to see Indian City at Anadarko and a man pointed out that nearby Binger was the birthplace of Johnny Bench, though he admitted there wasn't a whole lot to see there. I asked him where the best fishing was and he said, "Normally the Canadian. But it's dang near dried up," and shook his head regretfully. "Best bet would be some of the farm ponds. Nice catfish round here." He told me a couple spots.

We left a nice tip and went to the Sooner Superette for ice cream. As we were coming back out to the car, a middle-aged woman with hair curlers peeking from under an aqua hair net stopped me and pointed to the Ronniemobile. "Say, how's that thing runnin'?" she wanted to know. I told her it was running real nice, excellent air, nice smooth ride — I was beginning to sound like Rick England — a steal for somebody who really liked mustard.

"My cousin Nora almost bought that car," she said with a serious expression, and then cackled merrily. "Till she decided it was uglier than a cross-eyed baby."

Maggie plopped on the bed with a ring pop to watch *Hook* on The Disney Channel and I took Amos out for his evening constitutional. The sun was a bloodred disk hovering above Jim Seurer Field, where the Hinton Comets were finishing their afternoon football practice. I watched the final scrimmage and paused and chatted with a man whose son was playing guard for the team. He said his son was small but had legs like a bull, just what you need to play pulling guard. His son had his heart set on going to Oklahoma State but he'd have to grow something awful this winter and get through advanced algebra first. He was going to eat nothing but steak and potatoes. I asked him how the winters were out here on the Oklahoma plains.

"Long and lonely," he admitted with a low smile. "Good time for puttin' on weight."

The son jogged over, puffing. He was sweating profusely and appeared to have no neck, legs like a bull. His eyes flicked at me, then back to his father behind the grillwork of his face mask. "Dad," he grunted. "Can I have the truck after practice? Jen wants to go over to Weatherford."

His father considered a moment, then nodded almost imperceptibly.

"Thanks." The baby bull jogged away.

"Who's Jen?" I asked, knowing already.

"His new girlfriend." His father shook his head, lit a Marlboro Light. "She's about all that kid can talk about lately."

The next morning we drove to the Hinton Historical Museum and found Elsie Gray, the volunteer host, just opening up. She seemed to be the only person in town who didn't know who we were and who hadn't waved but she quickly led us on an escorted tour of the museum, a delightful pink Victorian house with white gingerbread railings. She showed Maggie old photos of the town, French bed dolls, and dresses made from flour sacks. "That's what those of us who grew up out here wore as kids way back then."

Elsie was seventy. She could remember the Dust Bowl years of the Depression like it was yesterday. "The crops dried up; it was so blamed hot and dry and dusty you just wanted to die. My mother used to wet down sheets and hang them over the windows to try and cool off our place. People were leaving this place right and left but she was some tough lady and not about to give up."

Elsie's father died when she was sixteen and her mother gave birth to her baby sister eight days later. "There were farm men round here who wanted to marry my mother but none of them were good enough for her children. That's what she used to say. We were so poor we didn't even know it and this land out here looked nothing like it does now. Talk about a desolate place. This was it—when that drought finished with it. There were no trees in sight. Just burned-out grass and dust. Edge of the world. You really felt for some of the Indian families, poor things, who had even less than we did. We lived on faith and scraps. I think that's why Hinton has so many churches now. We're so grateful. Nine at last count."

I asked what changed it, what brought back trees and people.

Elsie smiled. "Funny thing, really. It was like a miracle. One evening there was this big gray cloud approaching. You could just see it coming. Guess what it was?" She looked at Maggie.

"Rain clouds?"

"Nope. Birds. Migrating birds. They just set down one evening and were gone the next morning. The rains came not long after that and a year later we started to notice all these little trees growing around town. Cedar trees and hardwoods, mostly. Those birds had come down from Missouri on their way to the Gulf. Their droppings had seeds in them. Those trees are huge today. People always remark how lovely our trees are. Those trees, I tell 'em, are our blessing from the Lord."

She asked if we'd seen Red Rocks yet and I said we'd seen and admired it from one end to the other.

"You know, that was where the Dalton gang used to hide out from the law," she said. "And, speaking of outlaws, I'll tell you another true story." I could see how interested Maggie was; Elsie Gray had a gift for keeping an audience. "My grandmother came here from Missouri, where their closest neighbor was Jesse James."

I saw Maggie's confusion and interjected, "He was the most famous outlaw in American history."

"Maybe so," said Elsie, "but you better not say an unkind word about Jesse James in my grandmother's presence. She thought the world of him, as most people did who knew him. He may well have done the awful things they said he did but my grandmother said he was the soul of politeness and gentleness. He had superb manners and treated his wife royally and raised his children to be proper. He gave money to his neighbors, they say, and helped anybody who really needed help. Funny how history sees a man one way and the people who really knew him see him another way."

She led Maggie off to show her a turn-of-the-century bake oven and I wandered around looking at pictures of rawboned farmers and the Hinton of Dust Bowl days. I knew a fair amount about Jesse and Frank James and wondered if the militia groups that were their spiritual descendants and had possibly blown up the federal building in Oklahoma City knew they were attempting to lay claim to the same hard mythological turf as Jesse James.

Products of the sectional violence that turned the Missouri-Kansas border into a scorched battleground, the James boys began their dubious ascent to fame in the last days of the Civil War under the tutelage of Confederate guerrilla fighter William Quantrill, killing Union soldiers, looting farms, and shooting at least as many innocent civilians as they did Yankees. After the war, other Confederates went home but the James gang turned to robbing banks and trains, sometimes handing out press releases to startled victims denouncing northern atrocities. An influential Missouri newspaper editor and unreconstructed southerner named John Newman Edwards portrayed the James boys and their partners in crime, the Youngers—Cole, Bob, and Jim—as American Robin Hoods, not ruthless outlaws but victims of Yankee oppression, creators of a "Chivalry of Crime."

Big-city newspapers back East quickly picked up the story and turned the James boys into living legends, the darlings of pulp novels and Brooklyn stage dramas. After an aborted bank robbery in Northfield, Minnesota, during which three gang members were killed and the Youngers were captured, public sentiment turned against the Jameses, who escaped and stayed on the run until two new members of the gang, Bob and Charley Ford, shot an unarmed Jesse dead at the Missouri home where he was living under an assumed name with his wife and two children. Six months later, a weary Frank James turned himself in to authorities, but a sympathetic Missouri jury refused to convict him. A rough-cut intellectual who read Francis Bacon and Shakespeare, Frank drifted through a succession of meaningless jobs—as a race starter at country fairs, a shoe salesman, a doorman at a strip joint, even a detective at a department store for a while—and finally returned to his mother's home, where he ended his days by conducting paid tours of the house. Rumors continued to circulate that his brother was still alive—sightings of Jesse were reported all over America—and Frank became so worried Jesse's corpse would be stolen by robbers, he instructed that his body be cremated and his remains kept in a bank vault.

I called Silent Sam later from the Sooner Superette. The sun was going down, Maggie was watching *Babe*, and teenagers were gathering out front to palely loiter in the dusk. He asked how the trout were biting. I explained that our fly rods were idle; we were waiting for an engine transplant and seeing the sights of western Oklahoma. Earlier that day, I said, we'd rambled over to see Indian City and driven back through Binger, birthplace of Johnny Bench. I threw in just for fun that we'd also met a woman whose grandmother knew Jesse James and told him that the citizens of Hinton still waved and that I'd waved to everybody in town at least once, some twice.

"Hope you're still laughing when you get fifty miles out of town and the engine blows up again," he said. "That's the oldest scam in the book. Sawdust in the driveshaft."

"Ye of little faith," I said.

"No. I'm a lawyer."

I asked how he was feeling.

"I don't know," he said, dismissing his ordeal almost offhandedly. "Comes and goes. But my headshrinker told me a funny thing yesterday. I guess it's funny. It's kind of like a Zen question. If a man is walking alone in the woods talking to himself, and no woman is present . . . is he *still* wrong?"

Sam chortled. He sounded like a man who'd either seen the light or made peace with his madness.

"I get the impression you're pretty happy out there in the middle of nowhere," he said.

"I guess I am," I admitted. "It's not every day you meet a woman whose granny knew Jesse James."

"Remember, though, that's twister alley. Nothing in the world to match an Okie twister, they say."

"Oh yes there is," I said. "A Maine divorce."

"How's that?"

"Either way the trailer's gone just like *that*."

Sam laughed again. He liked our college-boy badinage. But I wasn't kidding. Given his improved mood—or maybe mine—it seemed like the opportune time and place to tell him about my busted-up marriage. So I told him.

He seemed deeply surprised and genuinely sorry.

"Man, that's tough," he said with feeling. There was a pause and he asked if *he* needed to be worried about *me* driving into a bridge abutment. I told him I was fine, no chance of that, I had two kids to live for and a garden to get home to and a surfeit of trout and was strangely getting better with each passing mile though I couldn't really explain why. Maybe our trip had been just the thing for what was ailing me.

"How's Maggie taking it?"

"I thought she was doing beautifully with it. Then I learned she wasn't. Now I think she's just okay and happy to be going home."

"Yeah. Time and distance always helps." He was quiet again, then cleared his throat as if about to make a summation to the jury.

"It's weird," he said, almost offhandedly "I'm going to an AA meeting this Thursday."

"Good for you," I said. I hadn't known he had this problem. Perhaps it explained something. It was good to hear he was willing to face his demon. Maybe it would be good for his marriage, or at least his life, though both of us were apparently learning there was no quick fix, no magic pill you could take.

I told Sam I had to run. I had to walk an old dog and go catch the end of *Babe* with a girl who wouldn't be one for much longer. He seemed reluctant to let me go.

"We should talk more often," he said. "Not just when our lives are falling apart at the seams. Come duck hunting with me in the fall."

"Only if you'll read the complete works of Edmund Spenser aloud first."

"Who the hell is Edmund Spenser?"

"The only poet I hate."

"Skip the ducks," he said with a laugh. "I'll come see you. Maureen has always wanted to see Maine."

I told him they would be welcome and not the least bit disappointed.

We spent another day roaming around Greater Hinton. We hiked through Red Rocks and drove over to see the Kiowa Tribal Museum at Carnegie. A routine of sorts developed: I would call Jerry and, coughing a little, he would inform me that the wait would be just a bit longer, nothing to worry about, a part was still en route. He sounded vague, strained, even a touch agitated, and I'll admit wondering if he knew what he was doing. My faith began to waver. Was Sam right? I'd hoped we might swing down through Dallas and then along the Gulf Coast, where my father had briefly owned a newspaper when I was three and four. That sentimental route was out of the picture now and it would be a close shave, in fact, just to make it home for Jack's birthday. Maggie started second grade in exactly one week's time.

So much of our lives is spent waiting—for someone to finish a job or make a decision, for something to begin or end, a season to come or go, someone to be born or pass away. My truck was dead but a stranger assured me it would be reborn. The summer was over and school was beginning. The fish weren't biting but the evenings had a hint of autumn's coming refreshment in them. Sitting on the edge of my bed at the Hinton Motel, at loose ends, wondering when and if we'd ever get rolling again, I picked up Maggie's Magic Eightball from her Medicine Bag, gave it a shake, and consulted it for an answer.

I turned it over and the white-lettered answer floated into focus: *Don't bet on it,* it said. I put the Eightball down, thought a moment, then decided to give the durn thing a second chance, turning it over once again. *Home is where the heart is,* it sappily informed me. A silly child's toy, I thought, setting it down again. To be on the safe side, I picked up the phone and dialed the airlines and found out what flew from Oklahoma City.

On the evening of our third full day in Hinton, there was a sensational barn fire at the edge of town. Fire trucks from several towns whooped past the motel, followed by police cars and speeding pickups. We joined the caravan in the Ronniemobile to the edge of town, where a crowd of a couple hundred people had gathered to watch flames leap from the metal warehouse and smoke wreathe across the flat soybean fields. Several people asked us how we were enjoying Hinton and I eventually found myself standing by the woman whose cousin Nora nearly bought our car. It was now beginning to feel like *our* car.

She was holding a paper sack of vine-picked tomatoes and gave me a couple of the meaty monsters. I ate one of them on the spot. It was sweet and delicious and I told her as much.

"Reckon so. They're grown from heirloom seeds," she declared. "Here, hold out your hand." She reached in her pocket and brought out a folded packet of dried black seeds, explaining she was planning to start a new crop of tomatoes and move them indoors before first frost. She insisted I take a few seeds, which I did, placing them in my breast pocket. I told her maybe I'd try and grow them indoors in Maine and she threw back her tautly curled head and cackled again. "I tell you what, that blame car'll get your butt chased out of Maine if you take it home."

"Or elected governor," I said, and we both laughed.

We returned to the motel in full darkness, smelling of hay smoke, and I agreed to watch one of Maggie's favorite movies with her, Steve Martin's *Father of the Bride.* I'd seen this syrupy remake of the Spencer Tracy classic several times with my daughter but the part where the bumbling *père* realizes his little girl has finally grown up and is about to fly the coop for good and is ineptly trying to get through the wedding crowd to kiss his daughter good-bye—well, that scene never fails to nail me. A lump rises in my throat, my eyes embarrassingly begin to leak.

I was at precisely this moment in the film, eating my second heirloom tomato, when a knock came at the door.

I opened the door, wiping tears from my eyes. It was Jerry the mechanic, wiping grease from his hands. He looked positively triumphant. "By durn, she's done," he proclaimed, waving a hand at my rumbling truck. "Runnin' like a dream, too."

He probably thought I had tears of gratitude in my eyes, and maybe I did. Old Blue did sound different, as if her next stop might be the inside lane at the local drag strip. But more important, she was a-runnin' like a dream. I drove Jerry back to his garage and shook his hand. I asked him if there was anything I needed to know about the impressive transplant.

"Only that the wheels will fall off before that engine quits," he explained by way of fare-thee-well.

And so, several hours later, on the morning of the fourth day, we rose again and rolled out of town under the cover of morning darkness, reinvented if not reborn. To be honest, I was suddenly sort of sorry to see Hinton vanish in my rear-view mirrors. What a nice place, I thought, a town birds made green again with trees. I sort of wished I could have gathered the whole place together and waved good-bye to the town where everybody still waved. In one of those flash insights that come only when you least expect it, I realized that I'd enjoyed being a prisoner in Hinton—one of the best moments of a fishing trip where I never even fished.

It was just over an hour's drive to Oklahoma City and we reached the chain-link fence at the bomb site just about the time the sun was coming up. The sense of the missing building was almost physically overwhelming. The eerie orange sodium security lights were just stuttering off and I saw a police cruiser slide by and noticed that people were already out. It would be another fiercely hot rainless day in Oklahoma and as we drove slowly by the fence where family members and strangers had left hundreds of notes and flowers and teddy bears attached to the metal crosshatch, I couldn't help wondering what kind of world my children would inherit.

I pulled over and stopped the engine and asked Maggie if she wanted to get out and go up to the fence and read some of the messages.

She sat up slowly, blinking in the grayish light. She'd been sleeping and I'd awakened her. I couldn't tell if she was sad or simply wanted to sleep some more, but after a few moments she shook her head and laid it back down on the pillow. I sat for a moment watching a few early risers walk along the memorial fence. Amos watched them, too. Then I cranked Old Blue and we headed for the interstate.

CHAPTER FOURTEEN

....

South of Sorrow

WE REACHED MY mother's just after sundown two days later. She stood on the lighted porch holding the door open with one arm, her waist with the other. The crickets were singing. "I was getting so worried about you two. Goodness' sakes. Where on earth have you *been*?"

She wasn't really mad, just a little worried, proving I come by it honestly. I kissed her and apologized for making us later than expected, explaining we'd lost a couple hours nosing around Florence, South Carolina, the small town where we'd lived for a year and a half when I turned six and started school. It was only a little out of our way and Maggie, I explained, had been anxious to see the town and hear my memories of it. To tell the truth, I'd been mildly curious to see the place, too, because I hadn't been back since we left. That was going on forty years. So much had happened to our family that year. She nodded as if she fully understood, then turned to Maggie and declared, "Well, sugar pie, did you leave any trout for anybody else to catch?"

Maggie beamed at her and managed a toothy "Yes, ma'am. But I caught more fish than Dad."

"True. The kid is a regular prodigy. She did some pretty serious injury to the nation's Gatorade inventory and supply of hot dogs, too." Call me a son of the old South, but I was glad my daughter had remembered to use "ma'am."

We followed her into the kitchen. Supper was waiting on the stove. Molly, my father's yellow Lab, had been asleep there and suddenly got up and growled furiously at Amos and then, wildly thumping her tail, fell into treating him like her long-lost beau. My mother had made sugar beans and a Yankee-style pot roast, and after we'd washed and begun dishing up, Maggie started chattering about seeing my first school and the Purvis place and the newspaper where her grandfather worked and then slipped into a broader rapid-fire travel narrative about Colorado Trails and the Snake River trip and her old man the Eagle Scout falling out of Norumbega Girl. Hinton earned star billing, as did Amos's touching the buffalo, the bikers at Rushmore, Cody Rodeo Night, Luke the horse, almost meeting the president, Chaco Canyon, and going to the Frogtown Festival with my friends in Minnesota. Funny what her brain had processed as highlights. She didn't mention trout more than once—the cute little pencil trout she caught on the Snake.

My mother glanced at me. She was charmed. She lived alone with Molly, volunteered at the church soup kitchen, gardened, and went to early movies with her widow friends. I suspected she missed my father desperately. I sometimes felt guilty for living so far from her but something I couldn't quite name foreclosed my return to the South. I'd told her almost nothing about my unraveling married life, just that we'd been working on a few things like all couples who'd been married as long as we had. She loved my wife and I knew she sometimes conveyed the impression to her widow friends that we lived an idyllic existence on our little hill near the ocean in Maine.

Afterward, while Maggie was having a shower before bed, we sat in the living room with the lights low and glasses of wine. She asked me again how the fishing was out West and I said it was simply fantastic, better than I could have imagined, and I couldn't wait to go back to the San Juan with a load of Liberace flies and my camera.

She smiled; the language lost her a bit.

"Is that a town?"

"No, ma'am. A river where the trout have advanced degrees in philosophy." At least I remembered to say "ma'am," too.

"What made you go to Florence?" she asked mildly, shifting the conversation.

I explained that it was just off the interstate and Maggie seemed fascinated by the idea that I'd been her age almost exactly the year we lived there. It was clear, I said, as we pushed hard through the heart of Dixie from Memphis to Birmingham, and then on to Atlanta and toward Columbia, that the landscape and culture of the rural South interested her. We'd sung gospel hymns with the radio, listened to the "obituary of the air," stopped for late peaches and boiled peanuts and nearly purchased a huge purple martin house, and stopped to gas up in several towns with decaying mansions and sleepy courthouse squares that made Maggie think of the movie *Forrest Gump*.

I smiled and swirled the wine around in my glass.

"She couldn't believe people would build a whole town to look like something in a movie, as if Hollywood made it up."

"It's good she saw it then. I think that South is disappearing pretty fast."

I nodded and admitted I wasn't particularly nostalgic about it or sorry to see that South go. In my mind a feeling of heat and sadness seemed to hover about these towns. Maybe that's why I had avoided going back to Florence all these years, I said.

"But I thought you loved living there."

"I did. But I guess I associate sudden change with it—the way things ended, the way we left. It was like the entire world changed overnight."

"A lot did happen at once," she agreed, taking a slower drink of her wine. "I suppose you mean Melvin Purvis and all that."

I nodded. Amos wandered into the living room and stretched out on her Oriental rug to sleep. Molly lay down a few feet away, watching him.

Curiously, Florence had seemed like a small paradise to my brother and me. We lived in a brick house whose large backyard ended by the honeysuckle hedge of a large estate owned by a famous man named Melvin Purvis. We had a "colored" maid named Louise who came every day and ironed clothes, made our lunches, and taught my brother and me to "feet-dance." She would place our feet on hers and dance us around the linoleum of the kitchen to a song on the radio by the McGuire Sisters. This was "feet-dancing." I remembered how the distilled water sloshed back and forth in the Coke bottle Louise used to sprinkle our clothes before she ironed them and how she and our mother would stand together in the kitchen talking quietly while my brother and I were supposedly taking naps. My mother was a newcomer to town; she looked like a young Lee Remick. Louise had worked for several of the prominent families in Florence.

I lay on the bed, listening to their quiet voices but just unable to make out the words, staring at my bare feet, wondering if I could actually see them grow, wearing only shorts and a cotton shirt with horizontal stripes, feeling the intense heat on the yard out the screened window, wondering too how I might finally catch a glimpse of Melvin Purvis the famous G-man. My brother told me Purvis was the most famous man in the world and I had no doubt whatsoever this was true. Purvis was the FBI man who shot and killed John Dillinger, Public Enemy Number One, the legendary lawman who ended the careers of Pretty Boy Floyd and Baby Face Nelson and a host of other famous gangsters of the 1930s. He had three sons, all considerably older than my brother and me, including one who could be seen driving a small red pony wagon around the family estate. How I longed to know that boy. How I hungered to ride in his red pony wagon.

"I remember how you two talked of nothing else. It was Melvin Purvis this, Melvin Purvis that."

"We were sons of a newspaperman."

"That's true."

Our father was the paper's director of advertising and we often rode our bikes downtown to his office, stopping at the Piggly Wiggly on Cherokee Road to get cold drinks and enjoy the air-conditioning. The Piggly Wiggly and the newspaper were the only air-conditioned buildings in town at that time. "Come on in," a sign in the store's window read. "It's cool inside." We were mesmerized by a reporter at the paper who could do amazing tricks. His name was Burt. Burt could make coins appear from our ears and make his finger appear to come off.

"Something I always meant to ask you," I said to my mother. "How exactly did we end up in Florence? I know why, I just don't know how."

She thought a moment. "Well, as I recall, one of your father's friends from his days at the *Washington Post* knew about it. After what happened in Mississippi, Florence was like a resting place for us."

"But you were never really comfortable there. . . ."

"Well, it wasn't home. You're never happy until you find a place that feels like home."

What happened in Mississippi was this: My father had started his own newspaper with a wealthy investor who turned out to be a crook. While my father was away in Tampa purchasing a web press, his partner cleaned out the company accounts and left town. The paper had been run-

ning for a year. My father came home and emptied his own
personal bank account to pay his six employees a final
check. His life's dream had just gone down the drain. He'd
lost everything. He shut off the lights, handed the keys to
the custodian, and walked across the street to the courthouse to smoke a cigarette and make a few phone calls. He
was thirty-nine years old and calmly told me this story in
full when he was eighty. A few days after the paper folded,
a phone call from my uncle Jim came, reporting that my
father's mother had taken a nasty fall up in Annapolis. A
couple hours later, my uncle Bob phoned with the terrible
news that their only sister, Irene, the aunt I had no memory
of ever meeting, had been killed instantly in a head-on collision. All of this happened within a week. My mother had
just come home from the Gulfport hospital. She'd had a
miscarriage.

"That must have felt like the end of the world," I said to
my mother, wondering, not for the first time, how I would
have coped with such an avalanche of bad news. Death,
bankruptcy, and a miscarriage all within days—almost
hours—of each other.

"You know," she said, looking at her half-full wineglass,
"I had a lot of faith in your father. It was a difficult moment
for us, one of those times as a couple you know you'll either
get through together or fly apart. He must have been going
out of his mind, but he never conveyed any of that to me.
There was never a sense of panic with him. He said things
would be all right and they eventually were. That's the way
life happens, sweetie. Good times don't last but neither do
the bad times. Florence wasn't home but it wasn't a bad
place to rest for a spell."

Perhaps I'd lived in the North for too long. My mother's
choice of words—"to rest for a spell"—sounded so southern
to me now, an echo of my lost childhood.

"And, naturally," she added, "he did well."

I knew this. He doubled the paper's ad lineage within a year, was named to the Southern Newspaper Executives board of directors, started fielding better job offers. Meanwhile, I was doing my dead-level best to catch a glimpse of G-man Melvin Purvis. Maggie and I had just seen his house—a handsome redbrick home with a wide porch and tall white columns that faintly resembled Jefferson's Monticello, approached by a long sandy drive framed by massive magnolia trees. The place was astonishingly beautiful, as I remembered it, and hadn't changed much, it seemed, in forty years, I told my mother, except it was now owned by a man who imported wine. His name was Charles Ducker. He'd been a kid in Florence, too, though I hadn't known him or maybe simply had forgotten him, and he was perhaps even more obsessed with Purvis than I was. We'd visited with him for half an hour and he talked about a day both of us remembered like it was yesterday.

It had just snowed in Florence. Snow was a rare event in that part of the South and we'd taken a tea tray off the wall and walked over to the country club golf course with Louise to go sledding. Louise said snow in the South was a rare thing and meant something important was going to happen. I thought she meant something in the newspapers. I'd just begun reading and Louise would sometimes read the paper to us. There were protests in southern cities and someone had burned a cross in the Florence High School yard out on TV Road. An airplane had crashed, killing all thirty-eight people aboard. The largest steel strike in American history was ending and my father's boss had asked me if I knew what "NAACP" really stood for. When I shook my head, he smiled and said, *Negroes aren't acting like colored people,* and then laughed. I told this to my mother and she looked unamused and told me some people ought to know better and not to repeat a joke that was in such poor taste but I wasn't sure why it was a joke or what "poor taste" meant so

I repeated it to Louise on the way to the golf course and she didn't smile, either, but just shook her head slowly as we walked along.

The next day, I came home from school, opening the door just as my brother was flying out. He told me something big was going on over at the Purvis place. We leapt through the hedge and ran across the estate's broad lawn and I remember feeling thrilled about this because an elderly colored gardener was usually somewhere around to gently shoo us off the property before we got fifty feet onto the yard. We found a police car sitting in the house's front drive and Burt the reporter standing with a couple officers on the house's front porch. Burt looked worried and told us sharply to go home or he'd tell on us to our father and one of the policemen ordered us to leave, too, so we left, went home and had hot chocolate in the kitchen, and only later learned that Melvin Purvis, the world-famous G-man, perhaps the most famous man in the world or at least the most famous man in mine, had shot himself dead with the same revolver he'd used to bring down John Dillinger. That was the rumor, at least.

I never learned the truth about the gun because we moved to Greensboro two or three days later, a few days after my seventh birthday. Greensboro felt a world away from Florence. A few days after we arrived there, my father took my brother and me downtown to see a civil rights demonstration at the Woolworth's on Main Street. He told us not to be afraid, explaining that we were witnessing history as well as an event that was a long time coming. I remember being a little frightened anyway—all these colored people sitting on the sidewalks on a chill February day placidly singing sweet-sad church hymns while the white people stood and tensely watched. But to tell the truth, I was still thinking about Melvin Purvis and how I was going to miss him.

"Isn't that strange," I admitted to my mother, getting up to refill her wineglass. She watched me pour and smiled. "I can't unlink these events. They all run together like a ruined watercolor. I never even saw Melvin Purvis yet his death was the first one I ever felt personally. The old South was dying and I never even noticed."

"Maybe that was just as well," my mother reflected. "That way you wouldn't miss it."

"Maybe so," I replied, sitting back down again. "I did learn one amazing thing from our stop there today."

Watching me, she asked what.

I said Charles Ducker told me Melvin Purvis hadn't really committed suicide with his own service revolver—he'd been murdered by J. Edgar Hoover. Over the years, Ducker had collected ballistics reports, rental car receipts, all sorts of bits and pieces of circumstantial evidence that added up to a conspiracy theory that sounded like something only Hollywood could have dreamed up. Purvis, a former provost marshal in Africa and prosecutor at the Nuremberg Nazi trials, was apparently about to testify before a Senate subcommittee probing organized crime's reach into government. *Given what is now common knowledge about Hoover's association with crime figures,* Ducker told me, *that probably made Melvin Purvis a marked man.* Ducker said he was still gathering material on the case but Purvis's eldest son, now a professor of art at a Boston university, was going to write a book exposing the whole affair.

"Do you believe it's true?" my mother asked me.

"I don't know. As a reporter, I've come to learn things sometimes aren't what they appear. Then again, I've seen stranger things in America. Which may explain why I gave up reporting."

My mother thought about this a moment. "Did Ducker say what happened to the family?"

"I asked him the same question. Particularly about the

boy in the red pony wagon. Sad story, I'm afraid. The family sort of fell apart after the father was gone. The boy with
the wagon apparently later mysteriously died himself."

My mother shook her head and finished her wine. I could
see people taking an evening stroll out her living room window, a young couple wearing light jackets and walking a
white dog. The nights in Carolina were cooling down, too.

"The good news, however, is that you appear to be doing
splendidly," I said, shifting the conversation abruptly back
to the safer present. But then I realized it wasn't all that
safe, either, and quickly explained to her how she'd impressed all of us with her dazzling self-sufficiency, something that with all due respect none of us had really
anticipated. "You're a tough old bird for a sweet southern
lady."

"I miss your father," she admitted. "Sometimes I miss
him so much I could die. But then I realize I am doing
okay." She was looking at me with her fine blue eyes, Maggie's eyes sixty years on.

"Maggie seems to have had a grand time. She reminds me
of you at her age, the way she chatters so."

"Amazingly enough, in all those thousands of miles she
never once asked how long it would be till we got there.
That has to be a new endurance record for seven-year-olds.
I probably should call Guinness right now."

"Perhaps that's because she was already where she
wanted to be. With you."

"Nice to think. But you have to say that because you're
my mother."

"How's my Jack?"

"Fine. Probably grown a foot by now. I'm trying to figure
out how to work a rocket launch and a trip around Africa
into the same two-week vacation. I've learned you can't
break a pinkie promise."

"You'll figure it out," she said, then sat for a second or
two more before adding, "And how about you?"

"What?"

I'd been looking out the window after the couple and their dog, but they were gone.

"I asked how you were doing. But I really don't need to hear any more about the fish."

I smiled, finished my wine, and said, almost offhandedly, "I'm great. Just great. A nice long drive was good for what ailed me."

She didn't ask what ailed me. I sensed she already knew. She just sat there waiting, staring me down sweetly, waiting for me to spill the beans, as if she had all night to hear it. That's when I told her about the divorce.

I thought she might begin to cry or tell me I was a fool or we were a couple of cowards to finally give up. But she surprised me again, merely held her empty wineglass and studied me with concerned calmness. I tried to imagine what was going on in her head. She loved and admired my wife and I had never failed at anything in her eyes. Perhaps she thought we were both self-absorbed fools doing our children a world of harm, like many people would think.

She patted the couch seat. "Come sit beside me," she said quietly.

I got up and went over and sat down beside her and she took my hand. Her hands were rough but warm, like mine. "I'm truly sorry to hear about this. I won't ask you why because I frankly don't think it's anybody else's business but yours."

I said, "I appreciate that, Mom. But I'm not sure either of us knows exactly why yet. Between you and me, I thought this trip out West might give me some insights into this mess. How we got into it, and how we are going to get out without scarring our kids for life."

She shook her head, almost fiercely. "Don't worry about the children. They're much more resilient than you can even imagine. They won't be scarred if they know you two love and respect each other, even if your marriage didn't work.

Don't pay any attention to what other people think or say, either. Nobody can understand what you all have been through. Just take it day by day, minute by minute if you have to. You'll figure out the right thing to do in time. I have faith in you—both of you. More importantly, darling, your children do, too."

I smiled at her and squeezed her hand. I was sitting close enough to smell her Chanel and remembered that my father always gave her a new bottle every other Christmas. I made a mental note to send her a new bottle of Chanel and a lengthy thank-you letter when we got home.

"You really *are* a tough old bird," I whispered as I leaned over to kiss her cheek. "And I mean that in the kindest possible way."

"I'll cry when you're gone," she replied, and then blinked back tears as she managed a little smile at me.

There was a noise and we both turned. Maggie had suddenly appeared, pink, grinning, wrapped coyly in a blue bath towel. Down the hall the shower was still running. "Gammy?" she said. "Can I have some vanilla ice cream and look at that jewelry again before bed?"

My mother had set aside half of her jewelry to someday give to Maggie. The other half was going to my brother's daughter, Rebecca. She smiled at Maggie and then looked at me with raised eyebrows. Ice cream before bed was strictly taboo in our house. But we weren't in our house.

"Of course, sweetie," she said, patting my hand firmly and then releasing it before getting up.

I drove the borrowed fly rod over to my old friend Pat's house. He asked me how the equipment had worked and I said it was simply lousy and he should seriously consider demanding his money back. I told him about not catching the biggest trout in the San Juan River and he grinned and offered me a consolation Scotch that I didn't refuse. I told him more about the trip and he asked me what I got out of it besides undersized trout and a secondhand motor from Oklahoma.

"I think I learned Maggie has the gift but not the passion for fly-fishing, whereas I have the passion but not the gift. Life's not a bit fair."

"No. But it's what happens while you're waiting to go fishing."

"God, that's such a ridiculous cliché," I told him.

"Yeah? So's God."

We sat on his screened porch and talked about our daughters, how they were growing up much too quickly and the hard part was knowing when and how to let them go. I told him about the difficulty our mutual friend Silent Sam was having in this respect, letting his daughters go and trying to make sense of his well-made life that hadn't worked out the way he'd expected.

"Whose life has worked out the way he expected?" asked Pat, whose own father was dying by painfully slow degrees of a rare nervous system disorder. "I always expected to be president of the United States by now."

"That's funny," I said, "I always expected you to be in prison."

"Very funny. So what did you tell him? To get some serious help, I hope."

"Nope. I gave him a couple poets to read, though."

Pat laughed. "That must have made him decide to get well fast."

I ignored his dig. "The poet Mary Oliver says there are three things you must do in order to be happy in this world," I said. "You must be able to love what is mortal; to hold it against your bones knowing your own life depends upon it; and when it comes time to let it go, to let it go."

"Spoken like a woman who's caught a few undersized rainbow trout in her time," Pat said wryly.

I said it was probably too soon to tell but maybe that's

what this trip had done for me—allowed me to get my hands on a grief I once couldn't have even imagined, to hold it for a while, and with luck to begin to let it go. Sipping my Scotch, I added that I didn't know exactly what kind of new world we were going home to face, but it was damn good to be going home.

"My best educated guess is that you'll never move back here," said my oldest friend, as if that possibility had just sunk in.

I admitted that I didn't think so. I loved the South but there was just too much sadness there to get my hands around, I said. I'd finally found a home on a hill in the North, a life of children and roses, both of which required a lot of hands-on attention and watering. For the moment, I was clutching this life to my bones with everything I had.

I said I couldn't really explain it.

"I think you just did," Pat said. He smiled and took my empty Scotch glass. "Go home."

We left Greensboro the next morning before dawn, pulled by magnetic north and propelled by the road anthems of Patty Loveless and Trisha Yearwood, reaching the bridge over the Piscataqua River just before midnight. A few early travelers were going over the bridge into Maine, getting a jump on the long Labor Day weekend ahead. I glanced at my odometer and did some rough calculations. My daughter and my dog were both sound asleep and WGBH from Boston was serving up the Tommy Flanagan Trio. Six weeks, eight thousand miles, nineteen gas-ups, and six gallons of Wild Blue Raspberry Gatorade later, we'd come home. Our own sacred circle was almost complete, and I thought about how Black Elk had gone so far only to discover how good this feeling of homecoming felt. *Don't grieve,* the poet Rumi said. *Anything you lose comes around in another form.*

It was just minutes before my son's sixth birthday.

I carried Maggie upstairs to her bed, then went into his room and sat on his empty bed looking at the stars on his dormer ceiling. He would be home tomorrow and we would lie here and talk about storms and gods, rocket ships and roads to Africa. I went outside and sat on the front steps to look at the real stars, wondering what my fellow travelers would choose to remember from our trip West and perhaps, years on, my daughter from the complicated summer when she was seven. As my mother said, these things take time to really know. I realized I had probably been searching for big trout and big answers and that one had proved as elusive as the other. But a long drive is always good and my mother had been right that you're never really happy until you find a place that feels like home.

Amos went off into the woods to see how the place was holding up without him, perhaps to have a nice midnight roll in the Fern Bowl. It was a beautiful summer night and I was pleased to find, a short while later, when I went back inside, fresh flowers waiting in a vase with a note from Maggie's mother, welcoming us home. She'd been there to freshen up the place and, I later discovered, had thoughtfully watered my roses.

About the Author

JAMES DODSON is a regular columnist for *Golf Magazine* and an editor of *Departures Magazine*. His work has appeared in *Gentlemen's Quarterly*, *Sports Illustrated*, *Travel and Leisure*, *Outside Magazine*, and numerous other national publications. He won the Golf Writers of America Award for his columns in 1995 and 1996. His first book, *Final Rounds*, received the International Network of Golf's industry honors award for Best Golf Book of 1997.